Seven Story Mountain

Seven Story Mountain

The Union Campaign at Vicksburg

by

PHILLIP M. THIENEL

McFarland & Company, Inc., Publishers
Jefferson, North Carolina, and London

This is the first softcover edition (1998) of the 1995 library bound volume published by McFarland. The two editions are identical in every respect except the cover materials used in binding.

Cover: Two Union soldiers at Battery Sherman guard the road to Jackson, Mississippi (COURTESY LIBRARY OF CONGRESS)

British Library Cataloguing-in-Publication data are available

Library of Congress Cataloguing-in-Publication Data

Thienel, Phillip M.
    Seven story mountain : the Union campaign at Vicksburg / by Phillip M. Thienel.
        p.   cm.
    Includes bibliographical references and index.
    ISBN 0-7864-0014-5 (paperback : 50# alkaline paper) ∞
    1. Vicksburg (Miss.) — History — Civil War, 1861-1865.   2. Vicksburg (Miss.) — History — Siege, 1863.   I. Title.
    F349.V6T48   1998
    973.7'344 — dc20   94-32408
                                                                            CIP

Manufactured in the United States of America

McFarland & Company, Inc., Publishers
  Box 611, Jefferson, North Carolina 28640

To the memory of
J.I.J.T.

Table of Contents

List of Illustrations

MAPS

PHOTOGRAPHS AND DRAWINGS

TABLES

Preface and Acknowledgments

This work took form from a longtime interest in the Vicksburg campaign. Its particular focus is on the overland march of General U.S. Grant's army down the Louisiana side of the Mississippi River and the joint army-navy amphibious operations that ferried the soldiers across the river. Once on Mississippi soil, Grant's troops sought out and defeated the Confederate soldiers posted to fend off the Union attempt to seize control of the river.

The content of most published books on Vicksburg limits coverage on the amphibious phase of the campaign to a report that Grant marched his army down the west side of the river and, with the support of the navy, crossed over to the east side. With this methodology much history is omitted; Grant and his soldiers are denied recognition for their notable achievement. Also omitted are the dynamics, tactics, and details of the march itself, along with the historical importance of the strategy in the Vicksburg campaign.

In a longtime study of the literature about the campaign, I collected bits and pieces of information on the march. Piqued by the seeming lack of interest in the subject, I began to view the march as a neglected, complex story worthy of being told. I became interested in the stories of the obstacles the soldiers met on the route, the critical events, the organization of the march, and the culture and sociology of Grant's army.

The march evolved from the importance of the Mississippi River to commerce, and a Union strategy that would return control of the river to them. In response to the loss of such control in the early military operations of the war, Grant ordered his soldiers to undertake tactical operations based on the national strategy to regain the river.

The first six attempts to reach Vicksburg were unsuccessful. These were followed by a successful seventh attempt, which with determination and manual labor achieved the objective.

This work approaches the subject from the perspective of the Union strategy to wrest from the Confederate army its control of the Mississippi basin, an area that stretched from the Yazoo River north of Vicksburg to Grand Gulf to the south. This objective was to be achieved by the defeat of the Confederate army posted in and around the targeted areas. It fell to Grant's subordinate corps commanders and the soldiers in the ranks to carry out the battle orders with their energy, loyalty, and determination.

This book also approaches the subject from the perspective of the natural environment wherein the army camped and conducted military operations. The variable climate, soil conditions, vegetation, water (bayous, ponds, creeks, lakes), and disease-carrying insects severely affected the soldiers' health and their ability to perform their duty. These factors also aroused their sensitivity to their camp surroundings. The march brought out the men's individual personalities and characteristics, which are chronicled in their letters, memoirs, diaries, and official unit records. Through these documents, one can envision how the participants lived through the hardships of the environment and viewed their arduous foot march.

Today those who are fascinated with all aspects of the Civil War are indebted to the officers and soldiers for their personal recollections and official records that survived severe battlefield conditions. We are indebted also to the relatives who preserved the soldiers' letters and diaries and then placed them in public depositories.

Each participant who left us something in writing responded, with his unique creativity and expressiveness from the depths of his being, to events that impinged on a soldier's life in a difficult campaign. They expressed many positive qualities that sustained them: humanity, love of and yearning for family home, friendship with cohorts in arms, and humor and bitterness. Likewise, they viewed with repugnance what they perceived to be ugliness in army life and the war.

Through the participants' records today's readers learn how Grant's soldiers lived the tell-tale moments of their ordinary humanity. One can also discern their feelings and attitudes toward the environment, other soldiers, and the army's sociology and culture.

The soldiers were not demonstrative in boasting heroic acts, and at times they found that their army duty was in conflict with their personal beliefs and consciences. In the permanent qualities of their characters, there stood forth, as an infantry sergeant recorded, a core of the faithful who demonstrated steadfast courage, endurance, loyalty, a moral center, and fixed innate convictions to fulfill their duty to the Union.

I have been privileged to read through many of these personal recollections and official records. I had access to a treasury of social history of an interesting and important historical event, and a chronicle of soldiers' lives. I became impressed by the richness of the information the soldiers recorded. I also developed an admiration for the known and unknown soldiers who spent long hours and had the talent to meticulously record their observations. Their writings were prepared under varying weather conditions, in the field and in camp, on the battlefield, on the march, in defensive positions, and in hospitals and winter camps.

People today who are interested in reading or pursuing research on Civil War topics owe a debt of gratitude to the soldiers who created the memorable written legacy of that phenomenon and to the archivists and librarians who have collected and preserved the legacy over the years. The documents are a treasure of historical information. They are written in straightforward language that tells us where and how the soldiers under the stress of war "had their noses rubbed into it."

As I read Grant's written reports, images formed in my mind of the gruelling march he instigated. He determinedly pushed forward, testing every opportunity to reach his objective, making decisions, and issuing orders as circumstances required. As the leader of the march, he stands forth as a stalwart figure who possessed the determination and doggedness to keep the army plodding forward. Through the difficulties his army encountered on the ground, he focused on the capture of the strategic target assigned to him by President Abraham Lincoln. His leadership and motivational skills allowed his army to successfully achieve its strategic goal. He was supported by loyal officers, noncommissioned officers and soldiers who toiled at arduous duties, overcame hardships, and suffered debilitating diseases. These experiences seem to have reinforced their sense of duty to march on until they succeeded.

The difficult terrain on the west bank turned the operation into a tactical one carried out by soldiers serving as engineers and pioneers. The multifarious tasks required able-bodied soldiers to put down their guns and pick up axes, shovels, and hand tools to build a road to enable the army to march out of its encampment. On the march they built canals, waterways, paths, breastworks, and bridges. Their tasks were laborious, calling upon them to perform innovative feats and use local natural resources to pass the many obstacles.

This story of Vicksburg is an effort to portray what a soldier's life was like in the campaign, and answers, I believe, the questions a reader would ask about his life. Many facets of human behavior were found in the culture and sociology of Grant's army. All the critical events that transpired—the decisions of Grant and his generals to deploy the army in the strategical and tactical operations—are portrayed based on the records the soldiers left. From the story a reader can form a picture of the soldiers' camp life, both the seamy and the noble. The noble, though, persevered and led to the victory.

One can never capture the full emotions of Grant's soldiers from their written words. My efforts have attempted to show the deeper reflection of the experiences of the men involved in a historical event that is often taken for granted.

When the conflict between the states culminated in armed rebellion, ordinary men assumed the burden of the soldier's role. One has to be impressed with how they performed that role. Each soldier performed in the unique, quiet fullness of his own life, especially in the battle for Vicksburg. In the self-contained phenomenon of the battle, they endured physical hardship and contracted diseases that brought more deaths than did the gunfire. They grumbled and groused, but they also affirmed and applauded their leaders. They exhibited many admirable character qualities that allowed them to win the battle.

The preparation of a manuscript is beyond the work of one person. I wish to thank the staffs at the archives and libraries who assisted me on technical questions and on locating materials: Alderman Library, the University of Virginia, Charlottesville; the George Peabody Library of the Johns Hopkins University, Baltimore, Maryland; Enoch Pratt Free Library, Baltimore, Maryland; Library of Congress, Washington, D.C.; National Archives and Records Administration, Washington, D.C.; U.S. Air Force Air University Library, Maxwell Air Force Base, Alabama; U.S. Army Engineer Center and School Library, Fort Belvoir, Virginia; U.S. Army Ordnance Center and School Library, Aberdeen, Maryland; and State of Kentucky Archives, Frankfort.

I am especially grateful to my sons, Norman and Stephen, and granddaughter, Stacey Thienel, for their interest in my writing, their instruction on the intricacies of the personal computer, and their help in the production of this work.

I also thank Mrs. Patricia Winter for her collaboration in the proofreading.

PHILLIP M. THIENEL
September 1994

"We are now attempting in fact to take a mountain."
Galway, *The New York Times*, April 6, 1863

The Theater of War in the West (Adapted from *Harper's Weekly*).

Introduction

In the following paragraph, a magazine editor in 1863 highlighted the two-sided importance of the Mississippi Valley region—symbolized by the town of Vicksburg—to the Civil War combatants. To the Confederacy, Vicksburg meant fastening control; to the Union, it meant capturing control of the metaphorical "Body of the Nation."

BODY OF THE NATION

But the basin of the Mississippi is the Body of the Nation. All other parts are but members, important in themselves, yet more important in their relations to this. Exclusive of the Lake basin and of 300,000 square miles in Texas and New Mexico, which in many aspects form a part of it, this basin contains about 1,250,000 square miles. In extent it is the second great valley of the world, being exceeded only by that of the Amazon. The valley of the frozen Obi approaches it in extent; that of the La Plata comes next in space, and probably in habitable capacity, having about 8/9 of its area; then comes that of the Yenisei, with about 7/9; the Lena, Amoor, Hoang-ho, Yang-tse-kiang, and Nile, 5/9; the Ganges, 1/5; the Rhine, 1/15. It exceeds in extent the whole of Europe, exclusive of Russia, Norway, and Sweden. It would contain Austria four times, Germany or Spain five times, France six times, the British Isles or Italy ten times. Conceptions formed from the river-basins of Western Europe are rudely shocked when we consider the extent of the valley of the Mississippi; nor are those formed from the sterile basins of the great rivers of

1

Siberia, the lofty plateaus of Central Asia, or the mighty sweep
of the swampy Amazon more adequate. Latitude, elevation,
and rainfall all combine to render every part of the Mississippi
Valley capable of supporting a dense population. As a dwell-
ing place for civilized man it is by far the first upon our globe
[Editor's Table, *Harper's Magazine*, February 1863].

CHAPTER 1

1861–1862

First and Second
Attempts to Take
the Mountain

The River's Lifeblood Sets the Strategy

"If the Mississippi could not otherwise be opened," Union Brigadier General John A. Logan declared, "the men of the northwest would hew their way with their swords to the Gulf if the opportunity allowed."[1]

General Logan had good reasons to proclaim publicly why the men of the Northwest would hew their way with their swords to the Gulf. The Confederates followed their military attack on Fort Sumter on April 12, 1861, with the closing of the Mississippi River from New Orleans northward to Columbus, Kentucky, and Belmont, Missouri, cutting off the lifeblood of the Northwest's commerce. General Albert S. Johnston, adept at defensive tactics, also posted soldiers along the Ohio River from Louisville to the Mississippi River. He grasped the importance of the river to both contestants; thus he foresaw the strategy of the Union would be to attack and disperse its soldiers to secure control of the rivers in order to deploy its army into the Confederate states. To the Union, restoring control of the Mississippi would not only provide natural benefits, but it would also cut off the transportation of goods to the Confederate states from states west of Mississippi.

Union leaders assured the men of the Northwest there would

be an opportunity to "fight their way to the Gulf with their swords."
President Lincoln, truly one of the men of the Northwest, had learned
of the Mississippi's importance in his youth on his flatboat trips
down the river to New Orleans. Control of the Mississippi quickly
became a national strategy.

An innate vision of the rivers was also instilled in Ulysses S.
Grant at an early stage of his life at Point Pleasant, Ohio, his birth-
place near the Ohio River. As a youth he had fished, swum, and ice-
skated on village rivers and creeks. He took boat rides on the Ohio
to Cincinnati, Maysville, and Louisville. In his adolescence, faced
with the choice of an occupation, Grant told his father one of his
preferences would be to be "a down river trader." His first choice
though would be to pursue a better education. Unable to help his
son in such a choice, his father sought the help of his district congressman, who responded favorably with an appointment to the
United States Military Academy at West Point, New York.[2] After
leaving the army at the end of the Mexican War and becoming a
storekeeper in Galena, Illinois, Grant became aware in his daily life
of the importance of the rivers, especially the Mississippi and its
tributary the Galena.

Lincoln and Grant were destined to play leading roles in the
Civil War. Lincoln would formulate the government's strategy;
Grant would conduct the army's military operations to regain con-
trol of the great Mississippi.

September 6, 1861. Upon his return to military service in the
Illinois Volunteers after the outbreak of the Civil War, Grant com-
manded troops in the first river battle in the West, securing the
Mississippi River at Cairo, Illinois. He boldly crossed the Ohio
River on September 6, 1861, and seized Paducah, Kentucky, gaining
possession of the junction of the Ohio and Tennessee rivers and the
Ohio and Mississippi rivers for the Union.

November 9, 1861. The scene shifted to Washington, where
President Lincoln involved himself in directing the national strategy
for the opening of the Mississippi. Commander David D. Porter,
who commanded the Union naval vessel *Powhatan* in the Gulf of
Mexico, reported to the outer office of the secretary of the navy on
that date. He took the initiative to tell Senators John P. Hale, of New
Hampshire, and James W. Grimes, of Iowa, who were also present,
his plan to capture New Orleans. According to Porter, they were
surprised there had been no follow-up actions on his plan. They

escorted him into the office of the secretary of the navy to meet with Gideon Welles. Informed of Porter's plan, Secretary Welles listened to his presentation and declared it should be laid before the president at once.[3]

The bureaucracy was simple at the time, and access to the president was easy to obtain. Welles unceremoniously led the party across the street to Lincoln's office. After listening to an outline of Porter's plan, the president declared his conception of Union strategy: "Mississippi [is the] backbone of Rebellion, [and] key to whole situation. While Confederates hold it they can obtain supplies and it is a barrier to our forces." Just as unceremoniously, Lincoln escorted the party across the street to the office of general-in-chief of the army, Major General George B. McClellan. He told McClellan the Mississippi River expedition was an important one and he was to spare what troops he could for a joint army-navy operation to take New Orleans and proceed on to Vicksburg, the key to all that country watered by the Mississippi and its tributaries. Before he left, the president ordered the army and navy officials to make their plans and send him a report.

February 6 and February 16, 1862. Grant's follow-up river tactics captured Fort Henry on the Tennessee River on February 6 and Fort Donelson on the Cumberland River on February 16. His decisive actions and victories in the opening stages of the war to capture control of the rivers were widely acclaimed. He terminated the Confederates' use of the Ohio River as an offensive or defensive position and drove Johnston out of Kentucky and western Tennessee.

March 11. To facilitate the army's western strategy, Lincoln placed the western armies under the unified command of Major General Henry Halleck on March 11, 1862. Halleck began to concentrate his soldiers against Johnston's Army of the Mississippi at Corinth, the important railroad junction east of Memphis where the east-west Memphis and Charleston Railroad and the north-south Mississippi Central Railroad crossed. He ordered Major General Don Carlos Buell to march to Savannah on the Tennessee River and Grant to march nine miles up river to Pittsburg Landing.

April 6. Johnston attacked Grant's forces at Shiloh before Buell could arrive. Caught unaware, the overconfident, poorly positioned Union soldiers were seemingly defeated.

April 7. Within a day Grant regrouped his soldiers, counter-attacked, and drove the Confederates back to Corinth, thus demonstrating his leadership qualities. Lincoln's critics made Grant their target because he had been caught unaware of Johnston's presence on the first day's battle, but Lincoln rebuffed them, saying, "He's a fighter, he stays on the battlefield."

April 24. The navy, in compliance with the president's strategic plan, commenced its operations to capture control of the Mississippi River. Navy flag officer David G. Farragut accomplished a great naval feat by attacking and capturing New Orleans. The army force committed by General McClellan at the November 9 meeting, which was under the command of Major General Benjamin Butler, accompanied the naval armada. After the navy's success, the army contingent occupied the city.

The President Orders an Attack on Vicksburg

May 18. President Lincoln at this point ordered Farragut to attack and capture Vicksburg. Farragut, who was apprehensive to sail up the Mississippi with his seagoing ships, questioned the commander in chief's decision. He reported he preferred to attack Mobile, but Lincoln's orders prevailed. Farragut then searched for experienced pilots to guide his fleet up the river.

Finding the spring water level to be high, Farragut's army-navy task force approached Vicksburg. Under a flag of truce, Farragut sent an emissary ashore in a ship's boat to demand the surrender of the town, but its civil and military officials refused to acquiesce.

May 22. Farragut's armada bombarded the town. Unable to bring about its capitulation, Farragut consulted with Brigadier General Thomas Williams, who commanded the army contingent of troops aboard the transports. Williams was unable to offer any attack plans to land his two ill-prepared, undermanned regiments on the east side of the river. Williams also reported that the ground on the west side of the river was too wet for his soldiers to land. In the face of the army's lack of preparation, Farragut decided to return the expedition to New Orleans.[4]

Sailing into New Orleans, Farragut found new orders awaiting him from the president and the secretary of the navy, repeating their instructions to clear the Mississippi River and adding Memphis as a new target.

May 30. Halleck, fulfilling his role in the strategy, marched his army steadily to Corinth. His soldiers, who had learned a lesson at Shiloh, entrenched their encampments every night. They arrived at the railroad center on the last day of May to discover to their surprise that General Pierre G. T. Beauregard had deserted the town.

June 6. Halleck called a halt to any further offensive action by his army force. Instead he focused on holding territory and sent Grant to hold Memphis, which surrendered to a Union naval force on June 6, and sent Buell to Chattanooga. Grant disagreed with the strategy, believing it best to keep his army moving steadily against the enemy's soldiers.[5]

The Union successes at New Orleans and Memphis raised the fears of the military personnel and civilian population at Vicksburg. They believed themselves safe from capture, but they recognized that the loss of New Orleans and Memphis made them more vulnerable to attack. Brigadier General Martin L. Smith assumed responsibility for building the town's defenses. Gun batteries were built along the bluff fronting the town at the water's edge to ward off Union attacks.

June 26. In compliance with his orders from the president, Farragut's fleet, followed by a flotilla under the command of Commander Porter and transports with soldiers from Butler's New Orleans garrison, returned to the vicinity of Vicksburg and commenced bombarding the town. The Confederates' tiered-gun emplacements on the bluffs before the town were ready to challenge the Union's naval and military presence.

June 27. The 3,000 soldiers in the expedition under General Williams were debarked onto a peninsula formed by the course of the Mississippi opposite the town. Williams, with orders from the president, set his soldiers and Negroes (who had either been taken into custody or had fled to Union lines) to work building a canal across the peninsula to enable naval vessels and army transports to bypass the Confederate guns positioned on the bluffs. Their hard labor turned out to be futile when the water level in the river rose and filled the excavated ditch. Williams, nevertheless, declared the project "a great one and worthy of success," but did not offer a plan on how to finish the canal.

June 28. The bombardment of the town by the Union's naval guns continued, and the Confederates gun batteries continued their return fire. Two of Porter's steamers were hit by the enemy.

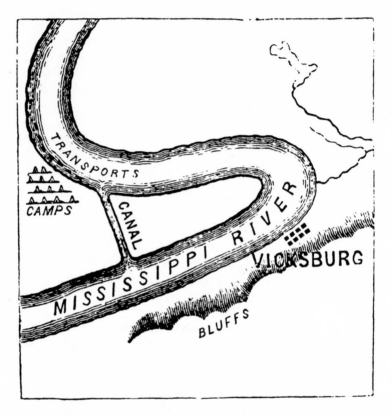

Proposed De Soto Canal (*Harper's Pictorial History*).

July 1. Naval ironclads from Memphis, under the command of Flag Officer Charles L. Davis, joined Farragut's fleet near Vicksburg. The two naval commanders conducted a reconnaissance of the target area and reviewed the president's strategy. They concluded that the task to capture Vicksburg properly belonged to the army, and they forwarded their conclusions and recommendations to Washington.[6]

Porter's fleet received orders to return to New Orleans, while Farragut and Davis' fleets remained in the vicinity of Vicksburg for two weeks futilely shelling the town. The navy's effort to bombard the town into surrender, and Williams' labor on the impractical canal then came to an end. The citizens of the town and Mississippi newspaper editors raised the North's ire by deriding the failures of the Union army and navy; they believed fervently that the natural terrain would protect them.

July 17. Even though the navy passed the Vicksburg mission to the army, the war in the West came to a standstill. Lincoln ordered General Halleck to Washington to become general-in-chief of the army and promoted Grant to command all the armies in the West.

September 20. The Confederates seized the opportunity to thwart Grant's plans to initiate an offensive action. They organized General Earl Van Dorn's Army of Northern Mississippi, and Confederate control of the military situation in the west reached a high water mark when Van Dorn forced Union soldiers into a defensive war. The Confederate successes were short-lived, however. Grant was able to place his offensive imprint on his soldiers and defeated Van Dorn at Iuka.

October 4. Grant followed up his Iuka victory with one over General Sterling Price at Corinth, and the Confederate soldiers retreated into Mississippi.

A conflict arose challenging Grant's command authority. As he started formulating his plans to deploy his army to Vicksburg, the relationship that governed him in the civilian-military hierarchy in Washington became a bit cloudy, with overtones of intrigue and strange top-level decisions. The conflict involved Major General John A. McClernand, a former Illinois congressman who had received a commission as a brigadier general in the volunteers after recruiting a brigade of soldiers in Illinois, he later commanded the brigade in the battles of Fort Donelson and Shiloh and received a promotion to major general.

In his short career, McClernand had been conceptualizing a strategy for the army. After the close of the Corinth campaign, he took a leave of absence from his command to travel to Washington to meet with the president and secretary of war, and to present his strategy to win the support of the West. He proposed to induce men to enlist in the war by sending a river expedition down the Mississippi to capture Vicksburg, accomplishing a popular Western goal by opening the river for commerce. The river expedition would, of course, be under his command. McClernand planned first to return to the West to recruit the necessary soldiers.

Looking for an opportunity to accomplish the Mississippi River strategy, Lincoln and Stanton—without staff advice—responded favorably to McClernand's proposal, and together they secretly worked out the organization of the force. Lincoln seemingly further stipulated that McClernand would resume work on Williams' canal project. Major General Nathaniel P. Banks, who replaced Butler in the Department of the Gulf and was another political general to enter the fray, would command a cooperative expedition that would deploy up the Mississippi from New Orleans to capture Port Hudson and then march overland to join McClernand's force in the capture of Vicksburg.

The strange decision was to be carried out secretly by McClernand, acting independently on the battlefield. A release provision for Lincoln and Stanton was included in the plan; McClernand would act under Grant's authority as commander of the Department of the Tennessee to countermand his orders.[7]

General Halleck recorded that he did not participate in the decision to launch McClernand's expedition, but when he learned of it he protested to the president about the awkward character of the civil decision in the military chain of command and the president's meddling in plans for the Vicksburg battle, a campaign that had been assigned to Grant's department. Halleck's protestations were to no avail.[8] Rumors of the decision spread in the unofficial information network and reached Grant. Professionally jealous of any infringement of a field commander's prerogatives, Grant was not pleased with the idea of McClernand having an independent command in his department. He suspected some intrigue taking place because of the strange stories he heard.

A Topographic Engineer Officer's Role

October 17. First Lieutenant James H. Wilson, Corps of Topographic Engineers, reported to Grant's headquarters for duty as staff topographic engineer officer. Wilson soon expressed his opinions about Grant's command situation and his belief in his destiny to exercise an important influence on Grant's tactical decisions. Aware of the difficult terrain in the West, he was eager to put his imprint on the battle.

The 25-year-old Wilson had graduated from the United States Military Academy in 1860. He spent his first year out of the academy as a topographic engineer officer at Fort Vancouver in the Washington Territory. When he returned to the East shortly after the outbreak of the rebellion, Wilson was eager for an opportunity to play an active leadership role and spent a few months in Boston recruiting soldiers for the Regular Army Topographic Engineer Company. Next he gained important experience as a topographic engineer officer on the staff of Brigadier Thomas W. Sherman, commander of the army troops in the joint army–navy South Carolina Expeditionary Corps that captured Port Royal as a base for the navy's blockading fleet. In September he joined McClellan's Antietam campaign, where he served as a staff officer in the Army of the Potomac, surveying the terrain and assisting in the deployment of troops on the line.

Upon completion of his assignment at Antietam, and in answer to his persistent requests for an important assignment, the chief of army engineers ordered Wilson to report to General Grant's army. After he met with Grant, Wilson wrote that he had formed immediate impressions. He assessed Grant to be "direct in thought and ways," which was one of the characteristics Wilson himself exhibited when he began to perform his duties as one of Grant's staff officers. He also recorded that Grant "invited no confidences nor repelled none." Grant and Wilson quickly developed a confidence in one another, however, and a successful commander–staff officer relationship. It was an opportunity for Wilson to demonstrate his ability as a topographic engineer officer, and to put into practice what he had learned about the effect of terrain on tactics at Antietam and in joint army–navy amphibious operations on the South Carolina coastline.

Wilson wrote that he related to Grant that Washington considered Vicksburg the strategic center in its military planning. He also told Grant that the capture of Vicksburg was assigned to Grant's theater of operations and military department in the West. Further, he did not hesitate to express a number of opinions to Grant concerning his right and duty to command all the troops in the attempt to capture Vicksburg. He told Grant to take command of the principal column for that purpose and urged him to go down river with his soldiers to save himself from a subordinate role. Wilson also reported to Grant on McClernand's duplicity in Washington, information he may not have known had already reached Grant.[9]

First Attempt to Take the Mountain

November 1. The assaults against Vicksburg up to this point had been conducted by the navy. Grant decided it was time to place his army in the limelight and launch an offensive. He focused his army's objective on Vicksburg, the target that then was most prominent.

The Union soldiers had outflanked every Confederate position on the Mississippi from Cairo to Memphis, and the river was opened to naval gunboats up to the stronghold at Vicksburg. The defeat of the Confederates at Vicksburg and Port Hudson, whose guns prevented river traffic 200 miles below Vicksburg, would insure the Union's complete control of the Mississippi River. After gaining control of the river, Grant's armies would be able to march east to Chattanooga, Atlanta, Savannah, and Charlotte, and join the Army of the Potomac in Virginia. Union control of the river would also stop the flow of war supplies and food across the river from the Western states. Such successes would enable Grant's army "to eat out the vitals of the country."[10]

Grant's offensive action focused on the Confederate army encamped near Vicksburg. Grant sent his soldiers on an uncertain march route that became in the ensuing months an attempt to climb the metaphorical seven-story mountain alluded to by correspondent Galway of the *New York Times*. Obstacles and difficult terrain had to be overcome in order to reach the enemy.

The enemy army would be difficult to reach. The difficult terrain formed a natural defense for the Confederate army posted in the vicinity of the town. On the river bank, a bluff rose as high as 250 feet above the water and traversed 100 miles north and south. The bluff reinforced Vicksburg's active military defense against Grant's army.

North of the town, the Yazoo River and its watery, swampy bottom-land delta, which stretched for a distance of 175 miles north and south and 60 miles east and west, formed an impenetrable barrier. South of the town, the ground remained swampy and impassable to the mouth of the Big Black River. Above the town, the Confederates fortified the bluff from Haynes' Bluff on the Yazoo River, and below, they fortified the 40 miles leading to Grand Gulf at the junction of the Big Black River with the Mississippi.

In spite of Wilson's recommendation, Grant first attempted to march his soldiers southward along the Mississippi Central Railroad tracks to Vicksburg. Grant reported to Halleck he would march to Holly Springs and Grenada with a force of 30,000 soldiers. General James McPherson would command the left wing and General William T. Sherman would command the right wing.

November 8. Major General John C. Pemberton, commander of the Confederate forces at Vicksburg, positioned his soldiers at Holly Springs. Grant's soldiers occupied Grand Junction and La Grange along the railroad tracks. Grant adhered to the military doctrine of operating from a covered supply base as the army moved forward. Repairs that had to be made to the railroad slowed Grant's march.

While the operation was in its early stages, there then arose one of the many human complexities Grant would face in the battle ahead. Lincoln issued orders to field commanders to protect Negroes when they involuntarily came into the army's lines. Humanity forbade letting them starve or be ostracized. With so many Negroes at Grand Junction, a delay occurred because, Grant reported, he had to stop to organize the Negroes to work on farms and to cut wood.[11]

Lieutenant Wilson received an appointment as a staff lieutenant colonel in the United States Volunteer Forces. Earlier in April he had been appointed brevet major for meritorious service.

November 12. Troubled by the conflict in command authority, Grant took the first step for clarification. He queried Halleck about the disposition of Union forces in his department, especially McClernand's, to assure a coordinated movement against Vicksburg. Halleck, relying on traditional military doctrine, replied to Grant that he was in command of all soldiers in his department and he had "permission to fight the enemy as he pleased with them."[12]

November 13. Grant's cavalry marched into Holly Springs and the enemy withdrew to the south side of the Tallahatchee River. Grant became concerned about the long supply lines from Columbus, Kentucky, to Holly Springs.

November 15. Grant sent word to Sherman to meet him at Columbus to discuss battle plans. At the meeting he ordered Sherman to march two divisions to Holly Springs and to march down the Mississippi Central Railroad corridor. Sherman promptly set out to comply with his orders.

November 29. Sherman marched his soldiers to Cottage Hill, 10 miles south of Oxford. McPherson had marched his soldiers 17 miles beyond Oxford. The two generals then had to halt the march while repairs were made on the railroad north of the Tallahatchee.

Arrival of Engineer Soldiers

December 1. Captain William F. Patterson's Kentucky Company of Mechanics and Engineers, attached to Brigadier General George W. Morgan's division, completed a journey by transport from Charleston, Virginia, to Memphis. The company's presence presaged the battle for Vicksburg would be one involving engineer soldiers and the company would fill a distinct need.

Patterson's company had been mustered into the service on September 25, 1861, with two officers, Captain Patterson and his uncle, Second Lieutenant Andrew Patterson, 45 years of age, two noncommissioned officers, and 28 privates, one of them Captain Patterson's father, Private William S. Patterson, 62 years of age. As a practice details from the infantry regiments augmented the company's work force.

In its year of service, the small company had performed significant engineer duties in the battle of Mill Springs, Kentucky, on January 19, 1862, in the occupation of Cumberland Gap on June 19, and in its subsequent evacuation on September 17.

In the engagement at Cumberland Gap, General Morgan, commander of the Seventh Division, Army of the Ohio, emphasized Patterson's company "performed most arduous service" building roads and bridges and laying mines. His report was also evidence that Patterson had made a mark for his company in his first year of service. At the evacuation of the Gap, Morgan wrote, "Captain Patterson of great merit."

December 5. General Joseph E. Johnston, the newly appointed commander of the Confederate forces in Mississippi, fell back to Jackson by December 5. General Pemberton fell back behind the Yalobusha River and the town of Grenada.

Grant had made a 60-mile march with his supplies that was part of a larger 180-mile trip from Columbus to Holly Springs. Rain made the overland movement of the wagon trains of supplies difficult. Grant's communications from Halleck led him to believe that he was receiving little support from Washington. He wired Halleck to ask how far he should march in view of his supply line difficulties. Halleck replied Grant was free to move his soldiers at his discretion. The instructions placed Grant in an uncertain situation.

Continuing to hear by word of mouth that McClernand's expedition down the Mississippi was inevitable, Grant discussed with Sherman a counter tactical operation sending Sherman's force to the mouth of the Yazoo River. McPherson's troops would press forward from Oxford and Grenada to the rear of Vicksburg, where the two forces would join.

Second Attempt to Take the Mountain

Sherman's deployment became the second attempt by Grant to climb the Vicksburg mountain. It was also an effort to finesse McClernand's maneuverings. Grant and Sherman recognized the potential danger of splitting Grant's force into two columns, with the railroad from Memphis to Grenada in such poor condition and the unavailability of any railroad beyond Grenada. Also they were in conflict with Halleck's military doctrine. Sherman acquiesced to Grant's decision, although for some time he had supported the water route to Vicksburg. Grant had turned this option down because of the failure of the earlier naval expeditions against the town, however.

December 8. Grant received approval from Halleck for Sherman's expedition to proceed down the Mississippi. Grant wanted Sherman to move expeditiously to insure that the operation would take place under his leadership. The idea of McClernand being in command of the expedition rankled Grant. He asserted his authority by sending with Sherman the soldiers McClernand had recruited in Illinois for his river expedition. A number of the recruits had already reported to Memphis.

Confederates Disrupt First Attempt to Take the Mountain

December 19. All the machinations of the Union civilian and military leaders became known to the Confederate authorities through the reports of watchful persons. General Nathan Bedford Forrest chose December 19 to attack and destroy 60 miles of railroad track north of Jackson.

December 20. General Earl Van Dorn attacked Holly Springs, captured Union soldiers, and burned Grant's supply depot. Grant became irate at the "disgraceful conduct in front of the enemy" that the commanding officer of the depot exhibited.

The raids of Forrest and Van Dorn, which destroyed Grant's supply lines, decisively impacted the inchoate advance on Vicksburg. For Grant, the raids resolved the conflict about where the starting point of an attack on Vicksburg should be. He decided to abandon his campaign along the railroad tracks, fall back to Memphis, and use the line of the Mississippi River for his route of attack and resupply.

While Sherman's joint expedition was underway at Memphis — after expeditious preparations by Sherman and Porter (promoted to flank rank and transferred to command of naval forces at Memphis) — Halleck telegraphed Grant that McClernand was to command the river expedition. Because the telegraph wires were cut, Sherman could not be informed and his expedition continued headlong on its way to disaster.

Another consequence of the disrupted communications was that Grant could not inform Sherman of his decision to fall back with McPherson's column to the Tallahatchee River. He had to leave the Yazoo expedition in a disastrous double jeopardy. Pemberton — without a threat from Grant — would be able to meet Sherman with his entire force. Sherman would be left to face a brouhaha with McClernand for usurping the authority delegated to him by the president.

Defeat of the Second Attempt to Take the Mountain

December 21. Sergeant Major Edward P. Reichhelm, 3rd Missouri Infantry, on duty with the Yazoo expedition, recorded in his diary that his regiment boarded the transport *Decotah* the night of December 20. He described the transport as the "imperial monster" because on board were 1,500 soldiers, 600 mules, 80 wagons, and an artillery battery.

December 22. Reichhelm wrote that the 70-transport expedition and six to eight of Admiral Porter's gunboats weighed anchor at 3 P.M. "A grand sight," he wrote, "inspiring us with confidence of success." There also existed the fear, he added, that the Rebels would "skedaddle" at the expedition's approach on the Yazoo, defaulting on a fight. The Union soldiers' victories at Paducah, Forts Henry and Donelson, Iuka, and Corinth had raised their confidence.

December 23. The expedition rendezvoused the previous night at Fryar's Point. At dawn the expedition of 35,000 "hardy and daring" soldiers started down the Mississippi River.

The expedition moved under the watchful eyes of Confederate spies along the river bank and came under cannon and musket fire by guerrilla parties lying in ambush on the river's shore at narrow bends.

Sergeant Major Reichhelm's diary relates that a brigade was put ashore to pursue the guerrillas and "there took their revenge burning houses, plantations, and villages." The river was lined with burning places, and he described the color of the flames as "beautiful but horrible." He added in his record that it was "deplorable, disgusting, wanton not a military necessity, but a vengeance to sack and burn."

December 24. The transport *Decotah* anchored while soldiers went ashore to collect and bring aboard pieces of rail fence for the boat's fuel.

Reichhelm wrote a question in his diary: "Do you want to know how I spent Christmas eve?" He answered it by recording, "the troops sang, the officers gave speeches, tobacco was passed around to the troops, and the officers drank whisky punch in their cabins." After he returned to his sleeping place, he mused on the rough life of a soldier.

December 25–27. At 3:00 A.M. Christmas Day the Yazoo flotilla reached Milliken's Bend. There Reichhelm recorded an example of the swiftness of military punishment—"the execution by firing squad of two marauders-house burners after conviction by a drum-head court martial." At noon the expedition departed for the Yazoo River.

The expedition started up the Yazoo River on December 26. At 4 P.M. the 3rd Missouri Infantry debarked and marched to a cornfield. The soldiers spent the night in a "cold piercing rain, soaken wet, blue with frost."

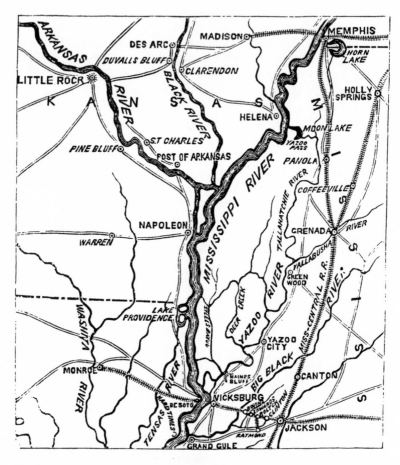

Operations on the Yazoo and Arkansas Rivers (*Harper's Pictorial History*).

The next day the soldiers reboarded their transports and moved four miles up the Yazoo to Walnut Hills and debarked. Sherman's soldiers became entangled in dense cockleberry hedgerows on the river's bank. A forward march ceased until the soldiers chopped out narrow paths to reach the causeways of dry land, and the delay in the attack dismayed the stymied soldiers. Captain Patterson's company set about supervising the pioneer soldiers in the construction of defensive earthworks, while Sherman's soldiers spent a cold night on wet, swampy ground.

December 28. In the first rays of the rising sun, Yankee soldiers looked to the crest of a high bluff where the Rebels were waiting behind prepared breastworks, daring Sherman's attackers to start the battle.

General Morgan, commander of the Third Division, ordered Captain Patterson to build a bridge over Chickasaw Bayou with the expedition's eight-pontoon bridge train. Assisted by an infantry detail, Patterson's engineer soldiers commenced floating the wooden pontoons, each one 18 feet long, 6 feet wide, and weighing 1,200 pounds, into position to form the bridge. Enemy troops immediately opened fire on the soldiers, splintering and rupturing the pontoons; water filled and sank two of them. Patterson's working party, in the face of severe musketry and shell fire, determinedly succeeded in positioning the other pontoons with flooring, but the bridge fell short of reaching the far shore. Patterson decided to abandon the task, the only time in the company's war service it would fail to build a bridge in battle.

Reichhelm wrote in his diary that his brigade, under the command of Brigadier General Charles E. Hovey, attacked in the face of withering musketry fire. After a brutal battle, the Yankees were repulsed. Dead and wounded soldiers were left lying in cornfields and furrows because the Rebels posted pickets to prevent Sherman's soldiers from recovering their dead and wounded comrades. The Rebels were set on shelling Sherman's soldiers back to their boats.

At night, Reichhelm wrote, his soldiers laid on the ground behind trees and hedgerows covered only with thin shirts and pants in a cold, howling storm. The cries of pain and anguish of their fallen comrades lying out in front of them on the battlefield only intensified their discomfort.

December 29. Sherman's artillerymen laid down a furious artillery barrage in preparation for a renewal of the attack. The Confederates countered with their own barrage of grape canister from a masked battery.

December 30. Convinced the enemy held an impregnable position, Sherman withdrew his soldiers. Rain and mud turned the day into a dreary one. Under a flag of truce, Sherman collected his wounded and buried his dead soldiers, who had for three days and two nights laid on the battlefield. His defeat demonstrated the futility of assaulting an enemy posted in strongly prepared earthworks and field fortifications.

CHAPTER 2

January 1863

Third and Fourth
Attempts to Take
the Mountain

January 1, 1863. The Yazoo River assault came to an end on the first day of 1863, when Sherman ordered his soldiers to give up on this second attempt to take Vicksburg. Sherman's casualties on the Yazoo were 119 soldiers killed, 982 wounded, and 756 missing.

January 2. Sherman's fleeing soldiers encountered Confederate fire from along the river bank until the flotilla left the mouth of the Yazoo River. Upon reaching the Mississippi, the expedition proceeded to Young's Point.

Sergeant Major Reichhelm wrote in his diary about his dissatisfaction with the commander of the expedition (name unwritten, but it seems obvious he was referring to General Sherman), who had led 35,000 brave men up to the batteries, forts, and rifle pits of Vicksburg surrounded by nearly impassable swamps. It was gross and unexplainable mismanagement of his own battle plans. Reichhelm concluded an army could not show more bravery than that shown at Chickasaw Bayou, a fortress that defied the "brilliant dash or sudden attack."

Although Reichhelm wrote about his fellow soldiers' bravery, he did not offer any information about how they reacted after suffering a whipping from the Rebels. In contrast, his earlier entries had noted the soldiers' fear that the Rebels would "skedaddle," preventing the Yankees from administering them a whipping.

Corporal John Griffith Jones, Company G, 23rd Wisconsin Volunteer Infantry Regiment, wrote in a letter addressed to his parents:

> On Yazoo river. I am well and happy. Thankful to be among living for among living there is hope. Have been on the boat four days. We left Memphis Sunday, December 21. After sailing three days we were ordered to go ashore and burn a railroad bridge that connected Vicksburg with Texas. A 55-mile march—there and back—left boat 9:00 A.M., reached bridge 9:00 P.M. Slept in cotton warehouse, soft bed, never slept better than I did on a bale of cotton. In morning ordered to take our beds to the bridge. General Burbrige [sic] [Brigadier General Stephen A. Burbridge, First Brigade, First Division] put torch to bridge. A large one. Set fire to everything that would burn. Ate as much as I could of honey and all manner of items. Cavalry put a town on fire same night. We put thousands of dollars worth of cotton on fire. Took more than 500 mules on our one day trip to Louisiana. Seven regiments in force.

Jones wrote home about the expedition to Dallas Station and Delhi, Louisiana. Essentially he told what he observed or heard by word of mouth, but the official record clarifies and adds specifics to the event.

General Burbridge, who commanded the expedition, wrote in his official report that he received orders from Brigadier General A. J. Smith, commanding general, First Division, on December 24 to conduct an expedition to destroy the Vicksburg-Shreveport-Texas Railroad. The railroad transported many agricultural products from Louisiana to Vicksburg, and it became Union strategy to cut off such resources.

Burbridge's soldiers were on transports underway with the Yazoo River expedition, but their course was altered to disembark them on December 25 for the expedition into Louisiana. The soldiers landed at Omega, the upper part of Milliken's Bend, at 9 A.M. At the outset Burbridge recorded he faced difficulty because of the lack of reliable maps. During the day's march inland, the expedition "thoroughly and effectually destroyed the telegraph line along the railroad."

Burbridge reported that at sundown after an approximately

Destroying Railroad Tracks and Burning Station (*Harper's Pictorial History*).

35-mile and 12-hour march, his expedition reached Dallas Station, where the main force, the infantry regiments, was concentrated. To carry out orders to destroy the railroad, Burbridge immediately ordered Lieutenant M. Whildin, with a detachment of the 6th Missouri Cavalry, to proceed 12 miles farther west on the railroad to Delhi. There his cavalrymen burned the depot and supplies stored therein and also burned a quarter of a million yards of newly manufactured muslin.

A cavalry detachment under Captain D.W.C. Shockley received orders to proceed to Quebec, a short distance beyond Delhi. There the cavalrymen destroyed the railroad for a half mile and burned the bridge over the Tallulah River and 100 yards of trestle. Encountering the enemy after his destructive work, Shockley believed it prudent to return to Dallas Station.

On the morning of December 26, the main force encountered 400 Confederate cavalrymen and four pieces of artillery on its left flank. Captain Ambrose A. Blunt, 17th Ohio Battery, dispersed them. The main force burned the bridge over the Tensas River, destroyed trestle work, and burned the depot and a large quantity of cotton, corn, and forage.

Its work done, the expedition marched back to the transports on the Mississippi, arriving at 10 P.M. Burbridge reported his soldiers were in the presence of the enemy for 36 hours and his infantrymen had marched to-and-fro 75 miles, but the cavalry had "dashed" 30 miles farther. He reported the accomplishments of the mission to be the capture of large numbers of horses and 101 mules (Jones reported 500) and the destruction of the telegraph line and so much of the Vicksburg-Shreveport-Texas Railroad as to place it beyond repair for months. The saw mills on the march route, he added, also were burned to hamper the railroad's repair.

While Burbridge's report omitted the dramatic anecdotes found in Jones' letter, he mentioned that on the expedition his soldiers and horses were exhausted from having pursued the enemy's cavalry on the expedition's flanks, but he noted that they had not incurred any casualties. It was a strenuous forced march, but Civil War soldiers were hardy marchers. To march 70 miles in 24 hours, roughly three miles an hour, could be termed quite a feat considering the climate, the soldiers' physical condition, their unfamiliarity with the terrain, the presence of the enemy, their need to stop for rest and food, and the wear and tear on their uniforms and footwear.

Confederate officials in the area, alarmed at the Union's unhindered penetration for a distance of 35-miles to Dallas Station and its cavalry's penetration 10 miles farther to Delhi, declared their enemy had disgraced them through outrages against their resources, bridges, and depots.

Corporal Jones' letter continued: "Reboarded boats, 25 miles to Yazoo river, in 10 miles landed and slept. In morning face to face with enemy. We the reserve on the right, fought two days. Many killed and wounded. Terrible to face. Five days and nights lying in woods on our arms. Retreated to boat January 1. They made the forts on top of high mountains, and had cut trees down across one another. It was a terrible place for the infantry to tackle. Health good."

On their return trip down the Yazoo River, Porter and Sherman discussed the advisability of a redeeming joint operation on the Arkansas River to attack Arkansas Post.[1] Concurrent with Sherman and Porter's Yazoo operation, Banks and Farragut commenced moving up the Mississippi River, but were blocked by the Confederate guns at Port Hudson.

January 3. At Young's Point Sergeant Major Reichhelm was ordered to round up a detail from the 3rd Missouri Regiment to bring aboard the transport 60 cords of wood. He reported it was a tough detail to complete in the rain and hail with a "dissatisfied crowd of soldiers" who grumbled and threatened to mutiny, but under his cajoling they completed the task.

January 4. When the transports arrived at Young's Point, McClernand met Sherman and showed him his orders from the president stating that he was to be in command of the river expedition. Sherman, outranked and determined to avoid conflict, acquiesced and resumed a subordinate command position.[2]

In a letter to his force, Sherman thanked the officers and enlisted men for their zeal, alacrity, and courage, though the expedition had failed to accomplish its purpose. He wrote that his army was but part of a combined movement in which others were to assist, but because of unforeseen contingencies the "others" must have been delayed. "We have attacked the defenses of Vicksburg," he added, "and pushed the attack as far as prudence would justify. Having found it too strong for our single column, we were drawn off in good order, and good spirits ready for any new move. A new commander is here to lead you. Chosen by the president. I know all officers and soldiers will give him same hearty support and cheerful obedience they have hitherto given me. There are honors in reserve and work for all to do."[3]

McClernand, after hearing of the Sherman and Porter plan to deploy 50 miles up the Arkansas River to Arkansas Post to attack the Confederate's Fort Hindman, gave his approval.[4] There is no record of any notice to Halleck or Grant of the expedition, or approval from them.

Lieutenant Allen Woods Miller, Company C, 36th Iowa Volunteer Infantry, posted at Helena, Arkansas, wrote in his diary, on Sunday, January 4, "No Sabbath in army except in name. Chaplain preached. How little attention—appreciation. Man's tendency unrestrained by purifying influence of woman downward."

January 5. Sergeant Major Reichhelm reported that the 3rd Missouri Infantry accompanied McClernand and Sherman up the Arkansas River, but wrote, "Half the regiment was on sick list, half unwell, and the mudsills left behind."

January 10. Grant completed the deployment of his army back to Memphis and received a telegram from Halleck that Sherman had met with defeat on the Yazoo River.

Lieutenant Miller, at Helena, wrote in his diary, "Had a peep at horrors of war—shudder. *City of Memphis* transport arrived with

750 sick and wounded from Vicksburg [Yazoo expedition]. Some have lain ten days without attention."

January 11. When McClernand and Sherman attacked Fort Hindman, 5,000 Confederate soldiers surrendered. The successful battle cleared the flank of the force to operate at Vicksburg and assured an enemy force would not march overland from the north to deploy in the Union army's rear. It also destroyed the safe haven of the Rebels' river pirates. The losses in the battle were 129 soldiers killed, 831 wounded, and 17 missing.

January 12. The *New York Times* editorialized that there was a disposition to be satisfied with the Western war in view of some gratifying successes, but the newspaper confessed it regarded the results against Vicksburg on the Yazoo River "with strong disfavor." In other remarks the editorial stated, "The country grievously disappointed in that quarter. We promised a speedy success and we had a right to expect it. The Sherman campaign a failure." The program was grand, the editorial continued, "but the performance has been lamentably puny."

January 14. Halleck wired Grant that he was authorized to command the operations against Vicksburg by the water route, and also, if he chose, to relieve McClernand from command. With his command authority clarified, Grant wired orders to McClernand to return his force from the Arkansas River expedition back to Milliken's Bend. The return of McClernand's and Sherman's soldiers, Grant declared, "stopped the wild goose chase of Union forces," and this statement intimated that his field commanders would stay close to the chosen battle target.[5]

January 17. Grant, accompanied by Colonel Wilson, journeyed down to Milliken's Bend to meet with McClernand, Sherman, and Porter and to settle the issue of command. He forthrightly faced a number of conflicting issues. Sherman and Porter had sent him a telegram asking him to supersede McClernand in command. Grant recognized there existed distrust of McClernand because he was a politically appointed general officer who had engaged in political maneuvering. There were also political jealousies in the officer corps between regulars and volunteers. Grant recognized that McClernand possessed military capabilities. He also recognized the need to temper his decision on McClernand's assignment because of his political ties to the president and the importance of the continued support of the Illinois Democrats for Lincoln, which

McClernand could influence. Grant had the authority to relieve McClernand, but overlooked his insubordination for the moment and retained him as a subordinate commander.[6]

Third Attempt to Take the Mountain

Grant made it clear to McClernand that he occupied the position of supreme commander. He also issued orders to McClernand to start work on the third attempt to take Vicksburg—the reopening of General Williams' canal where the Mississippi River impinged on the shore, "the swampy toe, and debouched below the bluffs on the opposite side of the river." This would permit Grant to move the army by boat below Vicksburg. He also ordered Sherman to provide details from his divisions to work on the canal. Sherman later reported that his two divisions alternately furnished a work detail of 500 men a day for what he termed "fruitless hardwork."[7] Grant, with the lines of communication settled, returned to Memphis.

Colonel Wilson recorded that he and Grant became more acquainted on this trip. Grant, he said, expressed to him his inclination to concentrate his army down river, as Wilson had recommended. He hoped that with the help his staff officers could give him, they could find a practicable line of operations.[8] Grant acknowledged what Wilson had already said to him and stated he was open to further recommendations. Wilson eagerly set about the task of finding the line of operations.

The president sent a message to McClernand, "For my sake and for Country's sake, you give your whole attention to the better work."

January 18. In accordance with War Department orders, Grant reorganized the Army of the Tennessee. He placed the 13th Corps under McClernand, the 15th Corps under Sherman, and the 17th Corps under McPherson, all to be posted at Milliken's Bend. The 16th Corps was placed under Major General Stephen A. Hurlbut and posted at Memphis and the outlying military posts to provide garrison duties and security and to protect Grant's lines of communication.

Corporal Jones, Company G, 23d Wisconsin, in a letter to his parents from Napoleon, Louisiana, wrote on his first night back from Fort Hindman that he heard rumors the regiment was to go to

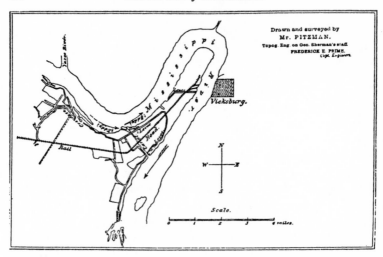

Layout of De Soto Peninsula Canal (*The War of the Rebellion, A Compilation of the Official Records of the Union and Confederate Armies*).

Vicksburg or Memphis. He also wrote that the regiment was sent after a band of 400 guerrillas six miles from the camp. "They fled," he told his parents, "before we arrived." He also wrote:

> We blew Fort Hindman sky high. I saw artist drawing picture of fort on top of a tree as we retreated to woods for rest [a staff member of Leslie's newspaper]. Our captain turned his back and ran from battle and second lieutenant took over, swearing as he did.
>
> There is much sickness in army, about half of men are sick. All the soldiers have suffered from dysentery. I escaped all afflictions.
>
> We think highly of our general [Brigadier General Stephen G. Burbridge]. He worked ten inch cannon himself. He is not afraid of work and he helps the boys to shovel and chop. He also showed great courage in battle.

January 20. Grant issued an order that all trading, trafficking, or landing of boats at points south of Memphis other than at military posts or points guarded by the navy, was positively prohibited. The order also provided that all officers violating the order would be arrested and placed in confinement. Also, all army officers passing up and down the river were to report violations; the navy was respectfully requested to cooperate in the enforcement of the order.

Sergeant Boyd, 15th Iowa Infantry, wrote in his diary as the steamer with his regiment aboard left Memphis, "Bands on each boat played and cannon on shore fired. Thousands of people on shore cheered and waved flags as fleet headed south. Great army which had never been defeated set its face for Western Gibraltar of Confederacy at Vicksburg. Everyone seemed hopeful."

January 21. Halleck sent a message to Grant stating he was not to rely on Banks and the naval flotilla in the lower Mississippi river for any support because Port Hudson stood as an obstacle to their movement.

January 22. Grant sent a message to McClernand: "I hope work of changing the channel of the Mississippi is begun, or preparations at least being made to begin. On the present rise it is barely possible that Yazoo Pass might be turned to good account in aiding our enterprise, particularly if Banks should be fortunate enough to get above Port Hudson."

The same day McClernand wrote to Grant from Young's Point:

> I arrived here safely at 2:00 P.M. with all my transports and command. Before nightfall I reconnoitered the country within three fourths of a mile of the canal and by nine o'clock this morning quite to and beyond it. The water of the Mississippi which is rising rapidly is in the upper end of the canal and must run through in a few hours if the rise continues. Further reconnaissances have been made today along the river bank some two miles below the canal. The line of the canal is now occupied by forces deemed sufficient to hold it. It is believed that by tomorrow night all my forces will have gained positions at the same time defensible and commanding.
>
> A Rebel force of 3,000 is said to be encamped at Delhi on the Vicksburg and Shreveport Railroad, some 40 miles from this place. The report is doubtless well founded. Another Rebel force estimated at 6,000 is said to be encamped on the Mississippi, some 80 miles below Vicksburg.
>
> Prisoners report enemy concentrating large force at Vicksburg, and he is determined to make a desperate stand there. I will immediately commence enlarging the present or cutting a new canal for the purpose of diverting the channel of the river as circumstances transpiring within a few hours may suggest. Additional implements however will be required to enable me to work efficiently in diverting the channel of the stream.

January 24. Lieutenant Miller wrote in his diary: "Orders to leave down river. Hearts will be made desolate there."

Corporal Jones, 23d Wisconsin, wrote to his parents:

> The question is settled. We are within eight miles of Vicksburg on *Ohio Belle*, have been for six weeks.
>
> I should think we have enough troops to capture any place necessary. Most likely we'll make a sweeping attack on Vicksburg one of these days. They are busily preparing for the move and it should be one of importance.
>
> Sick in regiment—deaths occurred. Diarrhea troubles soldiers greatly. Not me so far.
>
> We drew two rations of whisky last week.

Sergeant Boyd, 15th Iowa Infantry, wrote in his diary: "Arrived at Milliken's Bend. Weather wet and ground muddy. The flat space between river and levee is knee deep in black mud; levee 10 feet high and 20 feet wide at base, and top of it all the dry ground we can find. Walked down river two miles, saw many hospitals along levee and there are thousands of sick men here. Levee full of newly made graves [death from dysentery, fevers, smallpox]. Hard place for sick men here."

Boyd then wrote this prophetic statement in his diary: "Must have grit here or you die."

The 95th Illinois Volunteer Infantry Regiment reported the regiment's arrival at a campsite 15 miles above Milliken's Bend, where the men were "put to work digging a canal."

Frank Leslie's Independent Newspaper published a news item that same day: "Sherman withdrew from Yazoo attributing defeat to non-arrival of reinforcements from Grant and the absence of cooperative forces from Banks."

January 25. Halleck sent a message to Grant; "Give your attention to the work on the canal; President deems it important."[9]

January 26. Lieutenant Miller, Company C, 36th Iowa, wrote in his diary without mentioning the source of his information, "Message Sherman to Gorman [Brigadier General Willis A. Gorman, Twelfth Division], for God's sake send no more troops here. I can't find a place to land them on account of high water. Water's still rising."

January 27. Grant sent a message to Halleck: "Water is in old canal. The water is rising rapidly. Our Parrott guns will command the river soon. Banks is fortifying Baton Rouge."

Sergeant Boyd, 15th Iowa, wrote in his diary: "Men detailed to work on canal. They grumble it will be a failure. No fun working on canal knee deep in mud and water. I find them ugly, insubordinate, with little sense for discipline. I do not believe our commander knows what we are here for. Keep them employed until they can think up something. Rumor work on canal to be stopped."

January 29. Grant returned to Young's Point to assume personal command in the field and to commence the campaign. After a hasty observation of his milieu, he faced the truth: he was in a difficult position in swamps and mudholes and confronted with what he recorded as "terrible conditions." At the same time Confederate soldiers along the bank of the Rappahannock River in Virginia were jeering [Major General Ambrose E.] Burnside's cruel mud march with banners declaring, "Burnside stuck in the mud." Grant escaped the jeers of the Confederates, but his soldiers too were "stuck in the mud." Confederate spies were aware of the enemy's condition and were watching to see how Grant extricated his mud-bound soldiers.

Grant was tempted to return to Memphis, set up base, and move along the railroad, but a contrary voice told him, "that course a defeat; go forward to a victory." There were many critics waiting to pounce upon him at the occurrence of a turnabout defeat. He determinedly set his will to go forward. His first question was how to obtain the high ground. He answered that question by conducting what he termed experiments to find the proper answers. The answers would consume the time of his soldiers and divert the attention of the enemy. He admitted he had doubts about the success of his experiments, but he was alert and ready to take advantage of them if they did succeed.[10]

He discovered that the first imperative of the army was to construct a route for a return trip to dry terrain on the east side of the river. He also had to establish secure lines of communication and a supply base to store and distribute the immense amount of supplies and foodstuffs that would be required.

On a map it appeared the Army of the Tennessee's campground was approximately 20 miles northwest of Vicksburg. However, the long circuitous route that the soldiers would have to march to a ferry point for crossing the river measured approximately five times that distance.

The first challenge Grant's soldiers faced was the indomitable weather and the environment of bayous, swamps, and mud fashioned by the tricky Mississippi River. As the river flowed along its course, it continuously cut new channels and abandoned old ones, making it difficult to keep maps current.

Grant fretted as he set out on his third endeavor to take Vicksburg. Based on his observations of the terrain his army occupied, he recognized the task would take time and labor to accomplish. To move his army, he would need extra support from his engineer and pioneer officers and his soldiers. It quickly became apparent to Grant and his unit commanders that the movement of the army on roads and bridges would require more engineer and pioneer effort, skill, and ingenuity than had any of their previous battles. With the prospect of the huge amount of engineering work that would be needed to build all the bridges and roads to move the army, the army's officers and soldiers realized that the campaign's success would depend on the engineers' performances. Every soldier would also become an engineer-pioneer soldier with an ax, pick, and shovel.

There were only two engineer units in Grant's army: the 1st Missouri Volunteer Engineers Regiment and Captain Patterson's Kentucky Company of Mechanics and Engineers. These two understrength units would generally oversee the tasks and supervise the additional manual labor of each pioneer company in the infantry divisions, the infantrymen, and the contrabands.

The army's campsites on the west side of the river were on sparse dry ground on plantations amidst water and swampland, and the few roads in place were submerged and muddied. Rains during the winter of 1863 had raised the river to an unusually high level, which in turn raised the water level in the bayous and swamps, and the turbid and turgid water overflowed onto adjacent ground. Because of insufficient pieces of dry ground, the soldiers' camps were spread out for a distance of 60 miles along the banks of the river and bayous. More soldiers labored to keep the water out of the camps than labored on the canals and roads. The mounds of dirt forming the levees became the burial grounds for the daily ritual of burying the dead. At times high water overflowing the levees washed away the dirt, exposing the coffins or corpses wrapped in blankets.

Grant ordered his chief staff engineer, Captain Frederick E. Prime, Corps of Engineers, to take charge of the third attempt to open a route to Vicksburg. McClernand's soldiers ongoing work on the canal on De Soto peninsula was to provide a means for transports and gunboats to pass into the Mississippi River below Vicksburg. He would then land his soldiers on the east bank of the river on Pemberton's left flank.

Grant kept himself busy on other ways and directions to find high ground or waterways below Vicksburg. Based on his knowledge that Colonel Bissell's 1st Missouri Engineer Regiment had dug a canal in April 1862 to bypass Confederate-held Island Number 10 in the Mississippi River, he formed a plan to turn to canals. He ordered Captain Prime and Colonel G. G. Pride, a volunteer officer on his staff, to survey for similar canals on the bayous above or below Vicksburg. The two engineer officers reported to Grant that there were practicable canal routes. Above Vicksburg, Lake Providence, which was formed when the Mississippi changed its course in earlier times, could be joined to the Mississippi by Bayou Baxter and Bayou Macon. A route could be cut from the Mississippi through Lake Providence, into the Tensas, Black, and Red rivers to again join the Mississippi River 50 miles above Port Hudson. The Red River served as a supply route for Vicksburg from the resources of the West. Access to the Red River would also enable Grant to transport troops to Port Hudson to cooperate with Banks.

At Grant's camp, a *New York Times* correspondent wrote: "The opaline tints of dawn had barely made things visible when I arose from a slumber broken of dreams of contests, forlorn hopes, and the like, and glass in hand climbed to the hurricane deck to get a view of the points upon which the eyes of the nation are now centered. A soft blue smoke like that of an Indian summer was settled over the country through which the tall steeples and entangled bluffs of Vicksburg were plainly visible."

Fourth Attempt to Take the Mountain

January 30. Grant ordered McPherson to Lake Providence to initiate the fourth attempt to take Vicksburg. McPherson was to cut the levee there and open a channel for navigation to the Mississippi through Macon and Baxter bayous, then west through the Red River and on to Port Hudson and the Tensas and Washita rivers. To construct the 400-mile route would be a task of great magnitude,

Negroes at Work on De Soto Peninsula Canal (*Harper's Pictorial History*).

involving the cutting of trees under water, but McPherson, a former Corps of Engineers officer, had the professional capability to manage the project.

In a letter to Grant the same day, McClernand again raised the question of his being limited to the command of the 13th Corps. It

The Lake Providence Route (*Harper's Pictorial History*).

conflicted, he wrote, with the president's and the secretary of war's orders of October 21, 1862, which stated he was to organize the Vicksburg expedition.[11]

Captain Prime reported to General Grant that construction of a canal to correspond with the course of the current had been started. He added that he expected to dam the canal to obtain the approximate difference of the level between the water at the entrance and exit of the canal. "At present," he reported, "it is variously estimated from 28 inches to 3 feet. The velocity, as roughly measured today by using a floating body, was 422 feet in two minutes. Should circumstances require the expedition to remain here for some length of time, and the river continues to rise, there will be much trouble from the backwater in the swamps coming from the crevasses in the levee."

Corporal Jones, Company G, 23d Wisconsin, in a letter to his parents, wrote as Union troops approached Vicksburg:

> We drew 89 cents for 4 days rations due us after Fort Hindman. We have been in tents since the 24th; enough of riding boats. See Vicksburg from our tent, 5 miles away. See fortifications. Don't know when we'll attack. Gunboats will have to do most of the work. They are working on canal. We stand picket duty instead of working on canal. Burbrige [General Burbridge] preferred this. We stand picket duty once every 5 days, the main thing is to be out of old canal. 3–4 men in company died. 10 of us are alive and well. I had dysentery for 2 days—now well. My first sickness in army. Most of our sick are in Memphis hospital. Rumor we will receive our pay. Our camping ground is about 10 miles long and we are very near its southern end—and nearer Vicksburg.

January 31. Grant hastily replied to McClernand: "I take direct command of the Vicksburg expedition. You are limited to the 13th Corps."[12] Grant also sent a message to Halleck that he was pushing to gain passage to Vicksburg. "Prospects," he stated, "are not flattering at Williams' canal, where the work is diligently being pushed forward with the labor of 4,000 soldiers, but I am exploring other routes."

At his division camp at Young's Point, General Peter J. Osterhaus, commanding general, 9th Division, 13th Corps, published a memorandum to his division: "Your general has observed that mounted men frequently try the mettle of their horses by indulging in racing near our camps. Guards will stop any persons who shall amuse themselves as described above and arrest those who fail to obey sentinels."

CHAPTER 3

February 1863

Fifth Attempt to
Take the Mountain

February 1, 1863. Grant received a response from McClernand concerning his assignment to the 13th Corps: "I acquiesce to avoid conflict."[1]

Grant decided on his action for the fifth attempt to take the Vicksburg Mountain. He ordered Colonel Wilson to conduct a reconnaissance to determine if a boat passage existed through Moon Lake and Yazoo Pass, thence east through the Coldwater River to the Tallahatchee River, which joined the Yalobusha River about 250 miles below Moon Lake and formed the Yazoo River. If a passage could be found, this long, circuitous route would be used to outflank Haynes' Bluff, which commanded the mouth of the Yazoo River, and to land Grant's soldiers on the enemy's right flank.

The Yazoo Pass had been sealed off, forgotten, and unnavigable for a number of years. It had deteriorated into a stagnant, dreary, and wild place overgrown with snags and trees.

Sherman remained at Young's Point. There he laid off a due proportion of the dry ground of the levee for each division of his corps to encamp and assigned some units to quarters on the steamboats anchored at the levee. He established his headquarters in Mrs. Groves' house, "which had water all around it, and it could only be reached by a plank walk built on posts from the levee to the porch."

Prime reported to Grant on the De Soto peninsula canal project. The canal was closed in the afternoon by a dam of corn sacks filled with earth, resting against a wooden framework without any

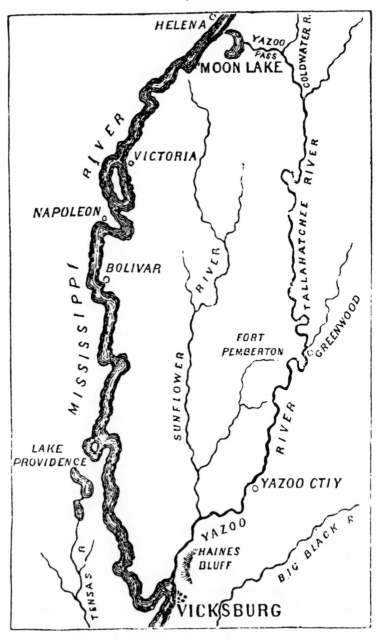

The Yazoo Pass Route (*Harper's Pictorial History*).

difficulty. Leveling showed the difference of the water at the two ends of the canal to be 2.62 feet. The river, he further reported, continued to rise.

The day being Sunday, generally a day of limited duties, General Osterhaus, commanding general, Ninth Division, ordered the field officer of the day to assemble the grand guards and reserves of three brigades near his division headquarters for inspection and parade at precisely noon. "The General," Osterhaus stated, "expects to find the troops in the best trim possible." He also ordered the detail of band and field music and added, "will be happy to meet brigade and regimental commanders."

February 2. Colonel Wilson reported to General Grant that he had started the Yazoo Pass reconnaissance. Brigadier General Willis A. Gorman had provided him with 500 men, two days' rations, and tools, and the expedition had arrived at the Yazoo Pass on the east side of the Mississippi at noon. He reported he found a favorable state of affairs. At 2 P.M. the men started cutting the 18-foot high and 100-foot wide levee.

"Tomorrow," Wilson reported, "will have waterway of 20 yards. There is a difference of 8½ feet in the water outside and inside the levee. Levee a heavy one and will require heavy work to cut through. But due to water level the crevasse once opened will enlarge rapidly. Back country north and south of pass is partially overflowed by water from crevasse in levee. Boats to go through in three days. The undertaking promises fine results."[2]

Lieutenant Herman A. Ulffers, McPherson's assistant staff engineer, made a study of Lake Providence across to Bayou Tensas. He reported Bayous Baxter and Macon, which connected to the river, were too crooked, narrow, torturous and obstructed by overgrown banks and timber to be made available for navigation of the river. In a seeming contradiction of his observations, he reported the canal could be made ready in a week, with a depth of five feet to give passage to Bayou Tensas. "No doubt of practicability of passage to Red and Mississippi rivers." He also informed McPherson of a Confederate battery at Monroe on the Washita River to defend salt works. He met no obstacles from guerrillas and captured some horses from fleeing horsemen who took to the swamps.

Sergeant Onley Andrus, 95th Illinois Volunteer Infantry Regiment, wrote a letter to his wife telling her his regiment had been moved from Milliken's Bend to Lake Providence to dig the half-mile canal from the Mississippi River to the lake. He wrote the canal was a "fantastic plan of some man who had been balked by Van Dorn's little band of cavalry at Holly Springs." On the destruction of Holly Springs, he added, "If I could have one tenth of its value I could live in ease the rest of my life whether it was a short or long time."

February 3. Grant wired a message to Halleck in Washington: "A ram ran the blockade at Vicksburg, and rammed an enemy steamboat tied up there. This is an important success as it cuts off the enemy's communication with the west bank. Work on the canal progressing."

Colonel George W. Deitzler, 1st Kansas Volunteer Infantry Regiment, First Brigade, of Brigadier General John McArthur's Sixth Division, 17th Army Corps, sent a message to Grant's head-quarters on his reconnaissance of the area west of Lake Providence: "Sent 100 able-bodied Negroes, all I can secure; collect more tomorrow. Planters sent Negroes into country. Won't be able to send many hands to work on canal. Water in Lake Providence lower, eight feet lower than surface of river. In six days hope to cut levee to connect lake and river, and with a 5-foot channel in Bayou Macon will have clear coast to Red River.

"At Raven's Lake Rebels have salt works where several thousand Negroes employed to supply whole southwest; should be destroyed. I can gobble up horses, mules, and cattle."

Colonel Wilson reported to General Grant: "Yazoo Pass open. River 75–80 yards wide running through with greatest velocity. At 7:00 P.M. discharged mine in mouth of cut, water rushed in. At 11:00 P.M. opening increased to 40 yards wide and water pouring through like nothing else I ever saw except Niagara Falls." He reported that logs, trees, and a great mass of earth were torn away with the greatest of ease, and he called the work a perfect success. On account of the great rapidity of the water, he added, gunboat captains believed it would not be safe to take boats through for four to five days. Wilson expected it would take several days to fill up the countryside enough to slacken the current and level off the water.[3]

McClernand, on instructions from Grant, issued orders to his corps to organize a pioneer corps in each division for hasty bat-tlefield construction and destruction of terrain obstacles. He also ordered a detail of one lieutenant and fifty enlisted men with mechanical skills and fitness for engineer work to report without delay to Captain Patterson's Kentucky Company of Mechanics and

Engineers located at the cotton gin on Ballard's Plantation. He also ordered his corps personnel to put their camps "in best possible conditions, bury their offal, and use the sinks." He ordered officers and enlisted men to salute and to look upon the practice of hand saluting as a compliment among military persons.[4]

February 4. Grant perhaps noted the contradictions in the reports of Ulffers and Deitzler on the second and third. He visited McPherson at Lake Providence on the fourth to observe for himself the channel being cut into the lake to connect Bayou Baxter and Bayou Macon for transports to pass through the Tensas, Washita, and Red rivers. A route in that direction would enable his army to be transported south to cooperate with Banks at Port Hudson and thence to march to Vicksburg.

Grant recorded he found a lack of progress on the work of his fourth "experiment." The water failed to flow from the river into the lake. "Scarcely a chance," he concluded, "this ever becoming a practicable route to move troops through enemy country, a 470-mile trip the enemy could obstruct." The work though had another aspect. He believed the manual labor of his soldiers performing engineer-pioneer duties, even though arduous and executed in an adverse climate and environment, was better than idleness and personal decay, especially with more troops present than could be employed to advantage at their camp grounds.[5] He passed on his conclusion in a letter to Brigadier General Lorenzo Thomas, the adjutant general in Washington, stating he had "no confidence in the canal opposite Vicksburg on De Soto peninsula."

Grant also commented in his letter to Thomas about two other projects (his "experiments") underway: (1) to turn some of the waters of the Mississippi through the old Yazoo Pass into the Yazoo River above Fort Haynes' bluff to reach Union gunboats of the Yazoo fleet above Yazoo city; and (2) to turn the Mississippi River into Lake Providence to enable its waters to follow the Tensas and Red rivers below Vicksburg without approaching any bluff or ground easy for Confederate defense. "This is a magnificent scheme and if successful will be a grand achievement. A glance at the map will show it at least probable." One must wonder about Grant's remark when his earlier observation in the day concluded there was "scarcely" a chance the Lake Providence project would provide a practical route to reach the enemy.

Aside from canal digging, Grant told Thomas, "We are idle.

The war against us by newspapers has reached large proportions. I hope it proves profitable to them."[6]

In an editorial on Grant's "vast army" opposite Vicksburg on the Louisiana shore, the *New York Times* commented:

> We do not imagine Grant will remain inactive long before Vicksburg. The West is anxious and impatient for speedy opening of the river. The region where Grant's army is camped is horribly unhealthy. His troops are of the fighting kind. He acquired fame on a memorable occasion by proposing to the rebels to move immediately on their works. Thunders of artillery will echo along the Great Valley and children of the Father of Waters will fight with the usurpers for their inheritance. The battle will soon be fought and won.

Sergeant Boyd, 15th Iowa Volunteer Infantry, wrote, "Men on levee have a fearful time in mud and water." He mentioned their camp life had a compensation: at Holly Springs they "captured" a fine library and it was in use as a circulating library in the company. He indulged in a bit of verbal quibbling in his use of the term "captured" for "looted.'"

February 6. Grant wrote to Admiral Porter his ideas for the expedition through Yazoo Pass. He suggested it proceed through Yazoo Pass into Coldwater, follow that stream to the Tallahatchee which, with its junction with the Yalobusha, formed the Yazoo River, the great object of the expedition. "Be cautious," he stated, "of gun battery at Greenwood on Yazoo River." Grant also mentioned to Porter the condition of the roads for wagon trains at Milliken's Bend. "No drainage; rain above and water underneath and all around, and a sticky slimy clay, all militate against roads."[7]

Sergeant Boyd wrote in his diary: "Beautiful day clear and warm. At crevasse men getting water stopped by putting brush and sandbags in break. Vicksburg proud and defiant dares us to come over. If Jack Frost would operate we would cross to fix them."

Charles Calven Enslow, Company C, 77th Illinois Volunteer Infantry Regiment, from his camp near Vicksburg wrote a letter to his wife:

> I finished washing clothes. "Darn gray backs" slay more than Sampson did. We have more "gray backs" than money. Hot water rids us of them. [Although the term "gray back"

usually referred to Confederate soldiers, Enslow undoubtedly meant lice.]

River so high water troubling us. Lay here till Banks cooperates from below. Things look encouraging. Sick getting healthy.

Found ice this morning to bear me.

At canal trying to stop water by damming it. 560 contrabands working there about. I hope they increase it a thousand fold and save our boys.

We blocked south and east. Soon as gunboats break blockade we can cut off Rebels retreat and whip them easily. When we surround them they will skedaddle. If we can run transports through canal we can let Vicksburg "rip."

February 7. In a letter to Brigadier General Samuel R. Curtis, a friend in Saint Louis, Sherman wrote: "Our canal here does not amount to much. It is full of water but manifests no disposition to change the channel. It is a very small affair and we can hardly work a barge through it for stumps. Even if it succeeds Warrenton Bluff lies below, next Grand Gulf, next Rodney, and so &c."

Colonel Wilson reported to General Grant in the morning:

Gunboat *Forest Rose* entered the Pass with great ease. [Gunboat captains were correct in their estimate it would take five days to enter Pass.] A mile inside levee we reached Moon Lake, traveled five miles to point where Pass leaves it and proceeded to reconnaissance. Stream not large or straight as it is nearer river. Went in about three miles and found no obstructions. Met three men in a dugout who came from Tallahatchee river and they reported people at mouth of the Coldwater discovered what we had done at levee and a force of 30–40 Rebels with 100 Negroes had worked several days in felling timber across the stream at intervals between its junction with the Coldwater and a point nearly five miles from Moon Lake.[8]

Corporal Jones wrote to his parents:

Rumor we will be going up river, no idea where. 5–6 in company passed examination to be discharged. 25 fit for duty in camp. Company had 100 when we left Wisconsin—now number 64. There has been considerable destruction of human life in many ways.

Getting very good cigarettes this past week.

Part of regiment goes up river today on an expedition. I remain to guard tent. No news. Quiet. Heard heavy cannonading from Vicksburg at *Queen of West.*

February 8. Colonel Wilson reported to General Grant:

I went with Captain G. W. Brown's cutter and crew and descended to Yazoo Pass nearly six miles; captured two men members of a company of partisan cavalry. They told me Rebels there in small force cutting timber but left night before.

I saw at different points 40 trees that had been cut to fall in stream, but in no place did they obstruct channel to prevent passage of boats. Some places drift timber collected against trees so as to contract roadway. A few hours work would open it so as to make passage easy. Timber I saw cut into water either sunk out of sight or drifted against shore so as to hurt nothing. I do not think trees will interfere with our navigation.

Stream 100 feet wide but very deep. Timber overhangs in many places. Will be necessary to cut out considerable to prevent smoke stacks of steamers from being knocked down. Tedious operation; many places banks of streams under water, but with all difficulties no one has doubts of our being able to work through.

General Gorman sent Brigadier General Cadwallader C. Washburn down yesterday with 1,000 men, and 500 sent today. They have begun operations.

Information passed to General Gorman the Rebels aware of our movement, and making arrangements for our reception. Where and how unknown.

We won't surprise enemy unless we get through in three to four days. If gunboats arrive we will make it unless obstructions at other end of Pass more serious than we think.[9]

February 9. Prime reported on the De Soto peninsula canal:

The water continues to rise at the rate of 2½ inches per 24 hours for the past two days. A dam has been erected at each point where the canal crosses the levee. The water in the intermediate space will be let out into the swamps and low ground as soon as the camps south of the railroad and west of the canal have been entirely removed, hopefully tomorrow.

This will make it practicable to remove the stumps and trees now in the canal, and to widen and deepen the canal to the necessary dimensions.

Few soldiers are at present employed on account of shifting camps, building roads, etc., and the delays which have prevented the canal from being emptied. Contrabands, approximately 550, are now here and are employed on the new entrance of the canal. The work on the canal between the levees will most probably be assigned to the details furnished by the troops. With fair weather and strong working parties, there is a fair prospect of obtaining satisfactory results.

The *New York Times* correspondent reported from Vicksburg: "The situation not definite here. Only chaotic preparations that precede the carrying out of some gigantic operation similar to that we are about to undertake goes on. Grant arrived January 28 to assume command and begins a task, if succeeds, will rank him with first soldiers on the continent."

Sergeant Boyd, 15th Iowa Infantry, wrote in his diary: "Contrabands fly for their freedom to our army. We can do little for them. Men in our camp brutal to them. Proclamation [Lincoln's Proclamation of Emancipation] increased prejudice, enemies of army and government say, 'Negroes shall not be free.'"

February 10. Admiral David D. Porter ordered the Union *Queen of the West* to sail down the Mississippi River below Vicksburg to the mouth of the Red River.

Sergeant Boyd wrote in his diary: "Regiment moved to camp at Lake Providence. Going up levee saw contrabands digging great ditch or canal from Mississippi out through levee to turn water into lake to enter Tensas Bayou, which runs into Red river, to flank Vicksburg." He reported they camped a mile from the work site, adding, "All the way from camp to river is one vast white field with ungathered cotton."

February 12. General Grant reported to General Halleck: "Continuous rise in river has kept army busy to keep out water, and much retarded work on canal."

Colonel Wilson reported to General Grant:

> With three days constant work we have made over five miles having passed and removed considerable obstructions of fallen and drifted timber.

In front of us for a half mile many trees reach entirely across the stream. Some cottonwoods and sycamores are four feet through at butt and will weigh 35 tons. Difficult to remove, plus country near stream overflowed. Nowhere is there more than a mere strip of land next the bank, and that only a few inches out of water.

But even so no doubt of our ability to remove the obstructions and make the Pass navigable for large boats. Our greatest difficulty so far has been to obtain tackle strong enough to resist strain, expect new six inch cables tomorrow. Will be able to lift heaviest logs. Saw-in-two larger trees and take out smaller section. In time remove obstructions. Narrowness and rapidity of stream requires everything to be taken out that will not float off or sink.

While we open Pass one end Rebels close it at other.

Seven miles from Moon Lake by meandering of stream some distance from Coldwater. Will take seven to ten days possibly longer to complete our work.[10]

An entry in Sergeant Boyd's diary: "Terrible rain last night. Water in all tents. Men lay in three inches of water."

February 13. General Halleck replied to General Grant: "Can dredges be used in canal? Four are idle at Louisville."

Porter's gunboat *Indianola*, with two barges attached for protection, sailed past the Vicksburg batteries, avoiding damaging projectile hits by enemy guns.

Sergeant Brown, 4th Minnesota Infantry Regiment, recorded in his diary:

Method of transporting troops unique. Wagons and stores in hold. The horses and mules and artillery crowded on boiler or engine deck. Above animals was rigged a staging covered with loose boards which allowed for ventilation from below. Four companies crowded in that cramped place about four feet high. Aroma indescribable, and at night when all still and the silence could almost be felt the music of those mules was demonstrated and anything but soothing to one's nerves.

February 14. The *Queen of the West* captured the Confederate vessel *New Era #5* on the Red River, but in the aftermath a steam pipe on the *Queen* blew up, forcing the boat to go aground and to be abandoned.

Sergeant Brown recorded in his diary:

Across river and through a ditch cut from the river across the levee by our forces his transport moved. River high. Fall 8½ feet in levee through which water flowed with great swiftness so much so we could not keep steerage way on the boat. We then had to make right turn but before we could make it we were forced side on to the bank with a force that made things jingle doing no harm. We followed lane of trees on each side submerged to height of 15 feet. Swift current. Steamer at its mercy. Striking trees one side they sprung so blow broken, then trees like whips rebound to other side. Troops breathless. Pilot pale. After a mile we in Moon Lake. Quiet sailing 5 miles. Came to pass. Took a long breath. Found hole of pass but could not get in as too much cross current and wind. Tied up for night. Blackguarded another regiment about its colonel affecting to make his commands like West Pointers.

February 15. General Grant reported to Halleck: "Steamboats have gone to within six miles of Coldwater. Express no fear they will reach it and Yazoo."

Captain Prime reported to General Grant about work on the canal: "Four companies of Colonel Josiah W. Bissell's 1st Missouri Volunteer Engineer Regiment arrived from Memphis and will be employed extracting stumps in the present canal, also in proposed enlargement, and in clearing a channel of 200 feet in width through the lowest part of the swamps and low ground between the canal and crevasse at Johnson's Plantation."

Sergeant Boyd committed some thoughts to his diary: "Storm last night; ground deluged. Five months pay due. Men with families at home discouraged. Hundreds would desert if had that pay. Discouragement thick and heavy. Men high in power reckless of their duty.

"Poor policy to carry on war or poor way of executing a good policy. Barbarous struggle laying waste the land."

Boyd also wrote: "More rain, today foggy. I with a squad of 28 men to work on ditch, so wet we could not work. Marie Deming brought in 400 contraband, men to work on ditch. Women and children pick cotton. Large force working on canal. We are almost through levee when river will flood all the back country on Louisiana side. Some think we only work here to cover cotton thieves. Cotton speculators follow army like vultures."

Captain Henry G. Ankeny, Company H, 4th Iowa Infantry,

wrote to his wife: "At camp near Vicksburg raining constantly, ter-
rific thunder, camp overflowed. What we suffered will never be
known outside these precincts. Work on canal going on. Some of us
work every day. Long time before we can do much on Vicksburg.
Tone of press up north, it is played out. Country drifting, war a
farce, no end in view. Frauds north and south for political power,
enrich selves and friends. My health good. Great deal of sickness
prevailing in army. Some new regiments have 300 sick. Many die.
72 left in my company."

Captain Prime reported to General Grant: "The water in the
river has been nearly at the same level for a week. Work on the new
entrance of the canal progressing. It is being done by contrabands.
Between the levees but little work has been done as yet by the troops
on account of the bad weather for the past two days. The water in
the canal has been drawn off by a cut leading into the low ground;
it is now about seven feet below the level of the water in the river."

General Washburn wrote to the Commanding General,
District of East Arkansas, who was responsible for the service support of the Yazoo expedition: "The men I have here I wish to retain
till the job is done and I have promised them that a paymaster shall
remain at Helena until they can get back and I request that you will
see that it is so."[11]

February 17. Sergeant Brown recorded in his diary: "Made it
into Pass, ran ten miles from Pass to Coldwater. Smokestack taken
off to go under limbs of trees. Smoke blackened everyone. Men
struck by trees hurt. Lines fastened to trees to prevent current making a wreck of boat. Met other boats. Got off boat for three hours
at farmhouse, walked a mile."

February 18. Grant reported to Halleck: "Canal work is progressing as well as possible. Excessively bad weather and high water.
Most of the time the soldiers can be out has been used to keep water
out of the camps. Five working days would enable us to complete
the canal, 60 feet wide inside, a sufficient depth to admit any vessel
here. Will take ten days to get the five days work. Three more should
be allowed as work being done by soldiers, most of whom under
most favorable circumstances could not come up to the calculations
of engineer officers."[12]

In contrast to Grant's criticism of the amount of work the
soldiers were doing, another voice spoke for them. The United
States Sanitary Commission reported that the soldiers "were forced

to lead a life for several months in a condition exceedingly un-
favorable to the preservation of their health and vigor. In unsuccessful attempt to reach Vicksburg they suffered terrible hardships."[13]

Grant's report continued:

> McPherson's Corps at Lake Providence doing work there.
> They could not be of any service helping on the work here
> because there are already as many men who can be employed
> on it. Then McPherson would have to march his soldiers 5 to
> 6 miles above to find land above water to encamp on. I am us-
> ing a few hundred contrabands here to work, but have been
> compelled to prohibit any more coming in. Humanity dictates
> this policy.
>
> Planters have deserted their plantations taking able-bodied
> Negroes; leaving old and very young. Here there is not shelter
> or transportation for them.
>
> I have sent a division of troops from Helena to join Yazoo
> expedition under Colonel Wilson. If successful will destroy
> the railroad bridge at Grenada and capture transports in
> Yazoo.
>
> Health of this army not what represented in public jour-
> nals. If it is as good as previous calculations believe there is
> confidence in success. Greatest drawback to spirits of men has
> been great delay in paying them. Many have families at home
> who are suffering for want of amount due them and they are
> bound for their support."[14]

Pay was an important and sensitive subject, particularly for the
many soldiers who sent their pay home to their families. One can
sense the importance from reading the soldiers diaries, letters, and
official records. The theme runs through all the complaints; families
at home were suffering because soldiers were unable to send money
from their meager pay. There is no information in the records,
however, to support soldiers' allegations that pay was withheld to
deter them from deserting, although some soldiers stated it did deter
them. If they were going home, they wanted to take their pay so they
waited for it. If the army did have such a practice, the officers would
not commit it to writing. Some Confederates spread the rumor that
soldiers would desert as soon as they received their pay. The pay
problem also existed in the Army of the Potomac, the Army of the

Cumberland, and in the Department of the Southeast, where some soldiers went on strike to force action on their pay.

Sergeant Andrus wrote to his wife that the canal from the Mississippi River to Lake Providence was finished, but when the levee was cut the bayous did not widen or deepen. In a pensive and forlorn mood, he said, "The dream faded. The 95th kept there to watch water run out of river in canal, soldiers sickened and some died."

Sergeant Brown wrote, "Into Coldwater, 2:00 P.M. 18 miles in 5 days, 130 feet wide."

February 20. Captain Ankeny wrote to his wife: "Last week raining. Scurvy breaking out, 5 to 6 in our regiment. Smallpox appears to run. Roads muddy. Cannot set around. Only pleasure letters from you."

Sergeant Brown wrote in his diary: "175 miles from where we are to Fort Pemberton. We run 20 miles a day, lay up at night."

February 21. Rain continued to slow work on the canal. Captain Prime reported that there had been only two days of favorable weather in which to work since the sixteenth.

Captain William Kossak, assistant engineer officer, was dispatched to examine the Confederate batteries opposite the outlet of the canal. He reported that there were three, one in casemate, and that they nearly enfiladed the canal. One of the batteries had opened fire, and it appeared that each of the three batteries had but one gun.

Prime made some changes in assignments for the engineer units. Two companies of Colonel Bissell's Missouri Engineer Regiment were relieved from duty at the canal on the De Soto peninsula and transferred to McPherson's 17th Corps to work on Grant's Lake Providence "experiment."

Company D of Bissell's Engineer Regiment reported that the company was employed building pontoons (a term widely used for, and generally considered interchangeable with, the then-official term ponton) for a ponton bridge train from wood collected in the area during January and February. There is no record that Bissell's regiment brought with it a pontoon bridge train from Memphis. The pontoons they built at Milliken's Bend were evidently used for transporting soldiers, supplies, and equipment across the bayous, and for future river crossings. The Corps of Engineers' authority on floating bridges classified them as pontoon bridges.[15]

Company I, under the command of Lieutenant Christian Lochbiler, 35th Missouri Infantry, was assigned to pioneer duty at

Milliken's Bend. There were a number of soldiers in the company who were skilled in hand-tool occupations and crafts and were experienced with boats.[16] Captain Prime assigned Lieutenant Lochbiler's company to assist in building the canal's casemates, batteries, gabions, and fascines to enhance its defense. Prime later reported that they had prepared 30 gabions and 120 fascines.

February 21. Colonel Wilson reported that work was completed removing obstacles in the Yazoo Pass at 5 P.M. on February 21. Sergeant Brown recorded that the regiment had moved into the Tallahatchee River and found burning bales of cotton floating down the river to impede the boats.

A correspondent for *Frank Leslie's Independent Newspaper* wrote, "Everything shows the approach of a deadly struggle at Vicksburg which will soon be environed by our troops on land as well by our gunboats."

February 22. Captain Prime reported little or no work done on canal because of rain. Colonel Wilson reported to General Grant that the steamers *Henderson* and *Mattie Cook*, entered Coldwater with a regiment and traveled two miles to Cole's Plantation.

Captain William F. Patterson, who arrived that Sunday at Young's Point with his Kentucky Company of Mechanics and Engineers, wrote to his wife:

> My bowels not act human—diarrhea—take no medicine—regulated by diet but you get few things you relish. So can't stop right place.
>
> Have excellent cookery for company. Teaching boys to make first quality hop yeast bread. I bought hops from sutler for $3.50. Have cow and calf will have milk in a few days.
>
> Lost so many items and seen so many articles destroyed I have become indifferent.
>
> Tomorrow have to go out to find timber to build road.
>
> Now head of pioneer corps per orders of General McClernand on February 3. General [McClernand] manifests great deal of pleasure in my success at different things assigned to me.
>
> Pair of Louisiana singing birds in my tent. Wish I could send to you. Best singing bird I ever met. A handsome bird. Try to catch some young ones.
>
> I dreamed of you last night. I kissed you and how gentle and kind you were.
>
> We have had an awful rain here.

Private Charles Enslow wrote to his wife: "It is immortal February 22nd of George Washington. Guns firing salutes to honor him. The future will also hold Abraham Lincoln in sacred remembrance."

Captain Ankeny wrote to his wife: "Received your two letters of February 8th. No news. *Queen of West* lost."

February 23. Captain Prime again reported that little or no work was done on the canal because of rain. Colonel Wilson reported to General Grant that the Yazoo Pass was open for navigation for 10 or 12 more miles.

Sergeant Boyd recorded in his diary that General Grant issued an order against any more card playing and gambling. He also wrote that Lincoln called for arming 300,000 Negroes, which "stirred the boiling cauldron of treason." Boyd also noted, "Rain all night and still raining; mud here to river three feet deep."

Sergeant Allen Geer wrote in his diary that the 20th Illinois Infantry had arrived from Memphis and had camped on high ground near a fine plantation. He further wrote that there was a rumor the regiment would work on a detail to cut a canal from Lake Providence to the Mississippi River.

Sergeant Brown wrote that the regiment arrived two miles from the junction of the Tallahatchee and Yalobusha rivers after traveling 225 miles and was camped on Clark's Plantation.

February 24. Captain Prime reported to General Grant that because of favorable weather, work on the canal had been resumed.

Colonel Wilson reported to General Grant:

> I am confirmed in my opinion of practicability of route for military operations.
>
> In Yazoo Pass some difficulties will be met from limbs of overhanging trees not removed because of impossibility of cutting them down without letting whole tree fall in channel. If water falls 4–5 feet could be easily obviated by cutting and pulling inward the trees now partly in the way.
>
> Coldwater considerable stream after junction of the Pass, 120–150 feet in width inside of banks; now full and rising.
>
> Presently boats 180 feet in length and proportional beam and draught of water can be sent from Mississippi to Tallahatchee by this route in four days, less with good management. Period of use of water route depends on water level in Mississippi River.
>
> I call attention to difficulty encountered and arduous labor

performed by troops to accomplish. Because land overflowed 25–50 feet from stream communication impossible and work could only be done by small parties, no more than 500 men could be at work, frequently half that number. Obstructions at intervals all along Pass. The principal one a mile long composed of heaviest trees cut from both sides of stream so as to lie across and upon each other. Various plans tried to remove them all attended with breakage of cable and boat machinery. Finally, by cutting, sawing and pulling out upon the banks entire trees the way was opened.

Labor severe, exposure great, found it necessary to relieve troops several times by fresh regiments from Helena.[17]

A participant on the expedition described the journey through the Pass:

A more execrable place never known. Nothing on earth would compare with it. Realms of darkness and despair. Not one straight piece 200 feet long. Boats were to keep 300 yards apart, but there was not space in the Pass to do that. Nature put more obstructions there than the enemy could. Cypress and sycamore trees in abundance on banks. Cotton woods, covered with wild grapevines. Pass never 100 feet in width. Timber formed arch over it. Smokestacks toppled. Limbs jutted out from trees. Nature did not want Pass traversed. Pass 20 miles from Mississippi to Coldwater. Mississippi to east side of Moon Lake where Pass starts 8 miles. Moon Lake to Coldwater 12 miles, a 3½ days trip, 12 hours a day could not drift with current, would have dashed us into timber, torn boats apart. Small boats each side to pass out lines made fast to trees to check headway or ease around sharp bends. Facetiously called the "Stern Wheel Expedition" because only sternwheelers used advance by holding back. Could not save boats from damage. Could not check heading to save smokestacks. Iron cylinders crashed into cabin and light upper works. Huge limbs smashing and tearing along sides. Tearing off stanchions and bracing. Sometimes light bulkheads on upper works. Boats not damaged in machinery or hull. An exciting trip; a limb came down endwise and killed a man in sick bay.

The Confederates attacked the Union gunboat *Indianola* and, among other boats, the *Queen of the West*, which it salvaged and repaired. The *Indianola* surrendered.

Private Enslow wrote to his wife: "Learned of *Queen of West* ground on sand bar in Red river—Rebels took it. Fighting for principles of forefathers. Against peace proposals. I endure knowing some at home sympathize with us."

Sergeant Brown reported he was off the boat and camped in a field of dead trees. "Hard storm, trees and limbs falling. Skirmished with the Rebels and took two prisoners."

A correspondent from *Frank Leslie's Independent Newspaper* wrote: "Two brigades of McClernand's finishing canal commenced last year which when opened will throw Vicksburg back from the Mississippi."

February 25. Captain Allen Miller wrote in his diary: "Steamer lay in Moon Lake. Steamers have gone through the Pass. We try tomorrow. Rain. Beautiful silver lake. Men characteristically American—rush to destruction as to a feast."

February 28. Captain Ankeny wrote a letter to his wife: "I send this by Chaplain, 9th Iowa Infantry Regiment, who [is] sick of sins of army. I'm sick of loss of ram *Queen of West* and gunboat *Indianola*. Two of best in river navy. Mustered for pay today. I have six months due. Yet no money. Rain."

The correspondent for *Frank Leslie's Independent Newspaper* wrote: "At Vicksburg both parties preparing for the coming struggle which will most probably be a regular siege in the Sebastopol fashion [a prophetic declaration]. Canal some say a ruse, little promise of success." This was the first time that the idea of a ruse was put into writing.

The men of the 20th Ohio Volunteer Infantry Regiment, camped out on the wet ground of a cotton field at Milliken's Bend, used their ingenuity to make life comfortable. They found boards at nearby plantations for tent floors. A number of the more imaginative soldiers were able to find boards appropriate to build porches on the fronts of their tents.

A private in Company B, 8th Illinois Volunteer Infantry Regiment, Third Division, 17th Corps, wrote in his diary about a storm of wind and rain. "Our tent bent and reeled like a willow. The levee broke and water rushed in. The drums were beaten to spread the alarm. To escape the danger the soldiers ran to the top of the levee where they watched the wind blow their tents down and whip them to pieces."

There were some morale building factors at the Lake Providence campsite. The soldiers were able to bathe in the lake, although one regimental surgeon limited their stay in the water to 20 minutes. They were also able to fish, which provided something different on their menu. The soldiers hauled a small steamer from the river to the lake and put it into operation. The steamer became an excursion boat sailing around the lake, providing the soldiers with a relaxing diversion. At night a regimental band sailed around the lake on the steamer, offering musical entertainment. The soldiers also had to be alert for Confederate patrols in the area that were attacking unsuspecting parties of Union soldiers.

February weather recorded by diarists and letter writers:

1 rain, mud
3 cold
4 cold, rain, sleet
5 cold, high wind NW, snowflakes
6 warm, clear
11 warm
12 terrible rain
13 warm, clear
14 more rain
15 storm, deluge
16 rain
17 rain
18 rain ceased
19 sunny, windy, mud dried
20 clear
21 rain, drenched
22 clear, warm
23 beautiful
24 clear, warm
25 rain at night
26 rain, torrents, 5 inches, left surface like a lake, tents leaked
27 warm, cloudy
28 clear, warm

During the month of February, a number of diarists and letter writers recorded their concerns about sickness in their camps. The writers did not have access to official reports, but they observed the large number of ill soldiers in their ranks and received word-of-mouth information on the threat and extent of disease in the army. The soldiers had reason to be fearful. The Army of the Tennessee incurred 1,286 deaths from the five classes of diseases in one month, 909 deaths from Class 1 (zymotic-miasmatic) diseases. It also suffered 9 deaths per 1,000 soldiers, the highest rate of the five largest armies in the field. (See Table 1.)[18]

CHAPTER 4

March 1863

Sixth Attempt to Take the Mountain

Confederates Block Wilson's Yazoo Pass Expedition

March 1, 1863. General Halleck sent a message to General Grant announcing, "There is a major general vacancy in the Regular Army to be given to the first general in the field who wins an important and decisive victory."[1]

Halleck omitted any mention of the four contenders who were expected to achieve "important and decisive" victories in the spring campaigns: Major General Joseph Hooker, commander of the Army of the Potomac, was expected to defeat General Robert E. Lee on the Rappahannock River: Major General William S. Rosecrans and his Army of the Cumberland were to capture Chattanooga; Major General Nathaniel P. Banks and the Department of the Gulf were to capture Port Hudson on the Mississippi River and cooperate with Grant in the capture of Vicksburg; and the Army of the Tennessee under Grant's command was expected to capture Vicksburg, the symbol of the control of the Mississippi.

Captain Prime reported that the first day of March was a fine day at the canal on the De Soto peninsula; the wind blew from the northwest, and the mud was drying rapidly. Work outside of the main levees was at a standstill, however, because of the high water, and the river was still rising. The dams outside of the levees had been overflowing, and the pump had been unable to work. One steam

59

dredge was there and would go to work the next day. A thousand contrabands were also at the work site. The six-gun battery below the mouth of the canal was progressing favorably and would be ready for guns in about three days.

Corporal Jones, in a letter to his parents, wrote: "I have been about 200 miles up river chasing Rebels. We chased 300 for 13 days. Ate too much catfish. Fatter than I have ever been. Quite hot. Peach trees full bloom. Planters planting their gardens. Paymaster supposed to be on way here from Memphis."

March 2. President Lincoln sent General McClernand a congratulatory message for his January victory at Arkansas Post. "You add," the president declared, "laurels to our growing fame."[2] Mention was not made of the fact that neither Halleck nor Grant had authorized McClernand to conduct the battle.

Grant reported to General Halleck that the gunboats *Queen of the West* and *Webb*, both flying the Confederate flag, had attacked the Union gunboat *Indianola* 35 miles below Vicksburg. After a 45-minute engagement, the Confederates captured the *Indianola* and its crew; they had removed its crew and guns and then sank the gunboat. Another effort on the part of Porter to participate in the Vicksburg campaign came to nought.

General McClernand issued an order to the 16th Indiana Infantry and 90th Ohio Infantry regiments assigning each one a section of the canal to work on. Half of their available force was to work on the canal each day. A quarter of each regiment's force was to report for work at 7 A.M. and another quarter at 4 P.M. They were to work under the supervision of Lieutenant William P. McComas, 13th Corps staff engineer officer.

Allen Miller wrote dejectedly, "Little progress. O horrible how slowly the cause moves."

The *Frank Leslie's Independent Newspaper* artist reported by letter from the Yazoo expedition: "Rain, everything hidden by gloomy atmosphere. Heavy rainstorm left thick fog. Eyes rest on wet tent figures wrapped in oil cloth. Prospect dismal in extreme. Gunboats guarding entrance to Yazoo to prevent Confederates from sailing out."

March 3. Lieutenant Commander Watson Smith, commander of the Yazoo expedition naval force aboard the U.S.S. *Rattler* on the Coldwater, reported to Admiral Porter that he was advancing slowly. The stream, he noted, was not so much wider or clearer than the Yazoo Pass as to make much difference in either speed or the amount of damage inflicted on his vessels. In his report, Smith wrote:

> Our hull has suffered as much today as on any day yet, we can only advance with the current; faster than that brings us foul. Our speed is not more than ½ miles per hour, if that.
>
> Wheels and stacks have escaped through care; but with over 20 feet above water, and less than 3 in it, without steerageway, light winds play with us, bringing the sides and trees in rough contact. I imagine that the character of this navigation is different from what was expected. We will get through in fighting condition, but so much delayed that all the advantages of a surprise to the rebels will have been lost.[3]

Sergeant Boyd's diary entry reads: "Weather cool, windy and clear. Some men have wives and little ones at home who depend upon pittance of $13.00 a month from absent father to keep them from starvation and want while cornstalk colonel for his glory and name can thus grab from these little ones." He was referring to requirements that soldiers buy items of uniform out in the muddy camp so that they could be dressed up to pass in review.

The artist from *Frank Leslie's Independent Newspaper* wrote: "Day clear, saw whole countryside in long line of levees beyond which tents of our army dot the mud and terminate in southward by long line of bluffs on the sides of which Vicksburg lies in the sunshine. Smiling on us like the promised land."

March 5. Commander Smith's report from the *Rattler* was a bit more promising:

> The river is clearer, and we make better speed. If we reach the Tallahatchee this evening, which our advance may do, our total distance from Delta will be but 50 miles, not 6 miles per day. I am having an account of the number of navy rations in the expedition taken. No vessel has more than a month's supply at this date, and the *Chillicothe* but seven days, the *Lioness* thirteen, and the *Fulton* seven. The last reports one boiler badly burned. My first knowledge of the *Petrel, Lioness,* and *Fulton* being attached to the expedition was received after entering the Pass. They joined after reaching Coldwater too late for me to prepare them for the expedition,

which could only have been done by sending them to Memphis. We are better off than the army, however, and have a fair supply of coal. An organized part of army and navy collects beef for rations and cotton for defense. The people report rebels and batteries below. Gathered some cotton today; much that we find is so badly baled as to be dangerous. I hope to make better speed from this time through.

March 6. Grant sent Halleck a bold and optimistic statement (his first one with a specific time): "The canal is near completion. I will have Vicksburg this month or fail in the attempt!"[4]

In an unusual act, Grant prohibited his soldiers at Milliken's Bend from writing letters home. His stated purpose was to deny information to the enemy, which guerrilla forces obtained by intercepting the Union's mail. Grant knew, however, that his army was constantly being watched by Confederate army cavalrymen, who passed on their observations and the information they gathered to Confederate leaders. Thus Grant could not have harbored any illusion that whatever actions he took on the east or west side of the Mississippi River were carried out in secrecy. His prohibition had dire effects on the soldiers' families. Rumors circulated Grant cut off the mail because his soldiers were dying of disease, and these rumors prompted an inquiry by the army's surgeon in chief.[5]

Grant wrote to Surgeon General William A. Hammond that there was not a high rate of sickness, although among "the men who had to put up with straw for so long a time and then with camping on low ground and in most terrible weather ever experienced, there was for a time of necessity a great number of sick."[6]

Commander Smith aboard the U.S.S. *Rattler* reported that he had sailed 12 miles beyond the Coldwater into the Tallahatchee, stopped for the night, and waited for the other vessels to close up. He reported that intelligence collected at different places and from different people indicated that Yazoo City was being fortified, 3,000 Negroes were doing the labor, and a large army equipped with heavy guns was there for its defense. He included the information that the river was high and the current strong.

Alonzo Brown reported: "For two days there were bad storms, too much water to do anything, wet throughout our tents soaking everybody. We call camp Grand Lake."

March 7. Grant qualified the optimism of his previous day's report in a new message to Halleck:

> I telegraphed you on the 6th of near approach to completion of canal. Last night one of dams across upper end of canal gave way filling up where men were at work getting out stumps; thus setting back work for several days. I hope yet however to have this work completed as early as I could possibly take advantage of it if it was already done.
>
> The work of getting through Lake Providence and Bayou Macon, there is but little possibility of proving successful. Too late a start; water level recedes to a cypress swamp. Slow work to clear out timber.
>
> Yazoo Pass expedition is a much greater success. Admiral Porter sent in fleet of 10 naval vessels, 2 ironclads, (*Chillicothe* and *Baron De Kalb*), 2 rams, and 6 light draught gunboats, under command of Commander Smith, and I sent fleet of 14 transports with 6,000 soldiers. The gunboats were to approach as near Haynes' Bluff as possible and fire signal guns to warn the squadron in the mouth of the Yazoo of their presence. Last night Admiral Porter responded he heard a signal.
>
> I am now sending General McPherson with his army corps and enough other troops to make full 25,000 effective men to effect a lodgement on the high ground of the east bank of the Yazoo River. Once there with his entire force he will move down in transports and by land to vicinity of Haynes' Bluff. Our movements have served to distract the enemy and make him scatter his heavy guns. His forces scattered too but they can move to any one point.
>
> Health good; confidence felt by officers and men.
>
> Dredging machines brought here by Colonel G. G. Pride work to a charm.[7]

Commander Smith, aboard the U.S.S. *Rattler*, reported:

> I am obliged to leave the *Petrel* about 12 miles from the Coldwater, in the Tallahatchee. Her wheel is about destroyed by accidents and bad management. We will coal tonight, and go on to Greenwood with the gunboats and transports, leaving the *Marmora* at the junction of the Yalobusha and Tallahatchee, to guard the coal (two barges) and the steamer *Bayard* and an army transport with troops. The *Romeo* follows

with the mortar. The little provision that the army has is spoil-
ing. They have five days' on hand, and have sent for only six
days' in addition. I can maintain my party (those now drawing
rations) for one month. If all entitled drew rations, would have
rations for twenty-two days.

We have these disadvantages—that we must fight down-
stream, and that all are sternwheelers but one, and the rams
cannot reach a vessel with wide guards in a tender place
without bringing up against their own works in front of the
boilers. I have cut away their bitts, and made the most of those
vessels.

The *Lioness* has eighty-five bales of cotton for defense, two
deep before boilers; the *Fulton* cannot carry any on the sides
forward. The army have, I believe, sent for more provisions,
but they will be scant when those received. This delay has
spoiled our chances. There will be more of it, as they forage
for provisions and fuel, and every transport, I am told, has an
empty hold. I anticipate a rough time. Have made best
preparations that our time and means would admit, and go to
work trustingly.[8]

Captain Prime's report reflected Grant's message to Halleck.
The work on the canal had been progressing satisfactorily when the
upper dam gave way on the morning of the seventh. The opening
in the canal levee which had been used to drain the water was still
open; consequently, there was a heavy rush of water at that point
which was impossible to stop. The opening had enlarged to about
150 feet wide, double its original width.[9]

Colonel Wilson, aboard the steamer *Henderson*, reported that
he had entered the Yazoo Pass through Moon Lake. Before going
farther, he was informed by some citizens from Coldwater that the
Rebels had been busily engaged felling trees into and across the
stream since the second. General Pemberton had given orders two
months earlier directing the obstruction of the Yazoo Pass. A party
had been organized for the purpose and began work immediately
after they learned Wilson's force had cut the levee.

March 8. Wilson reported that he had descended the Yazoo
stream nearly six miles in an open boat, but realized it would be im-
prudent to travel farther without a larger escort. He did learn the extent of the obstacles. He also confirmed his view of the suitability
of the route as a line of operations against the country on the left

bank of the Yazoo River.[10] The next day he reported that General Washburn, with three small steamers and two regiments of infantry equipped with axes, cables, and tools, had arrived from Helena and entered the Pass two or three miles without meeting any serious blockades.

March 10. The ironclad *Chillicothe*, 160-feet long and 50-feet beam, the *Baron De Kalb*, 175-feet long and 50-feet beam, rams, and 22 transports, some of them as much as 220-feet long and 55-feet beam, reached Dr. Curtiss' plantation a few miles from the junction of the Yalobusha and the Tallahatchee rivers without incident, according to Wilson's report. He stated that the rams and ironclads could have reached the same point by March 3 and with extra effort by the first. The total distance traveled was 225 miles.

After a careful examination of the obstructions and their probable extent, Wilson reported that the work of removing the obstacles had begun. The obstacles had been formed by trees that the Confederates had felled into and across the stream. The trees were of the largest and heaviest kinds—cottonwood, sycamore, oak, elm, and pecan. Those trees, mixed with driftwood, rendered the barricade of no trifling nature and, even under ordinary circumstances, would have required great labor to remove.

To add to the difficulties, the rapid rise of the water from the crevasse at the entrance overflowed the entire country, except a very narrow strip of land next to the bank that did not exceed 50 yards wide in any place, and frequently was not even half that size. The working parties were necessarily kept on board the boats. There being no way of reaching the lower end of the Pass with troops and the necessary provisions and implements, the work had to be done from the upper end and the blockades removed successively. Initially the two regiments charged with clearing the Pass used windlasses and other machinery for removing the fallen trees and drift timber, but with the breakage of cables, tackle, and boat machinery, this proved to be entirely too slow. A plan for cutting off the limbs, sawing intwo the logs, and drawing out what would not sink entirely out of the way was adopted. In many cases, entire trees measuring 90 feet in length and 4 feet through the butt were drawn out by attaching a few six-inch cables and hauling them out with 250 to 400 men. By laborious work the pioneers, together with soldiers performing pioneer duties, cleared the Yazoo Pass and prepared it for navigation.

The width of the waterway was from 60 to 80 feet and the depth from 18 to 30 feet. The distance from Moon Lake to the Coldwater was about 15 miles. The Coldwater from its junction with Yazoo Pass was a considerable river, from 100 to 130 feet wide, running through a dense wilderness all the way. The Tallahatchee was a very similar stream, some 130 to 180 feet wide. From 30 miles below the mouth of the Coldwater, it afforded fine navigation for boats 250 feet long. There were about 50 plantations between the entrance to the Yazoo Pass and the mouth of the Tallahatchee, a distance of nearly 200 miles.

March 11. Grant recorded that Brigadier General Leonard F. Ross had confronted the enemy at Fort Pemberton at Greenwood, where the Tallahatchee and Yalobusha met and the Yazoo River began, some 90 miles from Vicksburg. Ross discovered the fort was inaccessible by land; his soldiers could not accomplish much in the way of an attack because they were blocked by geography and Confederate soldiers. The attack by gunboats failed with 7 men killed and 25 wounded.[11]

Captain Prime reported an order issued by Grant requiring half the effective force of each army regiment to work on the canal. Though this seemed to be a large force, in truth it was not. A statistical record estimated that the effective force of a regiment was 662 soldiers per 1,000.[12]

In his report to General Grant on the Yazoo Pass expedition, Colonel Wilson stated that the *Chillicothe* had moved within 1,100 yards of the battery erected by the Rebels in a loop between the Tallahatchee and the Yazoo covering the mouth of the Yalobusha and Greenwood. The Confederates had opened fire with a 32-pound rifle and several smaller pieces. One shot hit near the right-hand corner of the *Chillicothe's* square turret, denting the plate that was struck about four inches from the plane of its original position and knocking its 9-inch pine backing into fragments.

During the afternoon both the *Chillicothe* and the *De Kalb* returned to attack. But neither approached nearer than 900 to 1,000 yards, and their shots had no visible effect. The *Chillicothe* received a shot in her left bow port and withdrew.

Miller reported: "Landed on western side. Ordered into line to fight. Marched down till we got smell of powder, shot and shell, discovered rebel fort. Roll up our garments and clean it out tomorrow, darned thing."

March 12. Grant wrote again to W. A. Hammond in reference to surgeon J. R. Smith's letter inquiring on the sanitary condition of the army and asking for suggestions. He also asserted that a great deal was said to impress public and officials that his army was in a "suffering condition," mostly from neglect. "I say health of this army compares favorably with any army. Every preparation made for sick that could be desired," Grant wrote.[13] (See Tables 1, 2, and 3 on pages 76–79 for comparison of health of armies in the field.) Grant added he had sent a boat to the United States Sanitary Commission so that it could provide the soldiers with comfort items from its sanitary store.

The Sanitary Commission report stated that Grant assisted the good work of the commission by providing a transport for the storage and distribution of its supplies which the commission freely distributed to Grant's soldiers. The report mentioned Doctor Newberry, western secretary of the commission, who was indefatigable in shipping supplies from Louisville that "the people of western states contributed for the relief of their brethren struggling for control of the great river." The report also noted that it was not known how the 15,000 packages sent "ameliorated or influenced despondent, ill provided men's bodily wants, and gave assurance of care at home." Among the items sent were barrels of potatoes, ice, vegetables, fans, crutches, pillows, sheets, and clothes.[14]

Colonel Wilson reported that naval forces were not ready to attack. At night General Ross ordered the erection of a cotton bale battery at a point northwest of the fort, placing in it one 30-pounder rifled Parrott gun obtained from the navy. The materials were moved from Clarke's plantation house at night, and the battery was completed between 11 P.M. and 6 A.M. the next morning.

Sergeant Boyd wrote: "Weather beautiful and clear. Received commission First Lieutenant, Company B, 34th Iowa Volunteer Infantry, so flanked Colonel Reid who wanted me to stay but 34th came first; Reid had opportunity. Sad to bid farewell to Company G, and faithful boys of 19 months." He remarked that as orderly sergeant, he had seen all their faces before him at roll call and memorized every one.

In a letter to his wife, Captain Ankeny wrote: "Health is good. We'll soon take Vicksburg. So I can come home. River rising, levee at canal broken so we are in great danger of being drowned. We [are] under order to move on main levee. Paid for two months."

March 13. Colonel Wilson reported that the *Chillicothe*, the *Baron De Kalb*, and a mortar boat attacked Fort Pemberton, but he was not able to observe any damage. The closest the gunboats ever approached was less than 800 yards. The Rebel position was strong by virtue of the difficulty of the approach; it was not known how many troops were defending the fort. "*Chillicothe* did not stand to its work well. Commander Smith was not sanguine about going close up to Fort Pemberton."

The position of Fort Pemberton was unassailable by infantry, and therefore it could only be taken by a vigorous, determined naval attack. The site of the fort was only slightly above the water. It occurred to Wilson that if the Mississippi levee near Austin, about 18 miles above Helena, were cut, a large volume of water might be induced to take the line of the Coldwater and Tallahatchee and flood the country near both streams. Brigadier General Benjamin M. Prentiss, commander of the District of East Arkansas, cut the levee, but not sufficiently to produce the desired effect. In Wilson's opinion, if it had been destroyed for two miles, a rise of two feet would have probably reached Greenwood. The enemy could not have withstood more than one foot.

Events of the previous two days prompted Wilson to send a personal letter to General John A. Rawlings, Grant's adjutant general:

> I've just written a hasty note to the general; please apologize for its meager character. I've now been two days and entire nights without sleep, and am almost dead. The mail boat goes early tomorrow, so I can't give details; but my next will compensate.
>
> I'm disgusted with 7, 9, 10, and 11 inch guns; to let one 6½ inch rifle stop our Navy. Bah! they ought to go up to 200 yards and "make a spoon or spoil a horn." They are to attack tomorrow, but may not do much. I have no hope of anything great, considering the course followed by the naval forces under direction of their able and efficient Acting Rear-Admiral, Commodore, Captain, Lieutenant Commander [Watson] Smith. One chance shot will do the work; we may not make it in a thousand. No more troops are needed here till Greenwood is taken. I think we have troops enough to whip all the Rebels in this vicinity if we can only get by the fort. One good gunboat can do the work, and no doubt; the two here are no great shakes.

We are stopped no certain. Ross has done all in his power to urge this thing forward. If what he suggested had been adopted, the ironclads would have been here fifteen days ago and found no battery of any importance. So much for speed. Very truly, your friend, J. H. Wilson.[15]

Allen Miller wrote in his diary: "Not much fighting. Gunboats reply with fire. Commander Smith says he'll knock the fort into the river tomorrow. Hope he will. Afraid he won't. We can't get at it with infantry or we would tear it down."

March 14. Admiral Porter advised General Grant that he had made a reconnaissance in preparation for the sixth attempt at Vicksburg, a route up Steele's Bayou and partially through Black Bayou toward Deer Creek. So far as he had explored the water courses, he had found they were navigable for the smaller ironclads and light draft gunboats. According to information gained from Negroes in the area, Deer Creek could be navigated to Rolling Fork, and there was no question about navigation from there through the Sunflower River to the Yazoo River.

Miller wrote, "Cannonading without success on Fort Pemberton."

March 15. Following up on Porter's reconnaissance action, Grant accompanied Porter on the ram *Price* to confirm the route through Steele's Bayou to Black Bayou. Porter could suggest a route through the bayou, but Grant had the responsibility to make the final decision. Upon the completion of the reconnaissance with Porter, Grant returned with a confirmation of the efficacy of the route. As a first action, he ordered the pioneer corps of Brigadier General David Stuart's Second Division and its 8th Missouri Infantry Regiment to report to Porter to clear what Grant observed as the great obstacle to navigation—the overhanging trees. Porter sent Grant a message assuring him of naval cooperation.[16] To support this sixth attempt to take Vicksburg, Grant ordered Sherman to proceed as early as practicable up Steele's Bayou, through Black Bayou and Deer Creek, and thence, using the gunboats already there, to enter the Yazoo River by any route. Sherman's mission would be to determine the feasibility of deploying an army through the water route to the east bank of the Yazoo River between Yazoo City and Haynes' Bluff. He was to find a point where his troops could act advantageously against the right flank of the Confederate army at Vicksburg.

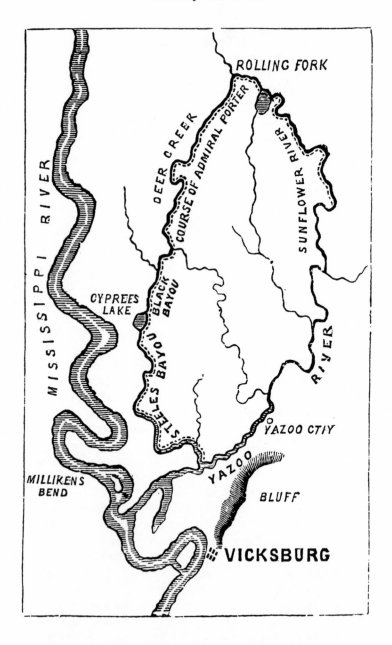

The Steele's Bayou Route (*Harper's Pictorial History*).

Grant's instructions were to have details from Sherman's army corps clear out the channels of the various bayous the transports would have to run through. Sherman was also to hold points that he judged should be occupied. Sherman issued orders the same day to the officer in command of detachments on board the *Silver Wave*: "You will proceed up the Yazoo to Cypress Bayou. In the bayou, now full and deep, proceed to clear it of the limbs of overhanging trees, or of trees which obstruct it for the navigation of steamboats of ordinary size and draught." The bayou, Sherman added, flowed 12 miles hence into another large bayou called Steele's Bayou, which was wide, deep, and clear. "You will clear out the first reach, say of 12 miles, so that a fleet of boats can pass through it."

A detail of 50 pioneers from Stuart's division was on board the *Silver Wave*, with 300 axes, saws, and all the tools necessary for the successful accomplishment of the assigned work. "Admiral Porter has already passed through this bayou," Sherman wrote, "and is now at a point beyond, working his way through to the Yazoo, and it is of vast importance that this part of the channel be cleared as fast as possible."

While Grant's orders to Sherman read "to determine the feasibility of the route," the problems Porter and Sherman were to encounter developed from their lack of knowledge or familiarity with the terrain they were to pass through. The expedition faced serious difficulties because of a lack of accurate maps and terrain information. The inordinate amount of time required to clear the obstacles on the water course was also a great problem. While the Yankees were spending time clearing natural obstacles, the Rebels observed the Yankees' movement in the bayous. The Confederate troops used their time and tools to build additional obstacles, such as anchored or floating tree rafts.

Porter and Sherman were moving into a wet wilderness. Land planters along the waterways did not believe naval vessels would attempt to pass through the bayous. They believed their obstacle-ridden waterways and isolated land formed a "Confederate snuff box the Yankees could not enter."[17]

The reconnaissance expedition was to proceed up Steele's Bayou, move through three miles of Black Bayou, and enter the Sunflower River. This would enable them to proceed south to the Yazoo River between Haynes' Bluff and Yazoo City, thus opening a route to turn the right flank of the Confederate army at Vicksburg.

Colonel Wilson reported to General Grant that the still ongoing Yazoo expedition, the fifth attempt at Vicksburg, was five miles from Fort Pemberton. Gunboat repairs were not completed, and the crewmen put off repair work out of respect for the Sabbath.

> I will try tomorrow, but I am not sanguine. I can see a disposition on the part of the Navy to keep from a close and desperate engagement. I tried to give them backbone but they are not confident. Smith not the equal of Lord Nelson.
>
> Rebels got ahead of us in obstructing pass and kept us back 10 days. Smith responsible for detention at this point. Consequent failure of expedition responsible for no other reason than his timid and slow movements. I ordered dispatch when we went into Pass. Other naval officers and General Ross agreed with plan. If had been done would have reached Tallahatchee in four days. I could have brought them in three.

This appears to be a bit of braggadocio when Wilson's time is compared to the difficult itinerary he previously reported.

Wilson continued in his report:

> I have erected a battery on shore 700 yards from the rebel fort. It is intended to embark a brigade on light draught gunboats and if rebel batteries silenced, soldiers will be landed at the fort and assault it and attack rebel infantry if it should stand. Program cannot be carried out unless the battery is completely disabled so that we can run down and break up the raft that lies just above the fort. Fort Greenwood [Pemberton] is constructed of cotton bales covered with sand and earth and would be very valuable to us.
>
> I am solicitous of my reputation. I would not have you or any one else imagine I have stood upon punctilio in matters that concern public welfare, but to the contrary I have not hesitated to tender my opinion upon a single occasion where I thought it worthy of attention, even to the naval authorities.
>
> I regret my own negligence or lack of foresight in not advising General Gorman to send a force down the Pass to Coldwater before we started at the levee in order to prevent interference with it. I was thrown off guard by appearance of the country being flooded from back water and crevasses. Indications were such, and it was so. Trees were cleared by men standing in boats. We might have prevented this, and might not.

As it now stands without two or three good ironclads soon, with a siege train, or fortune favors us, the game is blocked on us here as well as below.

Should it turn out this way Vicksburg becomes subordinate, our department secondary, and Rosecrans' army [Chattanooga] our hope in the West. In that event we will be required to furnish 50–60 thousand soldiers.

Rebels are making great calculations to "bag us" entire. They have battalion of volunteers to board our vessels. We can receive such gentlemen with bloody hands.

Difficulty of operations here arising from high water, nearly whole country under water. There is no way of our reaching fort except by landing against it with our boats after the guns are silent and the raft destroyed.[18]

General McPherson wrote to General Grant, referring to his dispatch on the Yazoo expedition:

The instructions to Brigadier General Isaac F. Quinby were to push forward the support of General Ross as rapidly as possible, which I am confident he will do, as he is fully awake to the importance of the matter. The First and Second brigades of General John L. Logan's Third Division are embarking this morning, and will in all probability get off this afternoon. There are not enough boats here to take the whole division.

General Logan goes up with his two brigades, under instructions to disembark near or at the Yazoo Pass, if the ground will admit, and send the boats back here for the balance of his command and a portion of Brigadier General John McArthur's. He is also instructed to embark on small boats, suitable to run the Pass, and push on to support of General Quinby as rapidly as possible. I shall go on the next trip of boats.

McPherson also issued orders to General Logan:

There not being boats enough to take the whole division at one time, you will proceed with the First and Second brigades to the entrance to Moon Lake, and if ground can be found in the vicinity to disembark the troops, do so immediately, and send the boats back to Lake Providence for the remainder of your command and a portion of General McArthur's.

> As fast as boats arrive suitable for going through the Yazoo Pass into Coldwater, you will embark your troops and push to the support of General Quinby. Your commissary and quartermaster's stores will be transferred to good, staunch boats, and also your ammunition. It is not advisable to have it all put on one boat, especially the last, but distributed on two or three boats, so that, in case of accident going through the Pass or down the river, we would not be seriously inconvenienced.
>
> Take with you a good supply of entrenching tools. You will exercise your discretion about taking the large boats into Moon Lake, and also in selecting the point of debarkation. If the whole country should be overflowed the men will probably have to remain on the boats they go up on, until suitable boats for the expedition arrive from the North. By the time you reach the entrance to Moon Lake, General Quinby will undoubtedly have selected a landing place on the Yazoo, which must be held until we can get our corps together, and ready for a farther advance.

Sergeant Brown reported that his regiment on the transport *City of Louisiana* attempted to enter Yazoo Pass. Engineer and pioneer soldiers were at work on scaffolds with saws that operated horizontally under water to saw off the trees several feet below the water to clear the channel. He also reported his company spent five days traveling eighteen miles.

Sherman also became involved in the inquiry about the health of Grant's Army of the Tennessee. In response to criticism of the medical service in his corps from Colonel R. C. Wood, assistant surgeon general, Sherman replied to him:

> Since January 20 we have been encamped on the low alluvial land on the neck opposite to and in sight of Vicksburg.
>
> To give an intelligent account of the hospital and sanitary arrangements would require statements of facts that you already possess in great detail, and I need not do more at this time than assert my belief that no army composed, as this was and is, partly of new regiments, ever had better hospital facilities, care and treatment. Our hospitals are now admirably supplied with everything that a generous and bountiful government could or should bestow. You can see this yourself, and every gentleman who has sought for proper information

has at all times had access to the proper sources; and during the whole period of time since we left Memphis we have been as well supplied with surgeons, medicines, medical supplies, and hospital accommodations as was to be expected. Doctor Charles McMillan has been all the time my chief surgeon and I know that he has labored unceasingly, has exhibited a wonderful foresight, and has not failed to avail himself of every means to provide for the wounded and sick soldiers. He has not lost an hour by sickness or absence, but has been all the time most active in providing for the wants of his department, and I avail myself of this opportunity to express to you, his proper superior, my unqualified approval of his acts. I have been in many battles, and I know of my own knowledge that the wounded at Chickasaw Bayou and Arkansas Post were removed from the field to the steamboats with a care and system provided by him in advance, that elicited my hearty approval on the spot, and better managed than in any other battle that I ever witnessed or bore a part in.

Individual exceptions have occurred, as they do in every city on earth, much more liable to occur in battles and on the field, where men's minds and passions are aroused, and the man who would enlarge on a single case of exception, and publish it to the world as a sample of the whole, is to be pitied as a miserable wretch, beneath the notice of government. Our morning reports exhibit the exact number of the sick in hospital and in quarters, and the dead. These go to the War Department regularly every ten days, and can there be compared with the statistics of other armies similarly composed and exposed. You may safely challenge a comparison.

Our army is admirably supplied in all respect, and no one deplores more than I do the spirit of falsehood and calumny that harrows the minds of our people at home, and has led to your visit to our camps. In a war we must expect sickness and death, but so far as your department is concerned, I feel assured all has been done and will continue to be done which skill, science, and foresight can accomplish. Our soldiers need far more the respect and confidence of their fellow countrymen at home than they do increased supplies of medicine and hospital stores.[19]

In spite of Sherman's umbrage and apologia at criticism, the medical reports in Tables 1, 2, and 3 recorded a different account of sickness.

TABLE 1
Total of Five Classes of Diseases*
Army of the Tennessee
January 1–April 30, 1863

	January		February		March		April	
	Cases	Deaths	Cases	Deaths	Cases	Deaths	Cases	Deaths
	41,820	837	35,506	1,286	35,376	769	29,567	628
Total Class I Diseases (Zymotic–Miasmatic) Army of the Tennessee								
Typhoid	653	181	666	288	716	159	405	104
Typhus	22	2	21	6	58	12	5	3
Typo-Malarial [sic]	409	21	493	59	371	35	358	46
Yellow Remittent	1,891	16	1,715	43	1,919	16	1,736	29
Quotidian	2,367	1	2,260	2	2,639	9	2,301	2
Tertian	1,820	2	1,982	6	2,050	0	1,991	0
Quartan	487	0	222	3	281	2	224	0
Congestive	97	26	102	30	106	25	179	22
Acute Diarrhea	10,788	43	7,699	67	7,615	7	6,963	8

TABLE 2
Surgeon General's Report
Total of Five Classes of Diseases
Union Armies
January 1–April 30, 1863

	January		February		March		April	
	Cases	Deaths	Cases	Deaths	Cases	Deaths	Cases	Deaths
Army of the Potomac	49,024	531	34,896	420	34,320	468	23,447	218
	(200,714)*		(177,856)		(176,638)		(149,182)	
Dept. of the South	2,187	2	3,477	8	3,802	10	2,844	10
	(14,646)		(26,348)		(25,538)		(23,514)	
Dept. of the Cumberland	23,482	410	23,983	365	25,358	334	23,949	333
	(90,543)		(103,298)		(102,453)		(104,885)	
Dept. of the Tennessee	41,820	837	35,506	1,286	35,376	769	29,567	628
	(143,942)		(141,158)		(146,790)		(143,367)	
Dept. of the Gulf	14,013	144	14,009	156	15,787	199	13,005	146
	(39,789)		(41,864)		(42,832)		(35,501)	

Numbers in parentheses indicate mean strength.

Chronic Diarrhea	2,352	51	1,820	140	1,822	147	1,386	136
Acute Dysentery	1,615	29	1,516	32	1,327	23	1,394	19
Chronic Dysentery	25	14	266	21	196	14	114	13
Erysipelas	314	24	198	25	235	11	223	14
Small Pox	291	19	230	35	281	19	212	24
Measles	1,189	93	556	75	153	20	67	0
Scarlet	0	1	1	1	2	0	8	1
Diphtheria	44	4	69	5	81	0	31	1
Mumps	639	1	459	1	273	0	225	0
Epidemic Catarrh	1,770	1	1,703	2	1,174	0	792	0
Other diseases of this order	795	5	513	68	382	5	251	3
TOTALS	27,568	534	22,491	909	21,681	504	18,865	425
Daily average all classes	1,349	27	1,268	43	1,141	25	986	21
Daily average Class I	889	17	803	32	699	16	629	14

*I Zymotic-Miasmatic; II Constitutional; III Parasitic; IV Local; V Wounds; Accidents; and Injuries.

TABLE 3
Rate Per One Thousand

Cases and Deaths Five Classes of Diseases
Union Armies
January 1–April 30, 1863

	January	February	March	April
1. Army of the Potomac				
Size	200,714	177,856	176,638	149,182
Cases	49,024	34,896	34,320	23,447
Per K	244	196	194	157
Deaths	531	420	468	218
Per K	3	2	3	1
2. Department of the South				
Size	14,646	26,348	25,538	23,514
Cases	2,187	3,477	3,802	2,844
Per K	149	132	149	121
Deaths	2	8	10	10
Per K	0	0	0	0
3. Department of the Cumberland				
Size	90,543	103,298	102,453	104,885
Cases	23,482	23,983	25,358	23,949
Per K	259	232	248	228
Deaths	410	365	334	333
Per K	5	4	3	3
4. Department of the Tennessee				
Size	143,942	141,158	146,790	143,367
Cases	42,820	35,506	35,376	29,567
Per K	297	252	241	206
Deaths	837	1,286	769	628
Per K	6	9	5	4
5. Department of the Gulf				
Size	39,789	41,864	42,832	35,501
Cases	14,013	14,009	15,787	13,005
Per K	352	335	369	366
Deaths	144	156	199	146
Per K	4	4	5	4
6. All Armies				
Size	489,634	490,524	494,251	456,449
Cases	131,526	111,871	114,643	92,812
Per K	269	228	232	203
Deaths	1,924	2,235	1,780	1,335
Per K	4	5	4	3

Sherman, based on information available to him, believed there was adequate care for his soldiers. What alarmed the public, officials, and families of soldiers—who had available to them information too—was the environment and its impact on the soldiers' health. A doctor writing on the subject concluded, "Sickness rate for Western Theater among men of frontier tended to run double that of Eastern."[20] (See Table 3.)

March 16. Colonel Wilson to General Grant:

> No nearer accomplishment of our object than yesterday. General Ross and Commodore Smith had an arrangement and we were ready at daylight to make the final effort. Ross selected three of his best regiments and embarked them on three light-clad gunboats ready to throw them ashore at the battery, provided the heavy guns of the enemy should be silenced and the raft broken so as to permit a landing.
>
> At noon our battery opened fire.
>
> Rebels covered their guns judiciously with cotton bales.
>
> In few minutes *Chillicothe* followed by *DeKalb* moved out with the intention of "going in" upon the well established principle of gunboat warfare, "close quarters and quick work," but *Chillicothe* struck with violence several times and had to retire. *DeKalb* also drawn out. Our battery kept up fire till night. I urged *DeKalb* to try close quarters; refused. Our sharpshooters pushed out and annoyed rebel gunners.
>
> A few more days of such policy as we have been compelled to adopt by a tardy unreadiness of the naval commandery will enable the Rebels to make Fort Greenwood entirely sufficient against any force than can operate against it from this quarter.
>
> With troops here without siege materials of any kind it is impossible to do anything without the gunboats first silencing the large guns. Enemy in isolated position. Cannot approach by land. Can only approach in front of his heavy guns. Can do no serious damage without direct approach. Can be taken with proper show of strength. I have no confidence in the snap or activity of present naval commander in this quarter and do not hesitate to say I regard him entirely responsible for the failure to take this place without a fight.
>
> The chance for us is if the river four feet or more it will flood entire country forcing Rebels out of their present position.[21]

Grant informed McPherson he had returned in the morning

from a reconnaissance some 30 miles up Steele's Bayou with Admiral Porter in a large gunboat, proceeded by four of the old "turtles."

The boats were pushed on, Grant said, with all dispatch to enter the Yazoo, and it was important that a force should enter there with all dispatch. He said he had information direct from Vicksburg and the Yazoo River, both from persons who had been there and from later papers, that Union gunboats (under Commander Smith) had been down to Greenwood and exchanged a few shots with the fort there. The enemy, he added, had sent up reinforcements from Vicksburg and some more guns:

> If we can get our boats in the rear of them in time, it will so confuse the enemy as to save Ross' force. If they do not I shall feel restless for his fate, until I know that Quinby has reached him. Quinby will have the most abundant force for that route with his Seventh Division and that of Brigadier General John E. Smith of the 16th Corps. I am now almost sorry that I directed the latter to join him. It seems impossible to get steamers of the class we want.[22]
>
> The route through Bayou Macon [Lake Providence, fifth attempt] may prove a good thing for us yet in some operation. But this one, to get all our forces in one place, and where it will be in striking distance of the enemy's lines of communication north, is the most important until firm foothold is secured on the side with the enemy.

Sherman reported to Grant that he had moved up Steele's Bayou and overtaken the fleet of ironclads just before they reached Deer Creek. He found Deer Creek not as large nor with as much current as he had expected, but found the water deep and the channel narrow. The ironclads, he wrote, pushed their way along unharmed, but the trees and overhanging limbs tore the wooden boats all to pieces. He found that the steamer *Diligent* with the infantrymen and pioneers he had sent up had nearly reached the fleet. They had been at work that day, but most of the time they were engaged in collecting rafts to stand on while cutting trees. "I don't think any boat can as yet come through this Black Bayou, but I will push the work," Sherman promised.

Sherman reported there was no high land there, nor was the route practicable for troops unless Admiral Porter cleaned out the

Yazoo and secured the mouth of Deer Creek. Then he might be able to use Deer Creek as the route for a diverting force. Only his small boats could navigate Deer Creek. He did not think he would make a lodgment on high land by such a route because of the difficulty of navigation.

"We are only 25 miles by land from Haynes' Bluff," he reported, "but I do not apprehend the enemy will do worse than send a party up to ascertain our strength and purposes."

To carry out Grant's instructions of March 15, Sherman ordered the 8th Missouri Infantry Regiment under Lieutenant Colonel David C. Coleman to proceed with all dispatch up the Yazoo and clean out the channel leading up to Steele's Bayou. Coleman subsequently received instructions from Porter to follow him up Steele's Bayou to Black Bayou and proceed to clear it of overhanging trees.

In his report to Grant, Sherman stated:

> Today I took the tug *Fern* and went up Steele's Bayou and met the gunboats as they were entering Deer Creek. I met Porter there, and proceeded with him in a tug up about three miles for Fore's Plantation, and then turned around and returned.
>
> My orders were to reconnoiter as to the practicability of moving my corps from Young's Point to some tenable position on the main land east of the Yazoo, from which to operate against Vicksburg and the Yazoo forts at Haynes' Bluff. Porter proposed to move up to the Rolling Fork, thence into Sunflower, and so on to the Yazoo below Yazoo City. I was to remain there.
>
> Tonight he sent orders for the gunboat *Louisville* to follow him. I disembarked the 8th Missouri at this place as a guard and set the pioneers to work in clearing away the trees and brush in Black Bayou, which is about four miles long, narrow, crooked, and filled with trees.
>
> The heavy ironclads could force their way through, pressing aside the bushes and trees, but the transports could not follow. The 8th Missouri passed through on a coal barge, drawn by a navy tug. Other pioneers and Negroes, including two companies of the 1st Missouri Volunteer Engineer Regiment, are busy and have so far progressed in their work. Yesterday the *Eagle* and *Silver Wave* came up far enough to land two regiments, 6th Missouri and 116th Illinois, at the first ground

above water from the Yazoo to this point. The two transports backed out and returned to Eagle Bend for more troops.[23]

Allen Miller wrote: "No guns fired; delayed. Oh, has lost many brilliant victories. Brigadier General [Clinton B.] Fisk is bustling around like an insane person with his long train of guards."

Captain Ankeny, in a letter to his wife, wrote:

> Moving camp in hot weather. Water drove us from old camp. Now below mouth of Yazoo. Be here a few months. Hear nothing of Lake Providence or Yazoo expedition. Know what we get only from newspapers. Canal I think a failure. Most troops gone. Grant may think differently. But canal has kept people up North quiet so has done some good. Troop health improving. Very few cases of smallpox. We might have fought two battles and not lost as many men as we have in past two weeks. [See Table 1. There were 50 more cases of smallpox in March than in February.]
>
> Since I received your last letter I know my duty to go to you and our child, and I know it is, but military law is tyranny itself. No sympathy. I cannot receive leave of absence. If you say my duty I will come. I am told man who will not do duty will meet reproach from friends. I would hazard all for you and Joey."

March 17. Grant reported to Halleck that since the dam at the upper end of the canal had broken, work with the dredges had progressed favorably, but all attempts to stop water rushing into the canal had failed. If necessary the canal would be able to pass boats of ordinary size in a few days. He also reported that the enemy kept busily engaged firing from the opposite side heights. "Yesterday and last night enemy shots hit the dredge nearest the lower end of the canal, but without any damage. Many of the large projectiles reached half way across the point."

In discussing the fourth attempt, or what he called an "experiment," Grant stated, "Ordinary Ohio river boats can now pass from Lake Providence into Bayou Macon and thence by easy navigation to mouth of Red river. I make no calculation upon using this route for the present but it may be turned to practical use after effecting the present plans." With respect to the third attempt, he remarked, "same may be said for the canal across the point." Speaking of the fifth attempt, or experiment, he related: "Information shows enemy moved several thousand from troops Vicksburg to Yazoo river. Besides gunboats I have Quinby's division there in the Pass on their way down. A division from Memphis should be on way up."

Grant also reported to Halleck that he had had a message the night before from Porter about the sixth attempt: "Ironclads pushed into Black Bayou," Porter told Grant, "became entangled in timber and could not move until it cut out." Porter asked Grant for 3,000 men to act with him. Grant wrote he had already sent all the boats at hand suitable for that navigation and he was sending the remainder of Sherman's division and would push troops through if Sherman reported favorably, as fast as his means would admit. The troops traveled up the Mississippi in large transports about 30 miles to where Steele's Bayou came within one mile of the Mississippi. Small class boats then ferried the troops from that point, which saved the distance from the mouth of the Yazoo, the most difficult part of navigation in Steele's Bayou. On the long, difficult, and circuitous route, the expedition bypassed the Confederate guns at Haynes' Bluff, the guns which had stopped Sherman the previous December.

"Reports of excitement in Vicksburg," Grant told Halleck. "Pemberton removing troops. I cannot satisfy myself to what point. Some may have gone up Yazoo and some to Port Hudson. I have no means of learning from below; occasionally through northern newspapers I learn."[24]

General Sherman reported to General Grant:

> I reconnoitered in a tug up Steele's Bayou to see if I could reach Rolling Fork by that route, but found it utterly impracticable for a small tug, much less a transport. All the country on both sides was deep under water. I next examined the left fork up to and beyond Tallulah bridge, but the bridge is swept away and the road deep under water. Indeed all the country bordering Steele's Bayou is submerged swamp. Satisfied that the only dry land in this climate was to be found here on Deer Creek, I returned and renewed the orders to push the work in clearing out Black Bayou.
>
> Deer Creek is a narrow, sluggish stream, full of willow bushes and overhanging tree limbs inhabited by animals, through which nothing but keel boats have usually plied. Porter's ironclads move like snails, but with great power, forcing all saplings and bushes and drift aside, but the channel is

useless to us in a military way. It cannot be used at this present stage of water. Its banks are usually from one to three feet above water and the road keeps upon the river bank a natural levee. There are a series of well-improved plantations the whole distance, and provisions are abundant; i.e., cattle, sheep, hogs, and poultry. The wagon road will be useless at this season, as the wheels would cut into the hubs in the damp, low places, on which troops can march very well. If we want to operate along this narrow strip, of course, the creek must be used to carry all articles of ammunition or subsistence other than what the men have on their backs.[25]

Miller wrote, "Nothing important to relieve tedium. Preparing for advance. Deserters say we had them whipped if we had only mentioned it to them last Friday evening."

The *New York Times* printed a report of a correspondent on the arrival of Porter's fleet in the Yazoo and at the outer defenses of Vicksburg. The correspondent also wrote he heard Banks' army had arrived at Baton Rouge for a simultaneous attack on Port Hudson. "If so," the correspondent prophesied, "the problem of the rebellion in the Valley of the Mississippi is likely to be solved before the close of the first quarter of 1863."

March 18. Colonel Wilson reported from his post on the Yazoo expedition:

> Military and naval operations are about terminated here for present. His excellency Acting Rear Admiral Commodore Smith left today for more salubrious climate, very sick giving it as his opinion that the present force of ironclads could not take the two rebel guns in our front. Lieutenant Commander James P. Foster, next in rank, has assumed command and insists on withdrawing his force. General Ross assented at first but has since determined to delay here till General Quinby arrives to assume responsibility of attempting to reduce the rebel works or of withdrawing land forces.
>
> Only way to take the fort is for gunboats to go up and hammer till they take it! We threw away magnificent chance to injure enemy. Culpable and inexcusable slowness of naval commander.
>
> If Porter sends right force could capture it. If not folly to keep force here. It will let enemy strengthen his force and bag our force.

It's provoking beyond measure to think that everything we undertake must be marred by incompetency and stupidity! I am intensely disgusted tonight.[26]

Miller wrote: "Mrs. General Fisk better go home and stay with the children. I guess fact of her having none is the secret of her being here. She divides the time of our general."

March 19. Captain Prime reported that an attempt had been made to stop the flow of water into the canal by making a dam where necessary by means of dredges around the opening through the main levee and some distance above it. A gap left to the east of the canal entrance and perpendicular to main levee was to be closed by a large barge filled with earth. An attempt was made to put this barge in place on March 14, but the effort was not successful because the posts yielded and some of the lines broke. The barge brought up against one of the dredges which had been placed within the dam for work on the canal. According to Prime's report:

> During the night as there was danger the dredge would be sunk, the remaining lines were cut. The next day as the current from the opening left for the barge was cutting through the canal levee, endeavors were made to change the course of this current by reopening the communication with the new entrance. This proved sufficient to throw the point of impact lower down, and, as the canal levee is being revetted with planks, it will probably not be cut through.
>
> One of the dredges has been employed strengthening the canal levee in the vicinity of the opening mentioned above. This has drawn the fire of the enemy's heavy guns in prolongation of the canal, which reaches nearly to the railroad.
>
> This greatly increased range of the enemy's artillery and the number of their shots that fall in the canal will probably render it necessary to alter the direction of the canal below the railroad.

Major General S. A. Hurlbut, commander of the 16th Corps, Memphis, reported to Brigadier General B. M. Prentiss, District East Arkansas:

> I regret exceedingly that the expedition to the Yazoo is in such a precarious position. I regret my inability to send you

the guns and ammunition you require. I have no guns. All boats are out or under orders to leave. I will order Brigadier General Eugene A. Carr, Fourteenth Division, 13th Army Corps, to you and you can order him to debark. Ross should never have been out of supporting reach, but he is though and must be saved if possible. The delay in boats is chargeable to others who will hereafter be answerable for it.[27]

General Sherman wrote to General Grant:

Learning that General Stuart's division of my corps had been sent up to the Muddy Bayou I proceeded down to see what progress they were making in getting across to Steele's Bayou, and found the division there, with two regiments, the 6th Missouri and 116th Illinois, embarked in the *Silver Wave,* which started out; General Stuart accompanied me. Our tug broke her rudder, and in the night carried away the smoke stack, which disabled her. She is under repair and will be used when serviceable in towing an empty coal barge loaded with soldiers as they arrive.

On the way up I met a messenger from Porter with a message written on tissue paper brought through the swamps by a Negro who had concealed it in a piece of tobacco reporting continued obstructions in his way and enemy infantry and artillery were giving him difficulty. They killed the men placed on bow of boats to shove them off of obstacles. He wants 10,000 men to hold the country, that he might remove the obstructions. I wrote him at once of the delays in sending forward men to this point, and that it was a physical impossibility for us to reach his boats with anything like that force, but I would hurry the soldiers of Stuart's division to this point, which is really the first high, or rather, dry ground. But it does not fulfill any of your conditions for we cannot reach the Yazoo from this point by land or water.[28]

Allen Miller wrote: "The most stupendous preparations for an immense strategic withdrawal for safety. Rumor of reinforcements played out. We are going to reinforce Helena I suppose. Grand move tomorrow 4 A.M."

March 20. Because of his concern about Vicksburg, President Lincoln sent a wire to General Hurlbut at Memphis (where a wire was then sent on to Grant's headquarters). "What news have you?

What from Vicksburg? What from Yazoo Pass? What from Lake Providence? What generally?"[29]

Halleck contacted Grant about the Steele's Bayou expedition: "In operations on Yazoo you have considered advantages and dangers of the expedition. Our information here on subject limited and unsatisfactory.

"One point discussed and I call your attention to it, danger in fall of water in Mississippi, having your steamers stuck in upper Yazoo unable to extricate them. Serious loss with our present shortage of steamers."

Another danger Halleck related was that the enemy would concentrate on Grant's isolated forces and Halleck would not be able to assist.

When the army was directed to one particular object, Halleck continued, it was dangerous to divide forces. All accessories should be sacrificed for sake of concentration. The great object was the opening of the Mississippi. Halleck emphasized that everything tended to that purpose, and that the eyes and hopes of the country were now directed to Grant's army. The opening of the Mississippi would be to the greatest advantage. "We shall omit nothing which we can do to assist you," Halleck promised.[30]

In Colonel Wilson's report on the Yazoo expedition, he stated that it was important to mention for the record that General Ross, who was commanding the Yazoo expedition, left Moon Lake on February 24. He arrived on March 10 at Fort Pemberton after a 225-mile trip. In justice to his services, Wilson wanted to explain the difficulties in navigation and delays that had occurred.

"To timidity, over cautiousness and lack of interest displayed by Lieutenant Commander Watson Smith, he commanding gunboats, and delay growing out of them, was attributable the failure of the entire expedition." Wilson added that Smith had been frequently urged by General Ross and ships captains Foster and Walker of the navy to move with more rapidity or to allow ironclads to go to Tallahatchee. Days were lost in the operation.

Ross' attack on Fort Pemberton on March 16 failed, but he remained in front of fort until March 20, constantly conducting reconnaissance with Colonel Wilson for a way to attack by infantry. They failed to find a feasible way, however. Because the ironclads were out of ammunition and no word was received on reinforcements, they thought it advisable to fall back.[31]

There is no record that Smith answered Wilson's caustic comments. He remarked in the record that he did not think enough planning was given to the preparations for the expedition. The difficulty of opening the Yazoo Pass, he recorded, could not be described. The task was greater than expected, and it became necessary to send in a party of 6,000 soldiers to aid in cutting away trees and removing logs that had accumulated in years gone by. Time was lost on the task. In Smith's opinion, "Soldiers and sailors worked as men never worked before and discipline and spirit of Mississippi squadron could not be better manifested than in witnessing efforts put forth by gallant fellows of fleet to overcome obstacles that were deemed by some insurmountable."

Smith also reported he had to save some ammunition and coal of the *Chillicothe* and the *De Kalb* for defensive operations when the fleet withdrew. He mentioned that his health had failed, but up to that time he had no fear for final success of expedition.[32] A naval surgeon reported Smith was in "precarious condition and recommended a leave of absence until he recovered his health." Porter approved.[33]

When he later wrote his memoirs, Wilson tempered his harsh criticism of Smith and revised his conclusion on the Yazoo expedition. He wrote that by incredible efforts a force of soldiers had exhibited strength in clearing a passageway and was in reach of Fort Pemberton at the head of the Yazoo River when the soldiers were stopped by an overflow which isolated the fortifications.[34]

March 21. Colonel Wilson reported that after marching 12 miles, General Ross met General Quinby coming up with his division; Quinby ordered Ross to return to the fort to attack.

Sherman reported to Grant from Hill's Plantation:

> About 3:00 A.M. I received another letter from Porter telling me that he was still in Deer Creek and that his passage was obstructed by the enemy, and asked me to hurry up to cooperate. As the bulk of my corps is still to the rear, it would be improper for me to pass beyond all reach of them, and I have accordingly sent up Colonel Giles A. Smith with all of his brigade with orders to march up the east bank of Deer Creek to the gunboats. He got off about daylight and has 21 miles to march. The Admiral is, doubtless, concerned for the safety of his gunboats, and with propriety. If the Mississippi water level were to fall they would be stranded in enemy Black Creek or mired in the mud.

In Deer Creek Porter optimistic about moving forward his remarkable expedition.

His ironclads rammed large oak trees lifting them out of the water to clear a passage. The banks of the narrow creek, with a one-foot clearance on each side, and shallow water, made a difficult task for him. The natives aware of the gunboats presence took steps to hinder them. They burned bales of cotton along the banks of the creek and the smoke and heat impeded the crews' work. Porter though pushed tenaciously through pouring water on his heated gunboats, and freed them with axes and saws when they became wedged between trees and in the willows.

The Confederates nearby felled trees with Negro labor on the creek. Animals in the trees, mice, rats, snakes fell onto the decks of the ironclads to the consternation of the crews. Soon Porter was stopped by the willows and its withes. They became Porter's albatross. It became a time of horror for Porter; he realized he could not sail anywhere. Rumor spread Confederate vessels sailing up Rolling Fork to carry out Pemberton's check of Porter. Confederate soldiers arrived and they routed Porter's sailors who had positioned themselves on an Indian mound, and closed in on the fleet. They also blocked Deer creek to prevent Porter using it as an escape route to the Yazoo river.

Porter also encountered trouble from an avalanche of water flowing from Rolling Fork and carrying logs the Confederates hoped would build a log jam as another means to snare Porter. The flood of water actually came from Colonel Wilson's act to cut the levee on the Mississippi to let water flow into the Yazoo in a scheme to flood the Confederate soldiers out of Fort Pemberton. It also had the unexpected consequences to make Porter's rescue more difficult.

My own impression is that the enemy has so obstructed Rolling Fork Bayou that it will be absolutely impassable to the Admiral's [Porter's] fleet, and it will be difficult and dangerous task to withdraw it safely back to Steele's Bayou and deep, navigable water. He must go through to Rolling Fork to turn his boats, but I understand the fleet is now within a mile of Rolling Fork. I will bring forward Stuart's division as fast as possible and get it here and it may be prudent to send [Major General Frederick] Steele's division to the same point, that we may have a force sufficient for any possible contingency.

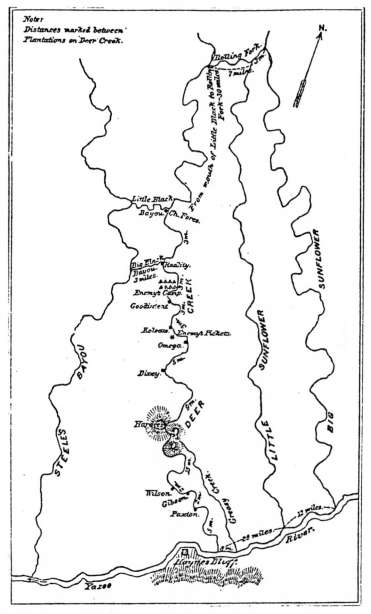

Steele's Bayou, Big Black Bayou, and Rolling Fork (*The War of the Rebellion, A Compilation of the Official Records of the Union and Confederate Armies*).

I have heard some considerable cannonading above this morning, which was doubtless the gunboats and not guerrilla operations, but it ceased after an hour. I suppose the Admiral was shelling the channel to protect his working parties. The enemy has a quicker route to reach Rolling Fork than we. Their boats can go from Yazoo City or Haynes' Bluff directly up the Sunflower, which is a large, good stream, and Rolling Fork is only seven miles long, and I understand the levee along it is continuous and above water. To reach this point, which is 21 miles from the fleet, we have to disembark at Muddy Bayou, march across to Steele's, ferry up 28 miles to the mouth of Black Bayou, and again transfer to a coal barge, and tow up about two miles before we find the first land. Thence to this point is 2½ miles, and 21 to the fleet. We were not and are not prepared to move troops this way, but will keep everything moving as fast as I can, but you know the difficulty of managing detached boats in small, crooked streams where overhanging boughs and submerged trees obstruct their progress at every quarter of a mile.

The three regiments which have gone up to Porter ought to reach him about 5:00 P.M. and if I can possibly get the Second Brigade up today or tonight, I will also send them forward as they will cover the advance of the fleet; but so far as accomplishing the original objective, viz, finding a practicable point on the east bank of the Yazoo whereon to disembark my corps, I pronounce it impossible by any channel communicating with Steele's Bayou. If the fleet push beyond Rolling Fork we can hold that point or this, and thereby enable the Admiral [Porter] to use his whole fleet. I only have the *Eagle* and *Silver Wave* to ferry troops up from Muddy Bayou and expect the *Diligence* up every hour; she is past due and will set her to work at once in bringing up men.

I take it for granted the five ironclad gunboats can fight anything that can be brought against them, and land forces are only needed to cover the ground, to enable them to clean out obstructions.

At night three steamboat loads arrived at the foot of Black Bayou. They were transferred to the first visible ground above water, at a point on the south shore to Black Bayou, about 1½ miles from its mouth and 2½ from Hill's plantation here. I conducted them through the dense canebrake by lighted candles to the plantation.[35]

Allen Geer wrote in his diary: "Weather continues hot. Times dull, false rumors, and disappointed hopes. Nothing happens to disturb dull monotony of camp life." Allen Miller wrote: "Another day's march nearer, nearer home. Met fleet of 6 transports. A countermarch is made, and we again find ourselves following the meanders of the current."

March 22. Sherman reported from Hill's Plantation about his operations to rescue Porter.

> This morning I had reason to believe from the sound of artillery in the direction of the fleet the enemy to be in force near the gunboats and without means of transportation or other facilities save what we carried on our persons I marched the soldiers over the same road which had been traveled by Colonel Smith. We went on double quick on the road along Deer Creek, entered some swamps, drummers carried drums on heads, cartridge boxes around necks. Soldiers were glad to see a general and field officers afoot. I gave them good specimen of marching, 21 miles by noon. Speed accelerated by sound of naval guns, more distinct. Met detachment of 8th Missouri Infantry under command of Captain Edward C. Washington, sent down to prevent obstructions being built below.
>
> I heard musketry. Running up the road I found Colonel [Americus] Rice [57th Ohio Volunteer Infantry Regiment] who said his column met force of Rebels with working gang of Negroes with axes. They ran into the swamps. I told Rice to deploy into swamps, sweep forward until he met gunboats. His movement was rapid and well executed.
>
> I came to large cotton field and could see gunboats in Deer Creek firing into swamps to hem in the enemy. Major [Dennis T.] Kirby, 8th Missouri, First Brigade, rode up and explained the situation.
>
> Major Kirby gave me a horse he picked up; I rode horseback to the levee. I pushed along the bayou road till I met Colonel Smith, First Brigade, Second Division, coming down to interpose between the Rebels and his outlying detachments. Our arrival was opportune. The two leading battalions of Kirby's 8th Missouri and Smith's First Brigade pushed the enemy along the swamp in rear of the plantation fields that bordered Deer Creek for about two miles, and until they were to the north and rear of the gunboat fleet. Sailors came out of the ironclads and cheered as our men swept forward across the cotton field in full view.
>
> As soon as possible I communicated with the Admiral

[Porter] and learned that he found the route far more difficult than he had been led to believe. Woods, he said, became full of sharpshooters who behind tree stumps, trees, levees fired at sailors who came out of protection of armor. Owing to enemy fire, and natural and artificial obstacles to his advance, he had abandoned the attempt to reach the Yazoo. At the time of my meeting he was in the act of backing down Deer Creek. It was difficult to handle boats in the narrow channel. One of Porter's barges at the tail of the flotilla going down sunk and had to be raised to clear the channel as going up river the vessels sailed in reverse order. A Rebel force of 6,000 anticipated Porter and obstructed Deer Creek with the placement of felled trees.

Because we had a force to protect Porter's fleet and fight off pursuing Rebels as it backed down Deer Creek, I accordingly made the necessary dispositions to cover his boats while engaged in the slow and tedious process.

I reported to General Grant, who, disappointed with the failure, ordered the expedition back to Young's Point.[36]

The sailors who were making it to safety with the aid of the soldiers were subject to the latter's words of derision. The sailors suffered their chagrin. (It would not be the only time in the war they would experience the chagrin of an army rescue of a fleet; later on Porter's fleet would be rescued by soldiers on the Red River.)

Secretary of Navy Welles commented that Porter's expedition was "an expedient without results."[37] Porter had experienced a number of expedients without success in his desire to coordinate and play a role in the battle for the Mississippi and Vicksburg.

General John E. Smith reported that on the rescue operation, General Sherman "exposed himself beyond precedent in a commanding general."[38]

Corporal Jones wrote in a letter home from Milliken's Bend: "Boy in regiment died. 3 sick. Feel fine. Hot here; raining today. Received 3½ months pay, $43.25. Pretty good living here. French bread. First rate need nothing. If you send anything send bottle pain killer."

March 23. Porter's fleet moved slowly as soldiers marched alongside Deer Creek to provide protection. Sergeant Snure, Company A, 48th Indiana Infantry, who was on the Yazoo expedition, reported that the regiment arrived with General Quinby's division at

Fort Pemberton, where the regiment embarked and camped a few miles above the mouth of the Yalobusha River. He added that Rebels had fortified the area, supposedly with six to seven thousand soldiers, and it was "a difficult place to go at." The gunboats, he reported, had attacked the fort several times before the regiment arrived but did not rout the enemy. Since then, the regiment had only engaged in some skirmishing.

Sergeant Geer, whose regiment had worked for a month on the canal at Lake Providence under severe climatic conditions, wrote in his diary: "Heavy rains. Boys want to leave this dull mud hole. Soldiers want forward movement before Rebels have time to circumvent us round about in rear." (This is an insightful observation not mentioned by officers in the records, although they might have disputed the soldiers' apprehension. The reason for Sherman's expedition against Arkansas Post might have been his anticipation of such an event.)

General Grant issued orders to his army to concentrate around Milliken's Bend as Colonel Wilson had suggested. He wrote for the record that the expedition to Steele's Bayou, Black Bayou, and Deer Creek, which was the sixth attempt to handle the problem of Vicksburg, failed more from want of knowledge about what was required to open the route than from impracticability in the navigation of streams through which the expedition was to pass. The commanders on the ground had to send back for pioneer and infantry forces; thus, the enemy was given time to impede the Union movement and progress. Grant concluded that the expedition had been withdrawn when it was almost near the open water of the Yazoo River. "All providential," he concluded, "in driving us ultimately to a line of operations which proved eminently successful."[39] (Grant's conclusion may have been true with regard to navigating Deer Creek, but Porter must have asked himself what he was doing on Deer Creek. Judging by Porter's difficulties with his ironclads, it does not seem possible that larger transports could have sailed through Rolling Fork to reach the Yazoo.)

Grant had to contend with the information passing outside of his chain of command from Milliken's Bend to Washington by General McClernand and the newspaper correspondents, but he seems to have brushed off such activity, concentrated on his army business, "and quietly worked out his own designs."[40]

Another informant appeared in Grant's department in the

person of Charles Dana, Assistant Secretary of War, who was sent by Secretary of War Edwin Stanton, to be his "eyes and ears at Grant's headquarters." To justify his presence, he was ostensibly on a task to investigate failure of the soldiers to receive their pay when due. While Lincoln professed confidence in Grant because "he was a fighter," Stanton did not share the president's judgment. He distrusted Grant and expected Dana to furnish him information if Grant were idle or unfit.[41]

Dana sent a message to Stanton from Memphis:

> A force on Yazoo, 4,500 under General Ross and 3,500 under General Quinby. They need small boats to convey reinforcements. The expedition is arrested at Greenwood where Fort Pemberton situated on a knoll made inaccessible by a swamp; heavy guns command the channel.
>
> The cutting of Lake Providence is perfectly successful. Bayou Macon full of snags; must be cleared out before Tensas river accessible. Canal at Vicksburg has broken through at upper end. River entered with great force. Health of Grant's army greatly improved. Sick list no larger than usual. This is not so well informed a place as I hoped to find it.[42]

(Dana did not give the source of his information, but the surgeon general's report does not support his assertion of army's greatly improved health. The number of deaths declined from the number in February, but not the number of cases of diseases.)

March 24. Sherman reported that Porter's fleet and his soldiers had reached Black Bayou, Hill's Plantation. "Not a shot was fired at the gunboats after we drove the enemy back at first encountering him. The enemy hung upon the rear of our column but would not come within reach."

Dana reported to Secretary of War Stanton:

> The Yazoo Pass expedition has retreated up Yalobusha 100 miles removing guns from battery planted against Fort Pemberton.
>
> Met Paymaster Major Edwin D. Judd who came from Young's Point, reported some small boats passed Pemberton. (He mentioned nothing on soldiers' pay.)
>
> The water is now flowing freely through the whole length of the canal opposite Vicksburg, but produces no effect in wearing

away the compact clay soil, which in lower half of its course is tenacious. Dredging machines inadequate to complete excavation, water too shallow for boats but too deep for men to dig in. Judd thinks it a failure.

Admiral Farragut came up Mississippi with Hartford and Albatross and drove *Queen of West* into Big Black river where he could not follow with his deep water vessels.

Brigadier General Nathan Kimball, 16th Army Corps, reports Lake Providence canal will now freely and safely pass the largest vessels through the Red river. Kimball thinks the enemy are already moving away material and preparing to evacuate Vicksburg.

Cutting of Mississippi levee has flooded whole country, and Confederates only avenue of supplies or of escape is now the Jackson railroad.

General Grant is dead sure he will have the place within a fortnight.[43]

(Even though Dana mentions Grant's second specific target date, he may not have quoted Grant correctly and his information was probably hearsay, as Dana was in Memphis, not with Grant at his headquarters.)

Hiram P. Howe wrote: "Struck camp. On board *Tecumseh*, started for Yazoo Pass. 1½ miles in pass we fast on snags. 5:00 P.M. free. 6 P.M. in Moon Lake."

March 25. General Hurlbut responded to President Lincoln's inquiry of March 20:

> Two divisions of General Sherman's command are in Steele's Bayou, above Haynes' Bluff, and two divisions in Yazoo Pass near Greenwood. Water runs freely into Lake Providence, but Bayou Macon is encumbered with trees. About 900 square miles of Upper Louisiana under water. Canal at Vicksburg deep enough but not wide enough. Enemy are repairing Mobile and Ohio railroad, and will run to Tupelo by next week. This road is strong guarded. All indications point to a steady abandonment of Vicksburg and concentration on Rosecrans, with a division on my left. Enemy's cavalry in front of Corinth are being strongly reinforced. This, I think, is a cover unless Van Dorn is driven across the Tennessee, when we may have some things to do.
>
> The troops in this command, 16th Corps, are in fine order and ready for what may turn up.[44]

(Evidence did not support Hurlbut's opinion that the enemy was abandoning Vicksburg.)

General Quinby, Seventh Division, 17th Corps, on the Tallahatchee River, sent this message to General McPherson:

> Present state of water cannot reach fort by land, or Yazoo river below it, on the west bank; but from position I hold on east bank we can easily get to Tallahatchee below the fort, and also to the Yalobusha. Both banks of the Tallahatchee about three miles below fort are several feet above the water and by means of a ponton [*sic*] bridge a force could be thrown in the rear of the fort and beyond reach of the guns.
>
> By crossing the Yalobusha just above its mouth and following down the Yazoo until we get below the fort we could cut off the supplies of the garrison and compel it to come out to fight or surrender. Either of these places will require a ponton [*sic*] bridge 250 feet long.
>
> Foster wants to return to Mississippi. One of great evils of our service that land and naval forces are left in a great measure independent of each other. The best concerted plans are liable to fail from this course.[45]

Dana reported to Secretary of War Stanton: "Hurlbut [16th Corps] has no intelligence. [What about the intelligence he passed on to president?] Rumor Yazoo expedition is definitely abandoned, but I can get nothing official."

A response on the withdrawal on the Yazoo is contained in a letter written by General Fisk, brigade commander, Thirteenth Division, to General Ross, division commander, on the Tallahatchee River:

> In obedience to orders from Brigadier General Quinby, communicated to me through your headquarters, the steamers *Citizen* and *Lebanon* have been placed in readiness to get under way for Helena tomorrow morning at daylight, and the detail of guards for each steamer ordered on board.
>
> Will you allow me, general, to suggest that it is hardly prudent to separate this amount of transportation from my brigade at present. I have just returned to my quarters from an interview with Acting Commodore Foster and Captain Walker, senior officers of the naval department of this expedition. I am assured by both of them that unless they receive

orders from Admiral Porter, directing them to remain here and wait for reinforcements of additional ironclads and ammunition, they will weigh anchor for the Mississippi river, via Moon Lake, on the 1st proximo, and quite probably before that date, and they have no expectations of receiving orders to remain. In the event of their departure, I suppose the army will follow. The transports leaving here tomorrow morning cannot make the round trip before the 6th of April under the most favorable circumstances, and some of them will without any doubt put themselves in condition not to return. My command now crowds the transports assigned to me, and the sickness in my brigade is fearfully increasing. It would be simply murdering my men to crowd them, as it would be necessary to do should we be ordered away before the return of the boats, and then is it probable that other transports will be sent into this expedition empty, to take the place of these which are expected to return with other troops? It seems to me that every foot of transportation now here should be retained until our situation is better known, or at least until our naval officers receive orders, or decide to remain here without orders.

Nearly two hundred new-made graves at Helena contain the bodies of men of my command who were murdered outright by crowding them into dirty, rotten transports, as closely as slaves in the "middle passage." It was a crime against humanity and Heaven, the packing of our brave soldiers on the White river expedition. You will, therefore, excuse me, general, if I earnestly protest against any probable repetition of such an outrage upon the gallant men who confidently believe that I will do all I can to insure their comfort and safety, without prejudice to the good cause for which they will cheerfully fight.

The company from the 29th Iowa, on the *Luella*, lost all their arms and clothing by the sinking of that staunch vessel, and one of my best officers, Lieutenant Nash, will doubtless die from injuries received thereby.[46]

(The White River expedition General Fisk referred to occurred January 13 when a large force under Brigadier General Willis A. Gorman, District of East Arkansas, proceeded up the White River to capture the town of Saint Charles, Arkansas. General Fisk commanded a brigade in the town's capture.)

General Ross sent General Fisk's letter to General Quinby with

the request that it receive careful consideration from the commanding general: "There is much force and pertinence in the suggestions.
It could scarcely fail to result disastrously should we be left without
gunboats and transports, as seems not improbable."

General Quinby sent the "protest" to General Grant, stating
that he was informed General Fisk was opposed to the expedition
from the beginning, and probably discouraged Lieutenant Commander Foster from withdrawing the gunboat fleet on or before the
first of the month.[47]

General Sherman reported to General Grant: "We remained at
Hill's Plantation all day. The enemy appeared at Fore's Plantation
about three miles above Hill's displaying three regiments of infantry
and some cavalry. I endeavored to draw them within range, but they
came no nearer. Porter left with the fleet; I propose to remain for
some days."

March 26. Sherman wrote to Grant: "I received a note from
you dated the 22nd and a note addressed to Porter by his flag captain, K. Randolph Breese, urging the immediate return to the
mouth of the Yazoo of the fleet for certain reasons outlined. Since
I sent scouts well to the front I concluded that the enemy had no
design to come nearer than Watson's, five miles above, I determined
to return. Accordingly at noon pickets were drawn in, all the men
and working parties were embarked on the gunboats and transports,
and we set out."

Dana reported to Secretary of War Stanton:

> I saw yesterday a Mr. Jordan, a very intelligent planter, who
> resides on Yazoo. He says river fortified and obstructed by a
> raft at Liverpool Bluff, 27 miles above Haynes', which is also
> obstructed by a raft.
>
> The fact reported by Paymaster Judd that boats above
> Greenwood passed into Steele's Bayou, he pronounced
> physically impossible.
>
> The Rebels think Vicksburg impregnable against any force
> but starvation.
>
> Let me suggest that I should be much more use farther
> down the river than here. At Grant's headquarters I can get the
> truth. Here it is difficult and uncertain.[48]

Hiram Howe reported, "Transport stopped to repair paddle
wheel—nigh unmanageable crosswise in stream."

March 27. Grant noted in the record that the original canal scheme had been abandoned and Lake Providence abandoned at the same time. Grant wrote that he had decided to open the Richmond-Carthage channel to afford a route for transports away from the enemy's guns. Roads in back of the levees would be used to carry troops, artillery, and wagon trains when the water receded in dry weather. Grant explained his strategy in greater detail:

> As early as February 4 I wrote to Halleck about this route more practicable by way of Willow and Roundaway Bayous, from Milliken's Bend to New Carthage. It would have been accomplished with much less labor if commenced before water inundated countryside. Dense timber to clear out before water let in, water receded and road to Richmond emerged. Some small steamers and barges through channel of bayous, but full river lowered water. No more successful than other experiments with which winter was whiled away.
>
> All failures would have been discouraging if I had expected much from these efforts but I had not. Rain, high water, dreary winter was one great hardship to all engaged. I would not divulge my plans, so called idle, unfit, other disparaging epithets. Sought my removal, but I did not answer complaints, continued to do my duty to best of my ability. President's support constant. At last waters receded. Roads beyond bayous emerged. Troops concentrated distant points at Milliken's Bend. I had in contemplation the whole winter the movement by land to a point below Vicksburg which to operate. Unless another success when waters receded. Did not mention it until needed to make preparations to start. Mentioned to Porter as needed his cooperation, and his fleet below Vicksburg. If troops there needed steamers as ferries. Porter assented to train sailors. Fleet concealed near Yazoo. Yawls and barges collected at Chicago and Saint Louis for ferries.[49]

Wilson wrote that as a staff officer he offered negative opinions agains* four of Grant's "experiments," the canal at De Soto peninsula, the canal at Lake Providence, the Yazoo Pass expedition, and Porter's Steele's Bayou reconnaissance. He noted, however, that even though they had failed, during their construction they served the purpose of worrying the Rebels about what tactical movements Grant might employ.[50]

Thus was set in motion Grant's seventh attempt to take Vicksburg, a method which Wilson had recommended at the time he reported to Grant's headquarters.

For Grant personally, his generalship had reached a critical point. He had not risen high in the hierarchy of fame and was on trial, as were the other army commanders. Paducah, Forts Henry and Donelson, and Shiloh he could claim as victories, but in the past twelve months he had failed to achieve notable successes. The Mississippi swamps had beleaguered him and placed him in limbo for the past three months.

Grant's seventh plan called for his army to march down the roads and move boats and barges down the bayous Duckport and Roundaway on the west side of the Mississippi. The Union gunboats and transports were to sail down the river and run past the gun batteries at Vicksburg. When the soldiers and sailors joined below the fortified town at a convenient site, his army would board the transports and other boats and naval vessels to be ferried over the river to its east bank.

Grant recorded that he had failed to succeed in the first six attempts to take Vicksburg because "God wanted him to use the road."[51] He issued orders to General McClernand to conduct a survey for a road.

When Sherman returned from the Steele's Bayou expedition to Milliken's Bend, he said it was the end of one of the many efforts to secure a footing to reach Vicksburg and added, "It became thoroughly demonstrated we could not divert the main Mississippi river or get practicable access to east bank of Yazoo by any of the passes."

The expedition's route had covered 30 miles through Deer Creek, 4 miles through Black Bayou, 20 miles up Steele's Bayou, 7 miles through Muddy Bayou, 5 miles through Cypress Bayou, and 12 miles to the Mississippi and camp.

In a message to Stanton, Dana said: "Report is Sherman has 20 regiments landed on east bank of Yazoo river above Hayne's Bluff and greatest enthusiasm throughout army at this success. The report he is supported by gunboats in Yazoo is repeated." Dana also stated that the channel from Deer Creek into the Sunflower River had to be enlarged by digging, but all reports on the subject were confused and doubtful. Dana concluded that the Yazoo Pass expedition had not been abandoned but had received supplies and had been reinforced by Quinby's division.

Company G, 57th Ohio Infantry Regiment, engaged the enemy at Rolling Fork, fell back to Hill's Plantation, boarded the steamer *Eagle*, and passed through Bayou Black, Steele's Bayou, Cypress Bayou, Bayou to Young's Point, where it encamped after a journey of 146 miles.

March 28. Sergeant Snure reported that his regiment conducted some reconnaissance that drew Rebel fire, which had little effect, except that a general's aide lost his hat. There was heavy rain at night that blew down the dead trees. He told his family he would write more perhaps, "if no preventing Providence," a statement that indicated his concern that he might become a casualty. He also offered his opinion that the Yazoo Pass expedition was proved a failure.

Frank Leslie's Independent Newspaper correspondent wrote:

> Operations Vicksburg uncertain. Work on canal interrupted by inflow of river. Yazoo Pass has promise. Advantage but we are not informed of what. Rumor expedition captured Yazoo City and destroyed Confederate fleet there.
>
> Canal great feat in engineering. Great human ingenuity in labor success questioned. Double object in view to punish Vicksburg rebellious city by diverting the channel of Mississippi thus leaving town comparatively isolated, and to allow gunboats to pass enemy's fire. Reports say 4,000 contrabands working on canal. Remember below sand is clay. Make canal durable when water flows. Correspondents say engineers cutting too near bend, should be two miles further from Vicksburg to take advantage of surge of current but increases labor. As is breaks levee of Vicksburg and Shreveport Railroad.

March 29. Captain Ankeny wrote to his wife: "Yazoo expedition has been a failure and returned. Canal work ceased. High water. Been having reviews, but what they mean I do not know. Generally they mean action against enemy. Cold for two days."

Secretary of War Stanton informed Dana: "Your telegrams have been received. Although information has been meager and unsatisfactory, I am conscious that arises from no fault of yours. You will proceed to Grant's headquarters or wherever you may be best able to accomplish the purposes designated by this department. You will consider your movements to be governed by your own discretion without any restriction."

March 30. President Lincoln set the day aside as a day of fast and prayer.

Dana reported to Stanton:

> Grant has sent for all steamboats that can be had as if he intended to move the bulk of his army from its present position.
>
> No gunboats have entered Yazoo river from Porter's fleet. They can't force the passage from Deer Creek into Sunflower.
>
> Porter himself while reconnoitering a bayou in a small steamer was caught by falling trees in his rear. Two regiments of infantry were sent to extricate him.
>
> Two newspapers here say Sherman has taken Haynes' Bluff, but I can find no foundation for the report.
>
> A spy of Hurlbut's declares Vicksburg fully provisioned for nine months.

When General McClernand received orders from General Grant to conduct a reconnaissance for a road south to attack the left flank of the Confederate army, he in turn issued orders to Brigadier General Peter J. Osterhaus, commanding general of the Ninth Division: "You will order one regiment armed and equipped with 40 rounds of ammunition in their cartridge boxes, an ammunition wagon laden with suitable ammunition, their camp garrison equipage, and four days prepared rations, to report opposite these headquarters by 8:00 A.M. tomorrow for further orders. I would suggest the 69th Indiana, Colonel [Thomas W.] Bennett, to be detached for the service contemplated."

McClernand issued orders to Colonel Bennett, 69th Indiana Volunteers, Milliken's Bend:

> Besides your own regiment you will have command of detachments of cavalry and pioneers for the purpose of the important expedition with which you are charged. The main purpose of the expedition is to open a practicable communication for our forces via Richmond, Louisiana between this camp and New Carthage. Of course the shortest route, whether by land or water, all other things being equal, would be preferable. It is certain there is navigable communication between Richmond and New Carthage by Roundaway and Vidal Bayous, and it is also believed that there is a road along the bank of Roundaway Bayou almost the whole distance.

That route which you can make available for the passage of troops and trains with the least labor and in the shortest time, you will select, and make available at the earliest practicable moment. The detachment of pioneers, as already mentioned, will be at your command for that purpose and Lieutenant William R. McComas, aide de camp and engineer, of my staff, will give you any assistance in his power.

If a practicable route be found, you will not only consider it with reference to passage, but also with reference to its capability of defense, and for this purpose you will select and report suitable sites for posts or garrisons along it. If no practicable route can be found, you will immediately report that fact.

March 31. In pursuance of his orders to conduct a reconnaissance, Colonel Bennett arrived at Roundaway Bayou, opposite Richmond, at approximately 2 P.M., where he discovered enemy cavalry pickets posted. Some of his cavalrymen crossed the bayou in skiffs and boldly attacked the Rebels. The Rebels fled precipitately, leaving two of their wounded to Union care, but carrying away seven of their other wounded. Thus Osterhaus' expedition engaged in its first skirmish with the enemy.

Captain Ankeny wrote to his wife: "Our orders are to be ready to march. Carry 14 days rations and no transportation; this indicated a move by water. No other mode of transportation here. No one knows where we go. I suppose some unknown bayou. Also dark what we are to accomplish. All side shows have played out. We will have to go far inland to take Vicksburg. This will be Grant's old line down Central Mississippi Railroad, taking Jackson tantamount to taking Vicksburg. We will leave our sick in camp. All in commotion here."

Frank Leslie's Independent Newspaper correspondent wrote from the Yazoo expedition: "Yazoo empties into Mississippi, 200 mile serpentine course. Rebels make lots of effort to obstruct Pass. Thrown away by nature. Nature put greater obstacles. Providence did not intend it for a military highway."

CHAPTER 5

April 1863

Seventh Attempt to
Take the Mountain

If at the beginning of the new month, Grant's soldiers found little change in the disposition of the Army of the Tennessee or their camp life, the *New York Times* correspondent Galway wrote of the sureness of change in the natural world. If nothing else was favorable or desirable, he wrote, the weather filled one's liking:

"Deliciously warm days and moderately cool nights together with the full, rich beauty of spring make our surroundings as delightful as could be desired. Under such circumstances, with cloudless skies by day and the undimmed glories of a full moon at night, with roads at once hard, dry and free from dust, provisions plenty, and no more to do than sufficient for purposes of digestion, campaigning among our troops is, at present, a positive species of enjoyment."[1]

April 1. Grant's reconnaissance orders to Generals McClernand and Osterhaus presaged the seventh attempt to take Vicksburg.

General Osterhaus made a personal reconnaissance in pursuance of instructions from General McClernand, and his observations convinced him of the necessity of a permanent occupation of Richmond, Louisiana. The town stood fast as a point where the necessary subsistence stores were forwarded to the besieged garrison at Vicksburg. The very rich and fertile regions between the Mississippi and Tensas rivers and Bayou Macon were easily reached by water from Richmond. Osterhaus' reconnaissance also removed all doubts about the main object of the expedition, the practicability of a road to New Carthage.[2] He reported that General McClernand shared his opinion about the importance of Richmond. Desirous of pushing forward the expedition of New Carthage, Osterhaus ordered reinforcements to be brought up from Milliken's Bend.

Osterhaus recognized in the absence of maps depicting the terrain on the west bank of the river the importance of his task to determine the existence of a road. He was aware too the task would have to be done by traversing the terrain step by step. The completion of his first step demonstrated to him the importance of Richmond as a point on the army's line of communications and the need to establish defenses before he set out on the second step to New Carthage.

General McClernand ordered Osterhaus to push forward a detachment of infantry and cavalry to reconnoiter as far as practical the road to New Carthage. He also noted the presence of Confederate cavalry in the area. "You will order all such parties to be boldly attacked and captured or dispersed."

Colonel Bennett of the 69th Indiana Infantry issued orders to his troops:

> Infantry to go into camp on Carthage road beyond town of Richmond and cavalry to go into camp on north side of the bayou.
>
> Private property will not be injured or destroyed. Soldiers will not molest or injure abandoned property. Provisions and forage to be taken on order of regimental commander.
>
> Commanders will enforce discipline of enlisted men and hold them in perfect readiness for action at any hour.
>
> This expedition is an important one, and if we all do our duty it will prove successful.
>
> Your corps commander has placed implicit confidence in the courage, discipline, and efficiency of this command. Let us not disappoint him.

Dana reported to Secretary of War Stanton that on March 28 after Sherman's return, Grant said confidentially that he had tried unsuccessfully every conceivable indirect means of attacking Vicksburg. Nothing but a direct assault upon the enemy's works remained. "This is also opinion of general officers of his army," Dana said.

The judgment of the general officers was divided on such an assault, according to Dana. "General Blair is reported to me as favoring it. I believe Grant himself opposed. Sherman too (the most influential of Grant's subordinates). Yet I have not positive information."[3]

Dana concluded by saying that he doubted Grant would move the bulk of his army back up the river. Grant was confident, Dana added, that by taking Vicksburg in cooperation with Admiral Farragut and General Banks, the Union forces would effectually cut off Confederate supplies from west of the river.

In his report, Dana also mentioned that deserters from Vicksburg who arrived in Grant's camp said that food, excluding meat, was plentiful in the town.

April 2. Grant wrote to Halleck: "In two weeks I expect to collect all my forces and turn the enemy's left flank. With present high water the extent of ground upon which troops could land at Haynes' Bluff is so limited that the place is impregnable. I reconnoitered the place yesterday with Porter and Sherman."[4] In this message, Grant intimated he planned to march his army south to cross the Mississippi River, but his target date proved to be overly optimistic.

Halleck addressed a lecture on military doctrine to Grant:

> While working upon the canal the division of your forces into several eccentric operations may have been very proper for the purpose of reconnoitering the country, but very important when you strike any blow, a maxim of military doctrine is you should have your troops sufficiently concentrated to make that blow effective. The division of your army into small expeditions destroys your strength and when in the presence of the enemy is very dangerous.
>
> What is most desired and your attention is again called to this object is that your forces and General Banks' should be brought into cooperation as early as possible. If he cannot get up to cooperate with you, cannot you get troops down to help him on Port Hudson or at least can you not destroy Grand Gulf before it becomes too strong? I know you can judge there much better than I. But the President is impatient about matters on the Mississippi; he has several times asked me these questions. I repeat them to you.

General Osterhaus deployed his reinforcements, sending the 29th Indiana Infantry and 22nd Kentucky Infantry, with one section of the 7th Michigan Battery, to Roundaway Bayou. He deployed the 69th Indiana Infantry and one company of cavalry by boats across the bayou to occupy Richmond and the road to Stanbrough's Plantation, three and one-half miles beyond. At that point the regiment would occupy a road reported to be above water and that led to Alligator Lake, where a force of the enemy reportedly was encamped.

At the same time, Osterhaus directed a reconnaissance to be made by cavalry as far as possible toward New Carthage. The movements were preparatory to an expedition in force intended to be made on the New Carthage road as soon as the 390-foot long timber-trestle bridge across Roundaway Bayou, under construction by Captain Patterson's Company of Kentucky Mechanics and Engineers with materials salvaged from nearby plantations, could be completed. He also ordered forward from Milliken's Bend to Richmond the First Brigade under Brigadier General Theophilus T. Garrard, together with the remaining two sections of the 7th Michigan Battery and a battalion of the 6th Missouri Cavalry, with four mountain howitzers.

Dana reported to Stanton that General J. D. Webster of Grant's staff [superintendent of military railroads] had arrived at Memphis and from him he had received authentic information that Grant had no intention to withdraw the bulk of his army to attempt a direct assault on Vicksburg.

Webster, according to Dana, said arrangements had been completed for beginning to open a passage (or canal) seven to nine miles long through a bayou emptying into the Mississippi at Duckport, Milliken's Bend, to reach a point below Warrenton. The bayou would be straightened and widened in what Webster said would be a two-week job.

Another plan was to float empty transports past Vicksburg in the dark with steam enough to save them from floating ashore but not enough to betray their presence to the enemy. With the transports below Vicksburg, troops would be marched down the Louisiana side, embarked below the Rebel batteries, and conveyed to the point where they would most effectually threaten the bridge over the Big Black River. (This message reveals that Dana did obtain information on Grant's plan to build the canal Walnut Bayou to connect Roundaway Bayou to New Carthage.)[5]

Dana also reported:

Our engineers have constructed two casemates on shore opposite Vicksburg whence with 30-pounder Parrotts they can destroy any building in the town, a distance of some 3,000 yards. Work done at night not to attract attention of enemy.

The Yazoo river expedition is definitely abandoned but the orders required a final vigorous attack on Fort Pemberton before withdrawing. Officers blame the captain of *Chillicothe* for not taking along sufficient ammunition; could have fought vessel longer. Fort might easily have been taken.

Paymaster Judd received today five million dollars which he distributed to his subordinates, who will leave for points of disbursement tomorrow.

General Hurlbut proposes to settle the Negro question here by enrolling for duty as pioneers, teamsters, &c all who are fit for service in this immediate vicinity and along line of railroad he is guarding, taking sufficient bonds for the good treatment and return of persons. Grant has approved plan.[6]

President Jefferson Davis congratulated General Pemberton for thwarting the Union army at Vicksburg.

April 3. General Osterhaus reported that the reinforcements he had ordered the day before arrived in the afternoon. Also, the cavalry reconnaissance he had ordered on the New Carthage road returned. The cavalrymen had advanced about ten miles when they were stopped by a rebel cavalry force at Holmes' Plantation. Captain Patterson's company finished the bridge across Roundaway Bayou at 7 P.M.

Grant's staff signal officer reported that a line of communications by signals had been opened from Milliken's Bend to the foot of the old canal. This system made it possible to transmit many important official messages to different points of line and to Admiral Porter's flagship, where an officer of the signal corps was permanently stationed.

April 4. Grant to Halleck:

> Porter has been in Yazoo river except a few hundred yards in Deer Creek near Rolling Creek where enemy placed obstructions and they are guarding and fortifying there. This will require enemy to throw in additional force and move some of their guns. My force had as well be there as here until I want to use them.
>
> A reconnaissance to Haynes' Bluff demonstrates the

impracticability of attacking that place during present stage of water. The west bank of the river is densely wooded and is under water. The east bank only runs up to the bluff for a short distance below the raft. The hillsides are lined with rifle pits with embrasures here and there for field artillery. To storm this but a small force could be used at the outset.

Grant also reported that because of the present batteries of the enemy, the canal across the point could be of little use. Grant then revealed his plan for the seventh attempt to take Vicksburg, a plan to employ a system of bayous running from the river (Duckport) and Milliken's Bend that would be navigable for barges and small steamers to pass around Richmond to move to New Carthage. Grant gave further details of his plan to Halleck:

> The dredges are now engaged in cutting a canal from here into these bayous. I am having all the empty coal and other barges prepared for carrying troops and artillery and have written Colonel Robert Allen [department quartermaster] for some more and also for six tugs to tow them. With these it would be easy to carry supplies to New Carthage and any point south.
>
> My expectation is for a portion of naval fleet to run batteries of Vicksburg whilst the army moves through by this new route. Once there I will move either to Warrenton or Grand Gulf, most probably latter. From either of these points there are good roads to Vicksburg and from Grand Gulf there is a good road to Jackson and the Big Black river bridge without crossing the river. This is the only move I see as practicable and hope it will meet with your approval. I will keep my army together and see to it that I am not cut off from my supplies or beaten in any other than in a fair fight. The discipline and health of this army is now good, and I am satisfied the greatest confidence of success prevails.[7]

(The end of the passage affirms that Grant had heeded Halleck's lecture on April 2 on military doctrine.)

Dana's statement on April 1 that Sherman was the "most influential of Grant's subordinates" can be seriously questioned. Grant passed over Sherman's proffered advice on the direction of the Vicksburg campaign. Sherman did faithfully support Grant's decision, however, which Grant outlined and sought approval for in his day's message to Halleck. Colonel Wilson, although he had expressed opinions against four of Grant's prior "experiments" at Milliken's Bend, exercised influence as a staff officer on Grant's decision.

Wilson recorded background information on Grant's plan. Early in the year Wilson had, in his discussions with Rawlins on the status of the army at Milliken's Bend, related his experience with the expeditionary force at Port Royal, South Carolina, in November 1861. At Port Royal, Wilson explained, naval gunboats and army transports developed and employed tactics to escape the fire of Confederate gun batteries in order to capture the fort guarding the entrance of the port facilities. Based on his experience at Port Royal as the expedition's staff engineer officer, he suggested Porter's fleet and army transports could emulate the same tactics and run the gun batteries on the bluffs at Vicksburg. Concurrently the soldiers could march down the west bank of the Mississippi to join at a rendezvous with the fleet and be transported across the river. Rawlins carried Wilson's proposal to Grant but reported back that Grant thought that the proposal was impractical and the boats would be destroyed.[8]

In his memoirs, Grant wrote that he planned to carry the expedition into effect as he proposed to Halleck and seemingly in the way Wilson proposed, if his expedients failed, but he did not mention Wilson's suggestion.[9]

Osterhaus left early in the morning on the second step of the reconnaissance expedition with detachments of the 2nd and 3rd Illinois Cavalry and 6th Missouri Cavalry and 49th and 69th Indiana Infantry regiments, totaling about 250 soldiers and four mountain howitzers. The occupation of Richmond and Stanbrough's Plantation was entrusted to General Garrard. Osterhaus' expedition crossed Captain Patterson's bridge over Roundaway Bayou at 5 A.M. and arrived at Holmes' Plantation, where the enemy's rear guard had been seen at 9 A.M. the previous day.

The last of the Rebels left Holmes' Plantation upon the arrival of Osterhaus' column and remained all day at a safe but observing distance. Osterhaus marched the expedition on to Smith's Plantation, where Roundaway Bayou entered Bayou Vidal. This plantation was about two miles almost due north from Carthage. The road was totally submerged, and boats became the only means of communication. "Seeing the enemy's pickets still in my front," Osterhaus reported, "I concluded to march past Smith's in order to find out, if possible, the locality of the rebel camp."

At Montgomery's Plantation Osterhaus halted the column, sending a cavalry patrol on to Dunbar's Plantation, six miles below Montgomery's. His soldiers saw the Rebels cross Bayou Vidal and learned that their main camp was on a high ridge on Judge Perkins' tract, between the Mississippi and Bayou Bridgeman, six miles below New Carthage and fourteen miles to the south of Dunbar's Plantation.

Osterhaus concluded:

> Further inquiry was unnecessary, volumes of water separating and protecting me from them. Leaving a picket of observation at Dunbar's, where the Rebels crossed Bayou Vidal, I encamped the detachment of 3rd Illinois Cavalry at Montgomery's, stationing at the same time pickets at such points between Montgomery's and Dunbar's as could control the enemy approach. The main body of the reconnaissance detachment I marched back to Smith's Plantation, with the consent and approval of General McClernand who had by this time arrived to join me.[10]

A reconnaissance conducted by McClernand and Osterhaus across the bayou toward New Carthage revealed that the water was over all the plantations between Smith's Plantation and New Carthage. They advanced along the levee running parallel with Bayou Vidal, and, proceeding around the break in the levee, they found their progress stopped by the fire of a skirmish with a Rebel picket force on the other side of the third and last break. The two generals were then in full sight of the inundated New Carthage, and it was evident to them that communication with the town could only be established by boats.

Serious about their assignment to find a route for Grant's seventh attempt to take Vicksburg, McClernand and Osterhaus on their return to Smith's Plantation immediately commenced preparations to secure a foothold at New Carthage to complete the second step of the reconnaissance. The enemy had collected all boats and flats, and the nearest one of any size they were able to learn about was almost eight miles down Bayou Vidal, below Dunbar's Plantation, and was protected by a rebel picket. McClernand and Osterhaus reported they received this information from a Negro who came into the lines with four others. These five men said they

General McClernand's Corps Marching Through the Bogs
(*Harper's Pictorial History*).

were willing to take the flat from the enemy. Osterhaus ordered
Captain Robert H. Carnahan to send the five Negroes and twenty
cavalrymen of the 3rd Illinois Cavalry to capture the boat.

A correspondent of the *New York Times* sent a dispatch reporting:

> Little has occurred to attract attention since the return of
> the expedition up the Yazoo. Important undertakings preg-
> nant with great results are frequently announced as under
> way, or about to be commenced. With the season fast march-
> ing toward the summer solstice, the breath of midday already
> fervent, the torment of mosquitoes at midnight unbearable
> without mosquito bars—which the commissary of existence
> doesn't furnish—while malaria, fever and dysentery are
> multiplying graves which convert their very camp ground into
> cemeteries; it is probably both expedient and necessary to oc-
> cupy the minds of the soldiers with the promise, at least, of ac-
> tivity in one direction or another. So far as one can judge from
> appearances, there is just now no definite plan or operations
> laid out for either the land or naval forces in this Department.
> Affairs are drifting. We wait for something to turn up. By the
> tone of dispatches to the press sent from this quarter, an im-
> pression seems to prevail at the north and east something to

turn up, and that we are driving a big business in this department. One day we see it stated that the Rebels are in their last gasp, being starved out. The next day they have evacuated Vicksburg, and a large number of Quaker guns have been discovered there. All false and deceptive. The truth, simple and undisguised, is so far as your correspondent can judge from actual observation, there is nothing doing here, except an occasional and fragmentary effort on the part of either the army or naval force to dig a canal, explore some bayou, or discover some creek or backdoor opening, by which to evade the Rebel batteries and get at Vicksburg, and take it, as it were by guile. These plans seem to differ as widely as do the mental and military qualifications of the men having command of affairs in this Department. At one time we are promised a brilliant triumph of engineering skill, by the opening of Lake Providence canal. But as soon as the water begins to rush through, and the work is pronounced a success, all further attempts are abandoned, the workmen and troops are withdrawn, and another grand scheme is projected in another quarter. The great canal that was to carry our troops and gunboats in safety by Vicksburg, and on which so much labor has been expended, seems just now to be abandoned altogether, and the opinion seems to prevail that no practical use can be made of it since its lower level outlet is within easy range of the rebel batteries on the Vicksburg side. If half or quarter of the labor which has been thrown away upon this stupendous humbug had been expended in the construction of a military road in the same direction, but out of reach of rebel guns, so as to connect the upper with the lower fleet, we should have had a highway on which troops and supplies, in any amount, could now have been safely passing the rebel strongholds on the Louisiana side, and all the canals have been rendered superfluous. Just at the present time, when the whole country is inundated and every little creek is swollen to navigable streams, it is comparatively easy to push our way in any desired direction, but as soon as these floods assuage, our gunboats and transports, if caught in these narrow and tortuous bayous, would be as high and dry as Noah's ark was upon Mount Ararat, and about as helpless.[11]

April 5. On their mission the 3rd Cavalry soldiers located and took possession of the flat. Returning to Smith's Plantation, they engaged the Confederates in their third skirmish when they encountered about 50 enemy cavalrymen on the east side of the bayou, who opened fire. The 3rd Cavalry returned the fire from their side of the stream effectively enough to gain the whole attention of the Rebels and thus enabled the flat to run the blockade without injury. Casualties inflicted on the enemy were one killed and one wounded.

Captain Patterson arrived during the day with his company of Kentucky Mechanics and Engineers and received orders to put his men to work immediately to arrange the flatboat to give protection against musketry fire and to carry one light gun and the requisite infantry force for the purpose of capturing New Carthage. He built bulwarks on the flatboat to protect the soldiers it was to transport from Rebel musketry fire and a casemate for the light gun emplaced aboard.[12]

Dana reported to Stanton: "I find no important information here reference Grant's movements. McClernand has moved from Milliken's Bend on April 3 and occupied Richmond on the railroad opposite Vicksburg. No part of Yazoo expedition has arrived here nor is there any information that the retreat has commenced."

April 6. Osterhaus marched out at 5 A.M. onto the flatboat bound for New Carthage. His expedition's advance caused the Rebel force to fall back down the Mississippi levee. Osterhaus disembarked the mountain howitzer and a company of 49th and 69th Indiana Infantry regiments to pursue the Rebels. The Rebels made a stand at the cotton gin on James' Plantation, about one and one-half miles below New Carthage. Osterhaus was determined to dislodge the enemy because the plantation's quarters, steam gin, and grist and saw mills covered 20 acres, and the acres for many miles around were the only dry lands in the area outside of the levee, which was effectually commanded by the gin. Osterhaus ordered the attack, the fourth skirmish of his expeditionary force with the enemy, and after a struggle of about an hour the Rebels were driven off.

In order to hold the important position at New Carthage, Osterhaus moved the entire 69th Infantry Regiment and two mountain howitzers to the gin to secure it against attack. A system of barricades and a deep, wide ditch across the levee were built. Osterhaus learned that the enemy's force of 700 to 900 cavalrymen at Perkins' Plantation had been reinforced by a six-gun battery and the 1st Missouri Confederate Infantry.

To secure his line of communications with Richmond and Milliken's Bend, Osterhaus redeployed his force, with the approval of McClernand. He protected the levee and roads, the line of retreat, and threatened the enemy directly by the force at James' Plantation and on its flank by the cavalry detachments at Dunbar's Plantation. The cavalry detachment at Dunbar's cut off the enemy from its resources for subsistence. Osterhaus' patrols extended over the country west to the Tensas River and obtained whatever was available for the benefit of the expedition enabling it to live almost entirely off the countryside. The Rebels kept a large force opposite Dunbar's harassing the Yankees by occasional shots. Osterhaus reported to McClernand that there was a continuous levee all the way from New Carthage to Saint Joseph and that the land adjacent to Bayou Vidal where it joined Perkins' Plantation was not submerged. "I have not the remotest doubt as to the practicability of the Bayou Vidal for boating purposes. It is a deep straight channel; only very light obstructions between the crevasse and the Mississippi. A few hours work will clear them away."[13]

Captain Patterson reported to General McClernand about his trip to New Carthage on Roundaway Bayou. In places there was a strong current, and in others the water was still. Near Holmes' Plantation driftwood slows passage and needs to be removed. At places trees are in the water and need to be cut and floated out. Near Smith's Plantation the floating timber occurred again with the downward current. Patterson stated that from Richmond to Smith's the army could run small flats the entire distance and then pass through the levee at Carthage into the Mississippi. After passing the main levee, the depth of the water was about three feet. Patterson reported: "Still General Osterhaus, who was along, thinks we will have no trouble to go through. We can land steamboats within 200 yards of the main levee, and there are cross levees reaching the river in several places to the main levee. There is no dry land save the levee. Small flats will be the readiest means of conveyance from Richmond to Carthage. We can construct these rapidly here with the help of these fine mills close at hand."[14]

Dana reported to Stanton:

> Arrived Milliken's Bend today at noon. Grant is very confident Vicksburg will soon be taken, not only from the result of the operations now on foot, but also from the starvation of the garrison.[15]

Grant reports supplies west side of the river cut off and
those from Yazoo country diminished.

McClernand's Corps occupied New Carthage. McPherson
ready to move from Lake Providence.

The new cutoff (Duckport Canal) is already half completed. Today 3,400 men are at work on it. Colonel G. G.
Pride, engineer, says that he will be ready for it just as soon as
necessary tugs and barges can arrive from up the river.

The length of navigation in this cutoff will be some 30 miles
and plan is to take through it small tugs with some 50 barges
enough to cross entire army with artillery and baggage in 24
hours. The channel will only be wide enough for narrow craft.

The half dozen steamboats protected by defenses of sand
bags and wet-hay bales will be floated down the river past the
batteries to serve as transports of supplies after the crossing is
effected. Land at or about Grand Gulf. Army operate on east
side of Big Black river. Enemy will be compelled to come out
and fight. The wagon train left behind at Memphis has now
been ordered down for the purpose of this movement.

Corporal Jones, Company G, 23rd Wisconsin Volunteer Infantry, wrote home, "Another death in the company. Sent overcoat
home without washing it. Expect another three months pay shortly."
Galway, the *New York Times* correspondent, filed this dispatch:

> The fact that our men are enjoying themselves does not
> altogether compensate for the entire lack of progress that
> marks the character of this expedition against Vicksburg. It is
> better than if they were dying by hundreds as they were a
> month since, or were suffering the privations and discomforts
> arising from lack of supplies and successive days of cold,
> pitiless rain; yet even this fact will not counterbalance the
> other—that we are beyond enjoying ourselves doing abso-
> lutely nothing; and that today we are as far from taking posses-
> sion of Vicksburg as when we landed here in the middle of last
> January.
>
> I don't say this to create discouragement on the part of the
> public, or a feeling of distrust against our commanders, but
> simply with a view of rousing inquiry as to our present position
> and of provoking discussion relative to the character of plans
> which keep a vast army in absolute idleness, without a single
> promise that this waiting will result in good.
>
> If it be a part of General Halleck's combinations to keep this

force here as a feint, with a view of amusing and keeping employed as large a number as possible of the enemy, while he moves against him at some other points, then the keeping here of our army may be of use, but under no other circumstances, particularly if they be connected with the hope that operations from this point may result in the capture of Vicksburg.

Massing men here amounts to nothing, for, whether we have ten men or one hundred thousand, there is always between us and the enemy a deep, swift river of a mile in breadth, to cross, which, in the face of the one hundred and sixty guns which frown upon us from the opposite heights beyond the reach of human valor, endurance or ingenuity. We must have firm ground upon which to approach that we may avail ourselves of those means of offense and defense invented by the skill of engineering.

As has been previously urged in this correspondence that kind of approach is only to be found in the rear of Vicksburg. We are now attempting in fact to take a mountain, surrounded by either wide deep rivers or impassable swamps. There is not with the exception of the narrow peninsula opposite, a single square rood of land within miles of Vicksburg upon which can be placed a cannon. Nature has rendered the approaches to Vicksburg fully as formidable and hazardous to a hostile force as art has made the actual defenses.

The original plan—that of penetrating south along Central Mississippi, and taking Vicksburg by a flank movement—was correct; and it yet remains to us as the only one which we can secure the reduction of that stronghold. Along that route we have high ground all the way; the rivers that cross the approach are narrow; a railroad connecting with Memphis furnishes a line for the easy transportation of supplies; the line of communication would be short and easily protected—in fact I believe it to be the only direction in which our present efforts can meet with success. All that we can do here is to amuse the enemy, keep him from sending reinforcements to Charleston, Murfreesboro or other points and to some extent cut off his supplies by blockading the river. But even admitting that we are here to employ the attention of the enemy, it is a matter of doubt that there is good sense in keeping, say 75,000 men, here for the purpose of hindering 25,000 of the enemy from reinforcing some other point. So far as the blockade is concerned, a half dozen gunboats can sustain it as well as though we had with them a land force of a half a million. In any case, a small force of three or four thousand would answer just as good a purpose as our present number.

One thing is certain, and that is every officer has long ago given up all idea that we can ever take Vicksburg from this direction. They are merely willing now like Micawber, hoping that the War Department will make an alteration in its plans or that some lucky accident will throw into their possession a point which has proved impregnable against their shrewdest plans and most ingenious combinations.

In view of these facts, which may as well be known as not, I think the sooner this army is taken from here, and a new base of operations taken up, the sooner the country will get rid of an enormous and useless expense, and the sooner it will begin to realize something substantial from the gigantic investment it has already made in the opening of the Mississippi river. We should have succeeded last fall in flanking Vicksburg by way of Grenada, had it not been that our line of communications was cut by a small squad of vagabonds under Van Dorn. If a department having an army of 100,000 men cannot keep uninterrupted a line of communications 70 miles in length, it is, to say the very least, most miserably managed; and yet it was the failure to keep open that paltry 70 miles of railroad, that rendered Grant's fall campaign a failure, that was to a very great extent responsible for Sherman's failure at Chickasaw Bayou that lost us a vast portion of Mississippi, and has cost us all the time and expense of the present expectations.

There has been no change of importance within the last few days. The battery on the peninsula has not commenced operations but will as soon as the skillful engineer who constructed it has had time to enlarge the embrasures, so that the gunners can work their pieces — a necessity in the work that did not occur to the contractor, until he had spent a couple of weeks in throwing up earth and in spiking on a hundred tons or so of railroad iron. By tearing it all apart, and rebuilding the defenses upon an entirely new scale, he might be able to correct this slight defect in the construction of his work.

General Grant has moved his headquarters from the steamer *Magnolia*, at Young's Point, to the dry land at Milliken's Bend.

The new canal is progressing and ere this reaches you will be finished. It commences about six miles above the original

canal and at a distance of a mile from the banks of the
Mississippi where it strikes a wing of the bayou that empties
into the Mississippi at a point called Carthage, a place about
thirty miles below Vicksburg. It will be used merely to float
supplies down to a land force that within a day or two has gone
across and taken possession of Carthage; and what this force
will do there I cannot tell. Without transports they cannot
cross the river, and hence will be limited in their efforts in
ravaging the country, and assisting Farragut in maintaining
the blockade of the river below Vicksburg.

The river is still rising and has rendered nearly untenable
every point below Milliken's Bend.[16]

Charles Enslow, Company C, 77th Illinois Volunteer Infantry,
in a letter to his wife wrote: "Everything is excitement today. See
thousands of troops pass by. We have enough troops to whip entire
south. Men stand up like men as God intended. Can't see how ragged
rebels hold out.

"Old Anaconda, which Scott told us so much about is beginning to tighten his coils and my opinion is that in six months he will
crush every bone in the body of the Confederacy. Here is Grant with
immense army hovering over Vicksburg."

"Old Anaconda" was a reference to Lieutenant General Win-
field Scott's alleged plan, Anaconda, for the armed forces to suppress the rebellion. Northern newspapers headlined their expressions of opposition to the conduct of the Civil War with the word
Anaconda, which became a catchword. Enslow probably picked up
the expression from reading some newspaper or by word of mouth.
The name of the creator of the expression remains unknown. There
is no reference to an Anaconda plan in the published *Official Records
of the War of the Rebellion* or in any of General Scott's reports.

It is interesting to note that Enslow used the expression in the
belief that it was an affirmative policy of General Scott. Unwittingly,
he turned around what he had heard to convey to his wife his own
thoughts on the progress of the war.

April 7. Osterhaus took action to stop the large Confederate
force opposite Dunbar's that was annoying his soldiers with occasional shots. He ordered Major Bacon Montgomery, 6th Missouri
Cavalry, to move his mountain howitzers to Dunbar's to shell at
daybreak their encampment. The order was carried out successfully,
completing the fifth skirmish with the enemy soldiers, who left pell-

mell. Osterhaus also published to his command the remarks from General McClernand, Headquarters, Advance 13th Army Corps, Smith's Plantation, acknowledging the expedition's service on the front. "Congratulate you on your success at Carthage, seizing the position, and pushing your pickets further down the river. You have reached a point further south than any other land forces marching from the interior towards the Gulf."[17]

Captain Ocran H. Howard, United States Signal Corps, Grant's chief signal officer, reported that a line was opened from General Grant's headquarters at Milliken's Bend, through General McPherson's headquarters, to General Osterhaus' headquarters at Richmond. The line was used as a means of communication between those points until the removal of General Osterhaus' command to Grand Gulf. From a point on this line, another line was projected to New Carthage and opened as far as Holmes' Plantation. While Grant's force was on the west side of the river, the lines were in use as a means of communication between different corps headquarters.

Allen Geer, 20th Illinois Infantry, recorded in his diary that the regiment continued to drill and put a guard around the camp to receive the adjutant general, Brigadier General Lorenzo Thomas.

Hiram Howe, 10th Missouri Volunteer Infantry, recorded in his diary an incident that occurred aboard the transport *Tecumseh* as his regiment retreated from the Yazoo Pass expedition under damaging fire from Confederate soldiers:

> *General Quinby to Tecumseh Captain*: "Move on—out and on! You had orders to move at 6:30 A.M. It's now 7."
>
> *Captain*: "We have to do some repairs—can't move an inch till."
>
> *General Quinby*: "This transport has troubled me many times on the expedition. I have a mind to take the regiment off and set fire to the steamer and burn her to the water's edge."
>
> *Captain*: "I own hull or bottom part—upper by firm in Saint Louis. I make my living running the boat. Fix her shortly—do not burn."
>
> *General Quinby*: "I'll give you voucher for your part and let company in Saint Louis worry about for their part—look out for themselves—they are a rebel set probably."
>
> *Captain*: "We'll repair. By time I get home and government

gives me money for voucher my family are in suffering condition. Repair in hour and a half."

General Quinby: "Then fix it."

General Quinby went ashore to talk to soldiers he permitted to go ashore: "Facilities to cook on boat poor."

Soldiers: "Yes, sir."

General Quinby: "Hurry and cook and get on board. Do not want to lose men in cane brake."

Captain of the Union gunboat following the *Tecumseh* starts argument with General Quinby about being delayed by transport.

General Quinby pulled out his sword and shouted, "Keep that gunboat back there!"

Gunboat Captain: "Why don't you get men aboard—won't wait!"

General Quinby: "Keep your gunboat back there!"

Gunboat Captain recognized he was talking to a general officer. "General, I owe you an apology. What remains of me. I'll send a yawl to take you aboard."

April 8. General Sherman wrote in his logbook: "I was at Grant's headquarters and they talked over campaign and personnel matters with absolute freedom. C. A. Dana was there. We all knew the notorious McClernand intriguing against Grant to regain command of expedition against Vicksburg. The newspapers in the north were raising a clamor. Lincoln and Halleck were shaken. None of us slackened our loyalty to our general."

Sherman also wrote a letter to Colonel Rawlins, assistant adjutant general, Army of the Tennessee, suggesting that General Grant call upon corps commanders for their concise plans for the best general strategy of a campaign in order to give those who wanted to offer their advice the opportunity to speak.

Sherman proposed that the Army of Tennessee, which he termed "far in advance of the other Grand Armies of the United States," be ferried back to the east side of the river and operate from a base on the Yalobusha River. He also suggested that an army force be left at Milliken's Bend to operate with the gunboats when the army was known to be near Vicksburg. "These ideas for Grant to read," Sherman continued, "and will cooperate and support zealously plan he adopts. I do not expect Banks to make an attack on Port Hudson this spring."

In later years in his *Memoirs*, Sherman said critics, when they learned of his letter, styled it a protest. He denied that it was and said it was a way for Grant to call upon McClernand for an opinion. Sherman added that Grant quietly worked out his own designs. Sherman had no criticism of him, but did think that the army could have moved on in November 1862 from its position in the highlands of Mississippi and that in not doing so it had lost six months.

When Sherman returned from the Deer Creek fiasco on March 27, he wrote in the record:

> I had always contended the best way to take Vicksburg was to resume movement so well begun previous November, i.e., march by land down country inland of Mississippi while gunboats and minor land force threatened on river. I believe Grant with four corps could move from Memphis, Grenada, Jackson, or down ridge between Yazoo and Big Black. Grant would not for reasons other than military, take any course which looked like a step backward. He concluded on the river movement so as to appear like connecting with Banks at Port Hudson [as the president and Halleck desired he do].[18]

Wilson suggested to Rawlins "he lay aside Sherman's letter on a council of war plan to return to the north to avoid friction. He also advised Rawlins a return of Grant's army to Memphis would be fatal to Grant."

Colonel William F. Vilar, 23rd Wisconsin Infantry, wrote that when Grant learned of Sherman's letter, he was unshaken by his suggestion of a council of war.

Captain Hains writing later on the Vicksburg campaign concluded that while there were fewer terrain obstacles on the Memphis-Mississippi Central Railroad route than on the march route down the west bank of the Mississippi River to Vicksburg, it was not feasible to follow Sherman's idea. The governing factor in the decision was not military but political considerations. Return to Memphis would have signaled a defeat of the Union cause to the country and foreign nations who were flirting with recognition of the Confederacy.[19]

Osterhaus reported: "At 11 o'clock this morning the enemy engaged his expedition in the sixth skirmish by attacking his position at James' Plantation bringing up two 12-pounder howitzers within 800 yards, and cannonading Osterhaus' soldiers for about three quarters of an hour. Nobody hurt. The enemy seeing no result, and afraid to come within range of my infantry, left for their camp again."

Dana reported to Stanton:

> Everything going cheeringly. The canal from Duckport to the bayou to let in water will be ready by night. A force equal to five regiments is at work digging. A strong body of pioneers is engaged in clearing the bayou.
>
> I learn when Admiral Porter was entrapped by the Rebels at Deer Creek week before last his situation was so desperate that when Sherman's forces arrived to relieve him they found he had already smeared his gunboats with turpentine preparatory to abandoning them and setting them on fire.
>
> Weather conditions cool here. Neither mosquitoes nor gnats have yet troubled men or animals.

Captain Patterson wrote to his wife:

> Just returned from New Carthage where I went with the advance. I regret I do not have orders from General [McClernand] of thanks for work we did on advance but will send when I return to quarters at Richmond where we moved company.
>
> People abandoned homes and property in hurried flight. They seemed seized with a sort of terror—leave everything—china—tea sets, that cost $300, furniture. Country from here to New Carthage in state of improvement. People lay out money for cotton gins.
>
> Crowding upon my mind is thought 10 years ago we wedded—welded link that made us one. Blessings of life have been showered upon us. Indulgent goodness of Heavenly Father.
>
> Sent $20 in letter and will express $200.

Allen Geer wrote in his diary: "Thomas appeared, ascended a wagon, positioned for a platform, and the old grey haired Roman nosed patriot addressed us in slow solemn imposing manner stating object and powers to dismiss unworthy officers from service and to promote meritorious from highest to lowest. Also to organize Negro regiments to place the old decrepit men and women and children on plantations deserted by their owners. Any soldier could apply for officer position in regiment over Negroes."

April 9. In a message to Grant, Halleck stated:

> Your explanation on sending back steamers is satisfactory. Embarrassing to Quartermaster not to have them to supply western armies.
>
> Important to keep General Banks advised of everything in your vicinity. You are well advised of anxiety of the government of your success, and its disappointment at the delay, to render it necessary to urge upon you the importance of early action. I am confident that you will do everything possible to open the Mississippi river.
>
> In my opinion this is the most important operation of the war and nothing must be neglected to insure success.
>
> General Charles S. Hamilton's resignation has been received but has not been acted on by Secretary and President. No doubt he resigns to get a higher command. This game sometimes succeeds but it also sometimes fails.

(Hamilton had engaged in a brouhaha with Grant for a corps commander's assignment, which Grant refused. Hamilton then uttered vitriolic verbal attacks on Grant for his personal behavior.)[20]

Osterhaus reported that Second Lieutenant Isaiah Stickel, 2nd Illinois Cavalry, who had been ordered to scour diligently all the country in front of the cavalry in a northwesterly direction, fell in with a Confederate army recruiting party consisting of two officers, two noncommissioned officers, one private, and one civilian. Stickel captured them all and brought them in, with the exception of a noncommissioned officer who attempted to run away and was badly wounded; afterwards he was paroled.

After arriving at Milliken's Bend and associating with the officers at Grant's headquarters, Dana formulated opinions about their attitudes and performances of their staff duties, which he passed on to Stanton. Wilson impressed Dana favorably. Dana reported to Stanton that Wilson was a person "unpopular among all who like to live with little work," but possessed of remarkable talents and uncommon executive power. Dana thought he would attract notice for his accomplishments.

Wilson probably would not have thought it relevant that he was not popular with all the soldiers. He was not a participant in a popularity contest; he was a participant in a war and had aspirations to perform a large role. Wilson's attitudes and motivations were indicated in a comment about his duty assignment as a staff engineer officer in the Antietam campaign. His job was to reconnoiter the terrain and place the troops in appropriate battle positions, and nobody but himself seemed to be in a hurry. "Corps and divisions move languidly to places as if they were getting ready for a grand review instead of a decisive battle," he wrote.

From his reading, Wilson had derived the idea that when close to the enemy there should be "bustle and push and rapid marching." His belief was not an unnatural one about battlefield dynamics, and he was discouraged to find different attitudes on his initial introduction into battle. His confidence in the military virtue of celerity and audacity was beginning to fade. Wilson made it clear at Antietam that he was in a hurry. At the beginning of the war, he had been isolated at Fort Vancouver and badgered the chief of engineers for a field assignment where he would have the opportunity to serve in a leadership position to make a mark for himself. After what he considered unfulfilling initial assignments, he received an opportunity when he was assigned to the staff of Grant's army. Dana's assessments of Wilson's qualities were borne out: he demonstrated initiative, he was ambitious, forceful, opinionated, courted the confidence of the generals, especially Grant, and freely expressed his opinions and discussed the army's tactical and strategical operations. He also demonstrated considerateness, empathy, and respect for the soldiers in the ranks.

Grant undoubtedly respected Wilson's skill and knowledge and the intense work pace of the 26-year-old staff officer. Within a year, Grant saw to it that Wilson received an appointment of brigadier general in the Volunteer Army.[21]

April 10. Osterhaus reported that McClernand recognized the practicability of the route to New Carthage; by other divisions were ordered to follow him. Osterhaus' line was then concentrated between Holmes' and Smith's plantations, preparatory to its final transfer to the Mississippi.[22]

Dana reported to Stanton from Milliken's Bend:

> Everything goes forward encouragingly. The Duckport canal will be ready for trial in two to three days as soon as the water is let in, which it is deemed advisable to postpone for fear the overflow may destroy the road hence to Richmond and Carthage before the remaining troops of McClernand's Corps have marched over it.

Preparations for running batteries by gunboats and transports are also nearly completed. Enterprise will soon be accomplished. Led by Admiral Porter in dark and cloudy night.

The actual length of the [Duckport] canal and [Walnut] Bayou now proves to be 37 miles and Captain Prime who explored the whole passage reports there will be no difficulty in making it practicable throughout if necessary by cutting the levee near the head of Walnut Bayou and flooding the whole country.

A depth of 15 feet of water can be reached throughout the entire passage. River men who have seen it pronounce success certain.

Sherman sees no difficulty in opening passage but the line will be precarious after army crosses the Mississippi river. His preference is for move by Yazoo Pass, landing army in region of Charleston and threatening Grenada and Jackson from that point to deprive enemy of supplies of northern Mississippi-Yazoo-Sunflower region, or to go to Lake Providence to Tensas-Red rivers and cut off western supplies.

I think his mind now setting on Grant's plan in favor of cross Mississippi, seize Grand Gulf.

Grant set on his plan. If canal does not work will move his force overland to New Carthage. Porter agrees on plan.

Uncertain if enemy suspects this plan. May think it a blind. Weather warm, uncomfortable; health of soldiers good."

General Osterhaus published an order appointing Major John W. Beekman, 12th Ohio Volunteer Infantry, to be chief consulting engineer of all work within the Ninth Division; the order stated that he was to be "obeyed and respected." The importance of Beekman's task was underscored by Osterhaus' orders:

The urgent necessity of the immediate repair of the levees and roads between Richmond and Smith's Plantation made the increase of the division's corps of laborers imperative without weakening the ranks by great fatigue parties; thus ordered all able bodied male adults not yet reported to division headquarters and retained in camps for any reason whatsoever must be turned over at once to Captain Schenck, Quartermaster, Ninth Division, and put to work under Major Beekman. Colonel Lionel A. Sheldon, 42nd Ohio Volunteer

Infantry Regiment, in executing the order would retain contrabands within his command and put them to work under an
experienced officer on the road from Richmond to Holme's
Plantation. Also, Captain Patterson will order all men belong-
ing properly to the Ninth Division to report to the division
with the exception of those skilled mechanics who can be of
any use in the construction of boats.

Allen Geer, 20th Illinois Infantry, wrote in his diary: "Great excitement in the regiment over who will get the commissions from the
applicants for the two Negro regiments to be formed. Enlisted men
who denounced Negro regiments now first in line to get commissions. Oh consistency, thou art indeed a jewel and scarcely to be
found."

Captain Henry G. Ankeny, Company H, 48th Iowa Volunteer
Infantry Regiment, wrote to his wife: "Returned here [Greenville]
after absence of six days. Our role lay down Deer Creek. Followed
some 40 miles. Richest country I have seen in Dixie. Plantations
with corn, beans, potatoes, large Negro quarters. We lived high. We
chased Rebels. All corn on route burned, three hundred thousand
bushels. Brought in one thousand mules and contrabands. One of
most successful raids."

April 11. Grant reported to Halleck that the Yazoo expedition had returned to the Mississippi. His force, he wrote, would
be concentrated at Milliken's Bend in a few days. "Grand Gulf," he
added, "is the point at which I expect to strike and send an army
corps to Port Hudson to cooperate with Banks. I will reach
Mississippi at New Carthage now in my possession with wagon road
and canal and bayous navigable for tugs and barges between here
and there."

Grant issued orders to Major General Frederick Steele, commanding general of the Eleventh Division, after the division's return
from the Yazoo expedition,

Remain with your division at Greenville for further orders.
It is a better place for your troops than your old camp, and to
some extent may serve to keep the enemy from getting provisions from the Deer Creek country. Rebellion has assumed
that shape now that it can only terminate by the complete sub-
jugation of the South or the overthrow of the government. It

is our duty, therefore, to use every means to weaken the enemy, by destroying their means of subsistence, withdrawing their means of cultivating their fields, and in every other way possible.[23]

General L. Thomas is now here, with authority to make ample provision for the Negro. . . . Whilst at Greenville, destroy or bring off all the corn and beef cattle you possibly can. The 150 bales of cotton you speak of may be brought in, and 100 additional bales if they can be taken either from neighbors to the Douglas' Plantation or persons holding office under the Confederate Government.

General McClernand reported to General Grant:

One brigade of General Carr's division went forward today as a detail to work on the road between here [Milliken's Bend] and Richmond. This division, as quickly as it can be made available, will relieve the detachments from General Oster-haus' division, stationed between Richmond and Smith's, so as to enable the latter to embark as soon as practicable after the transports reach Smith's.

A deficiency of wagons for the transportation of ammunition, &c., may cause some delay. If I find I can obviate this impediment by the use of boats on the Roundaway Bayou, I will do so.

I think it important that the supporting division should have sufficient time to put itself in readiness immediately to follow the advance division. Two field batteries with the advance division are scarcely sufficient to meet all contingencies.

In response to some discussions Grant and Porter held on the cooperation of the navy in the prospective operation, Porter wrote to Grant that he had received a communication from the Navy Department which would compel him to go below the batteries with the fleet sooner than he had anticipated. He asked Grant if the transports would be ready to go with him and how many would be available. "I would also urge the importance of throwing as many troops as possible without delay into Grand Gulf," he added, "that we may capture the guns there, and not let them mount them somewhere else." He added he could take the troops at Carthage, "and be upon the Rebels at Grand Gulf before they know it, shell them out, and let the troops land and take possession."

Captain Prime reported to General Grant:

> I have visited New Carthage following the bayous. Walnut Bayou takes the name of Brushy Bayou at Mrs. Amis' plantation where it receives Brushy Bayou proper; from that point to Richmond it has many bushes and large trees in the channel. The trees not being very close together can be removed without much trouble, to give the required channel of from 35 to 40 feet.
>
> A levee extends from opposite Smith's Plantation to New Carthage connecting with the main levee. There are three breaks in the Vidal bayou levee, each from 300 to 500 feet wide. The bayou from Richmond to New Carthage offers but little difficulty in obtaining the necessary waterway. At New Carthage where there is a break in the main levee, there is for several hundred yards but a depth of two and one half feet. This can be avoided by following Harper's Bayou, branching to the southeast from Bayou Vidal, and communicating with the river by the break in the levee about one half mile above New Carthage. General Osterhaus reports that this channel offers a depth of over seven feet.

General Osterhaus published an order to his Ninth Division soldiers: "It is the duty of all officers to take possession of all strayed government horses and mules and to capture properly from the enemy such cotton, mules, horses within lines of this command and turn same over to the Quartermaster of the Division."

April 12. Grant reported to Halleck:

> There is nothing now in the way of my throwing troops into Grand Gulf and destroying the works there, then sending them on to Port Hudson to cooperate with Banks in the reduction of that place. But there is the danger of overflowing the road from here to New Carthage when the water is let into the new canal connecting the river here with the bayous coming out at Carthage. One division is at Carthage and another is on the way.
>
> By turning in the water to the canal, water communication

can be opened between the two places in a very few days for barges and tugs. Of the former I have 15 and of the latter 3 suitable for this navigation. To use this route therefore it is absolutely necessary to keep open the wagon road to take over artillery and to march the troops.

In about three nights from this time Porter will run the Vicksburg batteries with such of his fleet as he desires to take below and I will send four steamers. Their machinery will be protected from shot by hay bales and sand bags to be used in transporting troops and in towing barges.

The wagon road by filling up the lowest ground, is now nearly completed and will be about 20 inches above to the water in the swamps. The river [Mississippi] where it is to let into the canal [Duckport] is 4.09 feet above the land. This though is 15 miles by the river below where the dirt road starts out. Had I seen nothing of the effect of the crevasses upon the back country I should not doubt the effect would be to overflow the whole country through which we pass. There has been a large crevasse just below where this canal leaves the river for a long time through which the water has been pouring in great volume. I cannot see that this additional crevasse is going to have much other effect than to increase the break in the bayou levees so as to make the discharge equal to the supply. I will have a map of this section made to send to you by the next mail which will make this more intelligible.

The embarrassments I have had to contend against on account of extreme high water cannot be appreciated by any one not present to witness it. I think you will receive favorable reports of the condition and feeling of this army from every impartial judge and from all who have been sent from Washington to look after its welfare.[24]

In the day's report, Grant outlined his plan to move his army and related the prodigious amount of labor that had been required to build the water route [Mississippi River to Duckport Canal to Walnut Bayou, to Brushy Bayou, to Roundaway Bayou, to Bayou Vidal, to New Carthage and the Mississippi River] and the parallel road, and the ingenuity and innovativeness of the officers and soldiers who served as engineers and pioneers in constructing the water transportation system.

Grant wrote to the adjutant general of the United States Army in Washington:

This is a report of Sherman's reconnaissance through Steele's and Black bayous and Deer Creek made in conjunction with a portion of Porter's fleet to find a practicable passage to the Yazoo river without passing the enemy's batteries at Haynes' Bluff, and if found sufficiently practicable to enable me to land most of my force east of the Yazoo river from which Haynes' Bluff and Vicksburg could be reached by high land, turned out to be an impracticable route.

The reconnaissance though did have some results. It carried our troops into heart of granary from which Vicksburg's forces are now being fed and caused alarm in enemy camp and caused him to move a number of their gun batteries on the river. Citizens fled from plantations and burned several thousand bales of cotton. Some of it not burned was brought away by gunboats. Much of their beef, bacon, and poultry was consumed by our troops and distributed among the Negroes. A scow loaded with bacon for the enemy was destroyed and probably two hundred thousand bushels of grain in the cribs were burned up. Several hundred Negroes also returned with the troops.

Adjutant General Thomas reported to Secretary of War Stanton:

General Grant has constructed a road to Carthage, half a mile of which has got to be raised 10 inches. He intends cutting the levee, which will open a water communication nearly parallel to the road, the shallowest place 7 feet, but this can be dredged if necessary. When the river falls 2 feet, he can cut with safety to the road, the road being necessary for the passage of artillery and troops. One division is at Carthage and another on its way there. About three nights hence Admiral Porter will run the Vicksburg batteries with such of his fleet as he desires to take below. General Grant will send four steamers, with machinery protected by hay bales and sand bags, when ready. The batteries below Vicksburg will be taken in conjunction with General Banks. This army is in very fine condition, healthy, and in good heart.

Dana wrote to Secretary of War Stanton:

Important modification of plans of operations from Halleck received on the 10th. After capture of Grand Gulf instead of operating on Big Black main force will operate against Port Hudson with Banks.

Dispatches will be sent to Banks to cooperate. Time of operation uncertain. Plan depends on canal to transport supplies and if necessary troops.

A week ago plan changed; decided to march troops to New Carthage via Richmond. Preparations made to improve road for purpose by raising it above expected level of the water. Now appears both canal and road cannot be relied upon. If water let in canal road will probably be overflowed. While a rainstorm which prevailed through last night muddied the road and proved a storm of 24 hours would render road impassable for days.

So canal probably will be used for men and supplies. Movement postponed until canal can be opened. Colonel Pride says need a week to let in water, finish dredging, and clear out all trees. Digging that can be done by hand completed in clearing of trees almost to Richmond. Barges and tugs are expected from Saint Louis end of week.

If Grant holds to plan to march thirty thousand troops to New Carthage water cannot be let into canal until they pass over road. No chance to find ground to camp on out of reach of overflow that the opening of the canal will produce.

If plan adopted Porter will take his vessels down next three days and transports run the batteries. Grand Gulf will be struck before canal is finished and its utility decided by experience.

Porter anxious to go. I think cautious course will be chosen. McClernand will lead attack on Grand Gulf and further one against Port Hudson.

I have remonstrated, so far as I could properly do so, against intrusting so momentous an operation to McClernand, and I know Admiral Porter and prominent members of his staff have done the same, but Grant will not be changed. McClernand is exceedingly desirous of this command. He is the senior of the other corps commanders. He is believed to be an especial favorite of the President and the position which his corps occupied on the ground here when the movement was first projected was such that the advance naturally fell to its lot; besides he entered zealously into the plan from the first while Sherman doubted and criticized and McPherson whom Grant would really much prefer is away at Lake Providence and though I understand he approves the plans he has had no active part in it.

> It is estimated ten thousand soldiers can take Grand Gulf, fortify it, and at same time make feints up Big Black river while twenty thousand more go down to Port Hudson. In this operation both McClernand and McPherson will be engaged. Sherman will stay here to menace Vicksburg and guard line of communications.

(Wilson stated that part of the reason Grant left Sherman behind was because he proposed the northern route to attack Vicksburg.)

Corporal Jones wrote in a letter from Milliken's Bend to his parents: "6 of us in tent at present—many sick. Our division [tenth] reviewed on 8th and 9th by General Grant, General Sherman, and Brigadier General Andrew J. Smith, the division commander, said 23rd Wisconsin Volunteer Infantry the best. Play ball every evening and Colonel plays with us. Quiet here. 100s of bales of cotton came in and shipped up the river. Drew new hats to protect us from the sun. Expect 300 conscripts to make up regiments. The heat will be enough to kill them."

April 14. Dana informed Secretary of War Stanton:

> Colonel Pride let water in canal yesterday at noon. Channel full, no reason to doubt its usefulness. Dredge deepening it. Major William Tweeddale, 1st Missouri Engineers, with working parties to clear out trees from bayou. All is done to within five miles of Richmond, but remaining distance more obstructed than rest of line. He needs four days to open for tugs and barges.
>
> Grant pushing troops to New Carthage by road. He doubts there will be an overflow. Brigadier General A. J. Smith's Tenth Division to march tomorrow. Brigadier General Alvin P. Hovey's Twelfth Division follows.
>
> Camp equipage of corps to be sent down in barges along with Porter's gunboats, which run batteries tomorrow night with three transports. Whole force embarked and the working of the canal insures supplies, movement to Port Hudson to commence.
>
> Grant to take risk to go to Grand Gulf before canal finished to get there before enemy.
>
> Now decided Grant will go to Port Hudson; McClernand to command at Grand Gulf. Enemy apparently unaware of this movement.[25]

(Dana's assertion was incorrect; enemy observers kept themselves fully aware of Grant's movements.)

April 15. Osterhaus' expedition engaged in its seventh skirmish with the enemy, as he reported:

> The importance of the possession of New Carthage was certainly not underrated by the enemy and on this day, after being reinforced by three more infantry regiments from Grand Gulf, he attempted a simultaneous attack on our front at James' Plantation and on our cavalry force at and near Dunbar's.
>
> At 4:00 A.M. a regiment had waded Mill Bayou a few miles west of Dunbar's, and attacked my outpost. My soldiers had to fall back on their reserves, who immediately provided support. I immediately sent reinforcements, and my soldiers successfully repulsed the Rebels. In the skirmish two men of the 2nd Illinois Cavalry were wounded; one later died. I could not ascertain the enemy's losses; we took two of them prisoners.
>
> On the Mississippi in front of James' Plantation large numbers of the enemy gathered, but on learning of the repulse of the attack on their left flank they withdrew, and since then we have been altogether unmolested by the rebel force.

Colonel Theodore E. Buehler, 67th Indiana Infantry, reported that his regiment with a strength of 360 soldiers of an authorized strength of 1,000 left its bivouac at daylight and after a day's march of 20 miles reached Holmes' Plantation at 5 P.M., where it encamped to drill and prepare for the active campaign.

April 16. McClernand reported one division had been ferried through the woods to New Carthage.

Grant with a party of his staff officers, including Wilson, late at night viewed from the deck of his transport the passage of Porter's fleet past the Confederate guns at Vicksburg.

General Thomas wrote to Stanton, "I ran down to Young's Point to take a position with a four-mile straight-line view of Vicksburg." He reported the sailing by of Porter's fleet of seven vessels protected with cotton and hay bales piled on board for protection. At 11 P.M., he wrote, the Confederates lighted fires on both shores to light up the river. They began to fire upon the Union vessels and kept it up until 2 A.M., but the naval vessels passed with little damage. The *Benton*, Porter's flagship, received a shot that killed one and wounded three crewmen. The transport *Henry Clay* received a shot in the stern and had to be abandoned; the *Forest Queen* received a shot in a steam drum and had to be towed by the gunboat *Tuscumbia*. Thomas added that the Rebels did not fire as many shots as he expected, and he closed his report with the observation: "It is a great success."

Secretary of War E. M. Stanton wrote to Dana: "Dispatches received. Allow me to suggest that you carefully avoid giving any advice in respect to commands that may be assigned as it may lead to misunderstandings and troublesome complications."[26]

Dana reported to Secretary of War Stanton:

> Vicksburg batteries to be run 9 o'clock tonight. Fleet of 6 ironclad turtles, 12 barges follow, 3 steamers. Our new batteries on the levee will participate.
>
> Grant goes to New Carthage in the morning to direct operations.
>
> Quinby's division of McPherson's Corps arrived yesterday; led by Colonel J. B. Sanborn. Quinby dangerously ill at Helena.
>
> McPherson here within five days. Weather perfect for marching or fighting. Spirit of troops all that is desired. Pride's cut off pushed with energy. Road to Richmond-New Carthage overflowed some but not impassable.

Corporal Jones wrote home he was bivouacked in the countryside 22 miles away from Milliken's Bend. The intention, he had heard, was for the regiment to go below to reach Vicksburg. He said he marched 17 miles on April 15 without his knapsack, and he felt as strong as ever. Jones wrote he had bought new boots, which had "hard work ahead for them," and sent his mother "five dollars to buy a new gown." He wrote that he expected Vicksburg to fall in two weeks at most and described the area: "I have seen some of the biggest snakes I ever saw, four to six feet long. Ten miles to go to reach Vicksburg. We are camping in hay 18 inches high. Plank fences cleared in no time to make floor boards for tents. Country here very beautiful."

Alonzo Brown wrote in his diary that his company had disembarked from the Yazoo expedition at Milliken's Bend, where it was very hot. He noted that the men in the company were getting sick fast and also said he had seen Fred Grant [General Grant's son] riding about the encampment on a pony.[27]

April 17. Two events intervened to change the course of events on the watery ground occupied by the soldiers in Osterhaus' expedition. Firstly, according to Grant and Porter's plan of joint operations, the naval gunboats had successfully sailed by Vicksburg early in the morning and anticipated joining up with McClernand's soldiers at New Carthage. Secondly, Grant arrived at McClernand's command post, accompanied by Wilson, and after assessing what McClernand and Osterhaus declared to be a successful operation and a practical route to ferry the army over the Mississippi River, he reacted with the clear declaration that they had failed to reckon with his tactics. His army stood inactive, hemmed in by bayous and pinned down by the Rebel cavalry. He calculated it would be a "tedious" and long drawn-out operation, given the dearth of boats and barges, to transport his army across the water to the transports at New Carthage and the Mississippi River.

Inactivity of the army was anathema to Grant. His generalship was characterized by the application of his energy to keep his army in motion. The winter was over; it was springtime, the time for the army to be in motion. He said a marching route must be found and reported that the water was falling, so that in a few days there would be insufficient depth for the boats in the bayous.[28]

McClernand readily responded that he had another route in mind for the third step of the seventh attempt to take Vicksburg; his route lay from Smith's Plantation, where the crevasse occurred, to Perkins' Plantation eight to twelve miles below New Carthage.

Grant ordered Colonel Wilson to examine the route McClernand had in mind by Bayou Vidal or Brushy and Negro bayous to Perkins' Plantation for the purpose of locating a more suitable line of communication to the Mississippi River. After completing his terrain survey Colonel Wilson reported to Grant that in his opinion it would be difficult to cross any number of soldiers greater than one division to the Mississippi levees at New Carthage and build a practicable line of communications. Wilson suggested that time would be gained by building two bridges on the route following Bayou Vidal and Brushy and Negro bayous. In polite bureaucratic language, he stated it would be quicker to march the army's soldiers down the road to another embarkation point than to attempt to ferry them to New Carthage.[29]

Reviewing Wilson's recommendation, Grant declared the ingenuity of the Yankees would be equal to the task Wilson laid out. The two men talked about the easy success of Porter's gunboats and the transports at Vicksburg and the prospects the event opened up for further success. They also discussed details of the campaign to follow. Wilson reported, "I counseled Grant again to give up all the work on canals and bayous as not only slow and fatiguing but useless."

The feasibility of running by the batteries having been demonstrated beyond further question, there was nothing left but to send the entire available force down the country as rapidly as possible, and this was finally decided upon. Supplies were to be left to follow by the river as needed. Wilson later wrote, "Upon returning to headquarters Rawlins told [by Grant] that he depended more upon my judgment on military matters than upon that of any one else in that army."[30]

To hasten the movement of his army, Grant ordered Lieutenant Hains to move forward the India rubber pontoon train for construction of the bridge over Bayou Vidal. It is to be noted though that in spite of Grant's instructions and the availability of the pontoon train, the soldiers serving as engineer-pioneers did not use it on the west bank of the Mississippi River to construct bridges. The cylinders were subject to puncture by tree stumps and debris in the bayous and to damage from Confederate musketry fire. Thus all the bridges on the west side were custom built by the soldiers to conform to the topography of the land and the bayous. They used wooden flatboats and trestles made from the timber collected from nearby buildings at the bridge sites.

By means of flatboats, 150 tons of ammunition were transported through the bayous to the Mississippi from Richmond. The flatboats were then used by Captain George W. Jackson, 34th Indiana Infantry pioneer company, General Hovey's division, to bridge Mound Bayou to Bayou Vidal, 630 feet wide. A squad of soldiers from the company remained in charge at the bridge to assure its stability until the army passed. There were no records of accidents or delays on the bridge.

Captain Patterson's Company of Kentucky Engineers constructed the next bridge where Gilbert Bayou joined Bayou Vidal. His engineer soldiers constructed it from a large flatboat 100-feet long and 24-feet wide that was anchored across the main channel of the bayou by a cable and chain on the south end and braced with wood against a tree on the north end. Ties of timber trimmed to eight inches were laid over the gunwales. On the timbers rested the

8"×12" stringers to support the floor planks. A span was built of 12"×12" timbers that were notched halfway into tree trunks and pinned and secured by chains from each end of the flatboat towards the shore. Three more spans were built toward both shores resting on trestles. The roadway was fixed in place by heavy beams pinned to the floor planks. The engineer soldiers finished the 790' bridge that was part floating and part fixed in just 14 hours.

A short distance beyond the bridge at Gilbert Bayou the 13th Corps pioneers built two bridges, totaling 150 feet, across a slough between Bayou Vidal and Mound Bayou. The two bridges were built entirely from logs cut from nearby trees. Split logs were used for the road planks.

Below the two bridges at the slough and between the mouths of Negro and Mound bayous, where they emptied into Brushy Bayou, Captain Patterson and his engineers built a 550' bridge. The bridge curved upstream and rested on 16 flatboats that were from 25 to 40 feet long and 12 feet wide, with piers and trestles on each end. The boats were anchored to a 2½-inch line that was stretched from shore to shore and supported in the center by a tree. Some of the boats were fastened directly to the cable passing over their bows; others were connected by short ropes.

Commenting on the bridges he had recommended, Wilson wrote that they "opened a practicable road, threading one of the most difficult regions that ever tested the resources of an army. The bridges were built by green volunteers who had never seen a bridge train nor had an hour's drill in bridge building. The same may be said of the quality of the men and officers who carried through that remarkable work."

Porter issued his "first report of the naval vessels that passed the batteries of Vicksburg on the preceding night for operations below." He reported that three army transports accompanied his large naval force. "I led the force in the *Benton*. 11:16 P.M. batteries opened fire on us. *Benton* returned fire as did vessels in the line. Enemy lighted both sides of the river and we were fair targets for them; we received little damage. Under fire two and one half hours. No one killed, but eight wounded. Army transport *Henry Clay* sunk. Transport *Forest Queen* temporarily disabled and was towed into safe quarters by *Tuscumbia*."[31]

General Osterhaus reported that the naval gunboats arrived and placed the position of New Carthage beyond dispute.

Grant's Transports Running the Batteries (*Harper's Pictorial History*).

An expedition was sent out by General Garrard toward Delhi for the purpose of intercepting Rebel subsistence stores collected at the point. The object of the expedition was frustrated because the enemy's force was largely increased. The operation as a whole, Osterhaus wrote, "may be looked upon as successful." He reported:

> Outside of the military importance of the positions gained, the enemy must feel his loss severely. He has been cut off from all supplies from this region, the resources are great: corn, molasses, bacon, and beef abounding along these bayous, and many captured letters give ample evidence of the importance of these supplies to the enemy's garrison at Vicksburg. From the last information collected it is estimated that over one million pounds of beef cattle have been sent to Vicksburg from this vicinity. All the advantages were gained by the loss of only one single life.
>
> During these operations the division not only subsisted itself, but at the same time secured large amounts of cotton for the United States Government. About one thousand bales have been sent by the Quartermaster to Milliken's Bend, and double that number of bales can be forwarded as soon as the necessary transportation can be had.
>
> Troops deserve the highest encomiums for their alacrity,

zeal, and good discipline during these trying and fatiguing operations. The military qualities they exhibited kept even pace with their sense of good order. Not a single case of wanton destruction has occurred within the lines of the Ninth Division.

Dana reported to Secretary of War Stanton:

> Porter left mouth of Yazoo just before 10:00 P.M., 16th, sailed down Mississippi silently and darkly, neither showing steam nor light, signal astern enemy could not see. 200 yard intervals. *Benton* in lead.
>
> Gunboats had doubled tongue of land in front of Vicksburg when flash from enemy's upper battery guns for one and one half hours, four miles in extent present. I counted 525 discharges. Bonfire in front of Vicksburg to light up the scene, direct enemy fire. 12:45 A.M. steamer *Henry Clay* burned, and abandoned by captain; only loss; one sailor stunned and three wounded.
>
> Our new batteries opened on Vicksburg public buildings at daylight.
>
> I go to New Carthage with Grant.

General J. C. Pemberton, the commander of the Confederate forces at Vicksburg, wrote to General Joseph E. Johnston, the commander of the Confederate army in Mississippi, to report that the Union forces were using the dredge boats from Milliken's Bend to dig a canal into Walnut Bayou, thence through Roundaway Bayou and Vidal Bayou into the Mississippi at New Carthage. He also reported the arrival at Vicksburg of the adjutant general, General Lorenzo Thomas who made changes in the Union's campaign plans. Pemberton noted that a large force of Grant's army had redeployed to New Carthage, below Warrenton on the west bank and at Richmond, and he also reported that five gunboats had passed the Vicksburg batteries early in the morning. "I am momentarily expecting a report," he added, "as to their character and condition. These five, together with the three gunboats and small steamer under Farragut, give nine vessels available for crossing troops or operating from above against Port Hudson."[32]

Alonzo Brown recorded in his diary that his division conducted a review for Adjutant General Thomas, who also spoke and said he was sent by the president to make known the government's policy on the Negro question. Brown wrote that Thomas made it clear that "the policy was to arm the best of them, organize them into regiments, which would hold points on the railroads, and the rest would be put to work on fortifications." Thomas also told them division enlisted men would be commissioned as officers and that he expected no opposition from men or officers in the West, but did have the authority to dismiss anyone from the army who opposed the policy.

Charles Enslow, Company C, 77th Illinois Volunteer Infantry, wrote to his wife from his camp 20 miles below Milliken's Bend:

> Struck tents yesterday at 10 and started a south course to Carthage. We had not gone more than a mile when I began to discover all manner of clothing, cooking utensils, etc. thrown away by soldiers and abandoned on account of bad roads.
>
> Marched 5 miles to Brush[y] Bayou, crossed and followed it directly for 7 miles where we camped for night, within a half mile of Richmond. Negroes say white folks herd us away to keep you folks from getting us. On a fine plantation [Holmes'] all kinds of machinery. A fine saw mill our men are running sawing wood for boats which we are building, small flat boats which are used to carry provisions and ammunition down to Carthage. We camped within eight miles of Carthage. Our advance within three miles of the place. Pray for me. We will need help from every source in our undertaking. Before you receive it we will be in deathly conflict with the enemy and if victorious camped in Vicksburg.

April 18. Grant returned to Milliken's Bend to prepare orders for the movement of his army. He ordered six steamers loaded to run batteries at Vicksburg, with twelve barges in tow loaded with rations because the wagons were unable to haul them. He wrote a letter to General McClernand: "I would still repeat former instructions, that possession must be gotten of Grand Gulf at the very earliest possible moment. Once there, no risk should be taken in following the enemy until our forces are concentrated. Troops first there should entrench themselves for safety, and the whole of your corps concentrated as rapidly as our means of transportation will permit. General McPherson will be closing upon you as rapidly as your troops can be gotten away and rations supplied." Grant also mentioned that all the wagons, including all the regimental trains, were to be kept constantly on the road between Smith's Plantation and Milliken's Bend. The number of wagons was increasing daily, he added, and troops guarding the different points on the road were to gather all beef cattle and forage within reach of them, but were not to destroy what they could not use. Grant closed his letter with the statement he would be back in a few days and hoped it would be his good fortune to see the corps safely in possession of Grand Gulf.

McClernand wrote a letter to Grant urging his consideration of the importance of immediately placing below Vicksburg a sufficient number of transports to carry the entire 13th Corps. "This Corps," McClernand continued, "has now gained a position that will enable us to capture Grand Gulf and cooperate in the reduction of Port Hudson. With these points in our possession the Mississippi would be open to New Orleans. With the combined efforts of both armies and gunboat fleets, we shall be able to attack Vicksburg in front and rear, and soon it must fall into our hands; and, with its fate, a virtual end will be put to the war in the Southwest, and a hopeful prospect of putting a speedy end to the rebellion."

Captain Prime reported that during the past 24 hours the water in Walnut Bayou had risen eight inches above the expected level. All the pioneer companies, he reported, had been put to work on clearing the bayou. Major Tweeddale reported that Colonel Bissell's four 1st Missouri Engineer Regiment companies and Captain Newell W. Spicer's pioneer company would clear the bayou to Richmond to the prescribed width by April 20 or 21. On April 19, Colonel Pride would start a small steamboat for Richmond. Two, and if possible three, barges of from 100 to 120 feet in length would be sent into the bayou at the same time, with pioneers on them provided with saws to cut six feet under water any obstacles they would encounter. Tweeddale stated, "I am afraid it will take them from three to five days to reach Richmond. When these barges have once passed it will enable all necessary supplies to be forwarded to New Carthage, unless prevented by a fall of the river. The river has been falling one half inch per day for the last two days."

General Hovey, Twelfth Division, issued an order that to prevent straggling and demoralization, a regimental roll call would be held at 6 A.M., 9 A.M., 12 noon, 3 P.M., and 6 P.M. He said his soldiers would soon be in a position requiring discipline; they must prevent plundering and house burning to keep from being a mob. He told his soldiers he had witnessed "disgraceful scenes since the march began, and he was not proud of the position of his division."

General Carr, Fourteenth Division, told his soldiers their division had the reputation of being the finest one in the army. He also told his soldiers per the recommendation of the medical officer they could bathe for 20 minutes in the bayou between 7 and 8 A.M. and between 6 and 7 P.M. "Cleanliness important and officers must enforce it. Medical Officer reported some men very filthy. Hope will not be amenable to charge in the future."

Allen Geer wrote in his diary that he had received four months pay but could not express money home because orders were issued to board small transports at noon. He said the regiment went down the Mississippi at dark in a gathering storm, and the gamblers kept him awake.

A correspondent of *Frank Leslie's Independent Newspaper* reported: "General Grant after feints and expedients has erected batteries within range of Vicksburg. A powerful rebel army there to oppose Grant."

April 19. Grant to Halleck:

> I returned to my headquarters at Milliken's Bend last night from New Carthage at and near the place where Porter's fleet anchored (6 iron clads and ram *General Price*) together with two divisions of McClernand's Corps. The whole of his corps is between Richmond and New Carthage.
>
> I had all empty barges here prepared for the transportation of troops and artillery and sent them by the Vicksburg batteries with the fleet. While under the guns of the enemy's batteries they were cut loose, and I fear some of them have been permitted to run past New Carthage undiscovered. They were relied upon to aid in the transportation of troops to take Grand Gulf.
>
> The wagon road from here to within New Carthage is good for artillery. From that point on the bayou levee is broken in a number of places making cross currents in the bayou; hence it is difficult to navigate with barges. I think however steamers will be able to run from where wagon road ends to the river. By clearing out the bayous from timber there will be good navigation from here to New Carthage for tugs and barges,

also small stern wheel steamers. This navigation can be kept good I think by using our dredges constantly until there is 20 feet of fall. On this subject though I have not taken the opinion of engineer officers nor have I formed it upon sufficient investigation to warrant me in speaking positively.

Our experiment of running the batteries at Vicksburg has demonstrated the entire practicability of doing so with but little risk. On this occasion our vessels went down slower than the current, using their wheels principally for backing. Two of the steamers were drawn into the eddy and ran over a part of the distance in front of Vicksburg three times. I shall send six more steamers when they are ready.

I sent a dispatch to Banks that I thought I could send a corps to Bayou Sara to cooperate with him on Port Hudson by the 25th. This will now be impossible. There shall be no unnecessary delay, however, in my movements. I hope soon to report possession of Grand Gulf with a practicable and safe route to furnish supplies to the troops. Once there I do not feel a doubt of success in the entire cleaning out of the enemy from the banks of the river.[33]

At least three of my corps commanders take hold of the new policy of arming Negroes and using them against the enemy without will. They are good soldiers as to feel the obligation to carry out policy in which they would not carry out with faith and zeal if it were their choosing. You may rely on me carrying out this policy ordered by proper authority to the best of my ability.[34]

The policy promulgated by President Lincoln was for the Federal government to deny to the enemy as much productive labor as possible. With the employment of the Negroes as farm laborers, the white males were available for the army. Halleck stated "every slave withdrawn from the enemy is equivalent to a white man put hors de combat." Thus the Union policy was to employ the Negro men of the south, as could be found practicable, in a military force to defend forts and depots. If their service proved worthwhile, Halleck stated, a larger force would be organized in the summer.[35]

Admiral Porter issued his detailed report of his fleet running the batteries at Vicksburg:

> Order of the vessels, 50 yards apart, *Benton, Lafayette* (with *General Price* lashed on starboard side), *Louisville, Mound City,*

Pittsburg, Carondelet, Tuscumbia, Tug *Ivy* lashed to *Benton*; three army transports and then *Tuscumbia* at stern to insure they did not turn back. Two transports when firing became heavy attempted to run upstream, but *Tuscumbia* drove them back and stayed behind until *Forest Queen* was disabled. Took her in tow and placed her out of reach of enemy's shots.

All vessels except *Benton* took in tow coal barges each with 10,000 bushels of coal, and all except *Lafayette* brought them safely past the batteries.

Having *Price* alongside the *Lafayette* did not manage well and the coal barge got adrift but was picked up at New Carthage.

Pilots deceived by large fire started on Louisiana shore to show vessels more plainly. We fortunate vessels had some narrow escapes. Saved by precautions taken to protect them, covered with heavy logs and wet bales of hay (excellent defense). Difficulties were strong currents, dangerous eddies, glaring fires every direction, smoke almost enveloping the squadron, and heavy fire of enemy. A transport burned and sank passing batteries; we picked up some of the crew and the others got away in a yawl.[36]

It is interesting to note that three high-level officials observing the passage of Porter's fleet reported a different number of vessels passing by: (1) General Grant reported 6 ironclads and 1 ram, (2) General Thomas reported 7 vessels, and (3) Dana reported 6 ironclads, 12 barges, and 3 steamers. Such a phenomenon accentuates the absence of coordination of information at Grant's headquarters or a staff officer who provided official information to persons authorized to receive it, and it raises the question whether officials like Thomas and Dana made inquiries of Grant for authentic information. From Dana's reports it appears he picked up most of his information by word of mouth from parties other than the commanders like Grant, Sherman, McClernand, and Porter or staff officers; much of his information lacked any reference to a source. Dana's presence presented an anomaly. To accomplish what Stanton sent him to do, he had to stay aloof from Grant; as a result his reports on Grant lacked authenticity. Grant also recognized Dana to be a pipeline to the secretary of war's office. For bureaucratic protection, he had to keep Dana at arm's length to avoid every word he uttered being telegraphed to the secretary of war.

Osterhaus issued an order to his division that commanding officers were to enforce the strictest rules to preserve all houses and buildings in the best order possible because the division would have to rely on them to shelter the sick. Officers of the day were to see that the order was carried out.

Osterhaus issued an additional order that the soldiers were to be well instructed by their commanding officers that in case of a sudden attack, day or night, they were to be brought out and formed in proper place in camp fronting the enemy. Every night, company officers were to see that clothing, shoes, accouterments, and arms were arranged in tents so a soldier could grasp them in the dark. Osterhaus also stated that the narrow ground of the camp rendered it necessary that the officers keep the soldiers well under control and prevent them from running about pell-mell. The wagon road through the camp was to be kept clear of all obstructions when emergencies occurred.

General Garrard of the First Brigade, which was camped at Smith's Plantation, ordered a regimental detail whose object was to help the wounded, so that men would not leave the ranks to assist their wounded comrades to the rear, thus exposing themselves to enemy fire.

Garrard also ordered that only soldiers of tried courage and of a high degree of intelligence should be assigned to the detail, as they would also be required to perform some primary surgical services to the wounded.

April 20. Grant issued orders for his army to march and thus launched the seventh attempt to take Vicksburg:

> The following orders are published for the information and guidance of the army in the field in the present movement to obtain a foothold on the east bank of the Mississippi river, from which Vicksburg can be approached by practicable roads:
>
> The Thirteenth Army Corps, Major General John A. McClernand commanding, will constitute the right wing.
>
> The Fifteenth Army Corps, Major General W. T. Sherman commanding, will constitute the left wing.
>
> The Seventeenth Army Corps, Major General James B. McPherson commanding, will constitute the center.
>
> The order of march to New Carthage will be from right to left.

Grant's order further embraced such subjects as the forming of reserves, bivouacking of soldiers until facilities were available to transport camp equipage, and providing only one tent to a company to protect rations from the rain and one tent for each regimental, brigade, and division headquarters. His order also stated that all the teams of the three army corps, under charge of unit quartermasters, were to constitute a train to carry the supplies, ordnance, and the authorized camp equipage. The order also provided for the establishment of general hospitals between Duckport and Milliken's Bend.

Grant also stated that the movement of the troops from Milliken's Bend should be so conducted as to allow the transportation of a ten-day supply of rations and half the allowance of ordnance required by earlier orders. He also stated commanders were authorized and enjoined to collect all the beef cattle, corn, and other supplies necessary for the army on the line of march, but wanton destruction of property, taking of articles, unless for military purposes, insulting citizens, going into and searching houses without proper orders from division commanders, were positively prohibited. All such irregularities were to be summarily punished.

Dana reported to Secretary of War Stanton:

> Colonel J. S. Bowen, commanding officer, Confederate army force at Grand Gulf, sent over three regiments to dislodge Osterhaus from New Carthage. A rebel steamer appeared before New Carthage. Porter sent *Tuscumbia* to shell out Colonel Thomas O. Benton's camp two miles below New Carthage.
>
> Bayou Vidal levee broke in three places, country between Roundaway and Mississippi overflowed, troops moved New Carthage by water. Scows constructed at saw mill on Holmes' Plantation. McClernand hard at work transporting troops and supplies to New Carthage. By same means, as well as scanty wagon train, supplied by ox wagons of the country, he is transporting supplies down from Richmond. Only very small boats accessible to Bayou Vidal.
>
> Pride's cut off worked at with energy but engineers differ in opinions as to when loaded barges can get through. Two small steamers and barge carrying pioneers with tools passed through the canal this morning into Walnut Bayou. Pride thinks in three days boats will go to New Carthage.

Colonel Wilson thinks it will take two weeks. The wagon road hence to Smith's Plantation is in very good condition and not likely to be overflowed. This road as well as Pride's cut off is protected against inroads of the enemy by overflow of country toward Tensas. Strip of dry land between two lines of water is nowhere more than three miles wide.

Officers in this army, who, three months ago, told me they would never serve along with negro regiments, now say General Thomas makes bad speeches to troops but that they shall obey orders.

Corporal Jones, 23rd Wisconsin Infantry, wrote home from Holmes' Plantation: "We are within 8 miles of New Carthage. Will cross one of these days. 2–3 transports ran the blockade, 6–8 gunboats. We hear rebs picking up their legs and getting out of Vicksburg as quickly as they can. Sent another $5. Would have sent more but needed a pair of boots. We have to march through wet places, water up to our knees, and sometimes our waists. Half boys losing health due to carelessness."

Captain Ankeny, 4th Iowa Infantry Regiment, wrote to his wife, "Considerable excitement is caused amongst the candidates for officers for the negro regiments. Negro of some importance now. McClernand below New Carthage. Transports below so we'll probably go other side of river."

Brigadier General John S. Bowen, who was commanding the Confederate forces of Major General J. H. Forney's division posted at Grand Gulf, wrote that Grant's army, which was under watch by Major I. F. Harrison's cavalry, obviously intended to move on Grand Gulf. Bowen's engineer officer advised him to meet Grant at Rodney or Bruinsburg, but Bowen replied he needed 15,000–20,000 men for such an engagement.

April 21. Grant informed Halleck: "I plan to move my headquarters to New Carthage tomorrow. Every effort will be made to get speedy possession of Grand Gulf and from that point to open Mississippi river. If I do not underestimate the enemy, my force is abundant with a foothold once obtained to do the work. Six transports will run the batteries tonight."

General Sherman informed his corps that General Thomas would address the troops on the policy of the war. The troops would be dressed in their best uniforms, and commanders would form them at a point facing the levee. Sherman told his men: "A single gun, from Hart's battery, will be the signal for attention, and officers and men will listen to the remarks of General Thomas, and heed them as the voice of our Government. Officers and men will preserve their places in ranks during the speaking, and conduct themselves as they know good soldiers should. A second gun from the same battery will be the signal for marching the troops back to their respective brigades."

With the completion of the bridges by Captain Patterson's Kentucky Company of Mechanics and Engineers and a detail of soldiers from General Hovey's Fourteenth Division, General Osterhaus issued an order for the 69th Indiana Infantry Regiment and 1st Wisconsin Battery to move early the next morning on the third step of the reconnaissance to Judge Perkins' Plantation. He also issued orders that soldiers would not move beyond the picket lines without a pass and foraging parties would go out under the charge of an officer who would be held responsible for any depredations the soldiers committed.

April 22. Six Union steamers ran the Confederate batteries at Vicksburg. When civilian crews refused to pilot the steamers, a call went out for military volunteers. They successfully completed the task. Grant later wrote that volunteers could always be found among his officers and soldiers to perform a difficult task.

Dana reported to Stanton:

> Yours of the 16th received the 21st. Its directions shall be scrupulously observed even in extreme cases.
>
> McClernand succeeded in moving transports up Bayou Vidal to Smith's Plantation so he can move troops to New Carthage with rapidity. At mouth canal depth is 15 feet. Four dredges work day and night. Alarm is felt at report of sudden and unexpected fall of Mississippi river at Memphis and above. A fall of 15 feet would leave canal without water. Barges could still traverse bayous. Coal for naval fleet would have to be drifted down Mississippi. Fall would also deprive line of protection of flood from Tensas river which it now enjoys.

April 23. In a report to Halleck, Grant stated: "Six boats and a number of barges ran the batteries last night. All passed more or less damaged. I think all the barges went through safely. Casualties so far reported two men mortally wounded, several wounded, more or less severely. About 500 shots were fired. I look upon this as a great success. At the Warrenton batteries there was heavy firing, but all the boats were seen to go past. What damage done there is not known."[37]

General Carr reported that after leaving Milliken's Bend on April 12, his Fourteenth Division completed the 30-mile march with its arrival at Perkins' Plantation. On the march it was engaged in making and repairing roads, replacing levees, and collecting and navigating boats of various kinds.

Medical inspector E. P. Vollum of the Surgeon General's Office reported after an inspection of medical facilities in Grant's army that there were enough medical supplies on hand to care for 10,000 men in the field for three months. He also reported: "Taking into account the field, convalescent, floating hospitals, and general hospitals at Memphis and other nearby cities there can be no doubt that there is ample accommodations for the Army of the Tennessee. Instead, I would say thousands of beds now ready or being prepared would never be occupied unless army suffers beyond precedent."[38]

Alonzo Brown wrote that the soldiers in his regiment discussed the speech General Thomas made about organizing Negro units. He wrote that the initial negative feelings about the use of Negroes as soldiers gave way when the men reasoned that it made sense to use them to suppress the rebellion when they were available in such great numbers. They recognized that the enemy used the Negroes for noncombat duties. Brown concluded, "Amusing to see change of sentiment among our men. Colonel Sanborn received four times as many applications for officer commissions as were needed."

The 83rd Ohio Volunteer Infantry Regiment, Tenth Division, performed provost duties on its march to Perkins' Plantation. It monitored the collection of beef cattle, corn, and other supplies and guarded against looting of personal property. In spite of the ban, one soldier reported that he entered a plantation house and took silverware, butter, chickens, and all the sweet milk he could drink.

The 5th Iowa Volunteer Infantry spent four days on the 50-mile march to Perkins' Plantation. Because of the muddy condition of the road and the limited number of wagons the regiment was allowed to use, each night it had to return its wagons to Milliken's Bend to bring forward the supplies it had left behind because of lack of wagon space. It was an arduous task for the animals and wagon drivers that required long hours of work. Commenting on the effects of the march, the regimental commander said his infantrymen had been inactive for so long that marching over bad roads with a heavy knapsack under a scorching sun exhausted many of them. Each night stragglers were picked up along the march route by ambulances and brought to the bivouac site.

Colonel Manning F. Force, commander of the 20th Ohio Volunteer Infantry, recorded in his diary his reaction to the march to Perkins' Plantation and the camp environment: "When the sun set the leaves of the forest seemed to exude smoke and the air became a saturated solution of gnats. When I sat down to eat the gnats got into my mouth, nose, eyes, ears. I placed a circle of cotton around us and set it on fire. The smoke brought water to our eyes, but we drove gnats away. At intervals at night I woke up and burned wads of cotton."

April 24. Grant discovered that there was a lack of dry ground at Perkins' Plantation for a troop staging area and also a lack of facilities for transports to anchor and embark troops. He also knew that his reconnaissance with Porter of the land above Grand Gulf revealed that it was impracticable to land troops on the bluffs. Grant thus issued instructions to Wilson to cross the Mississippi to conduct a reconnaissance for a landing on the peninsula between the mouths of the Big Bogasha and Big Black rivers as a means of marching to the rear of Vicksburg. Accompanied by an infantry regiment, Wilson crossed to the east side of the river by boat. He discovered that the terrain bottoms on the peninsula near Congo's Landing on the Big Bogasha were in places several miles wide and overflowed from four to ten feet deep, which made it practically impossible to climb to the highlands. On the Big Black River, he found a crossing at Cox's Ferry, but the river appeared to be too narrow for the gunboats and transports. Movement on the Big Black River would require Porter's assent. Wilson concluded from his reconnaissance that the army and navy would have to run the batteries at Grand Gulf and seek a landing farther down the Mississippi.[39]

Grant also issued orders to McClernand to reconnoiter the road around Lake Saint Joseph to Hard Times Landing, located 22 miles farther down the river bank. In compliance with Grant's instructions, General Osterhaus ordered Colonel James Keigwin, 49th Indiana Infantry, Detachment of Ninth Division, to be in readiness to command a division detachment for the purpose of

Corduroyed Road and Trestle Bridge (*Harper's Weekly*).

making a reconnaissance on the Lake Saint Joseph road to a point opposite the mouth of Bayou Pierre to ascertain whether a practicable road could be found near that point that would place the division in a position on the flank or in the rear of Grand Gulf. The detachment was also supposed to capture or disperse the Confederate command of Major I. F. Harrison, which was deployed somewhere on the road.

Dana reported to Stanton:

> Grant arrived last night at Smith's Plantation. He set out with Admiral Porter to conduct a reconnaissance of Grand Gulf. They observed four batteries, with three guns each, positioned there. A new work is being built in rear. There are rifle pits in works along the shore. Enemy zealously working and strengthening their works; the garrison is reinforced to 12,000 soldiers.
>
> Porter advises against frontal attack. Recommends troops march farther down to a place to be ferried over, or be embarked on transports and barges floated past Grand Gulf batteries at night. Five transports that ran batteries April 22 at Vicksburg anchored at New Carthage.
>
> Grant directed that two regiments from each corps shall remain to guard the line between here and Milliken's Bend, but if water falls so as to leave canal dry and uncover the country on both sides of road, it will require for that duty a division at least. [As Grant marched south the enemy would quickly

occupy the vacated area, if left unprotected, to disrupt the Union's line of communications.]

Fall of river continues. Probably road will be chief avenue of transportation. Weather hot. Troops in high spirit at prospect of fighting.

April 25. At 6 A.M., Colonel Keigwin marched his detachment out of his camp at Perkins' Plantation. The detachment consisted of the 49th Indiana Volunteer Infantry, under command of Lieutenant Colonel Joseph H. Thornton; the 114th Ohio Volunteer Infantry, under command of Colonel John Cradlebaugh; a detachment of the 2nd Illinois Cavalry, under command of Major Daniel B. Bush, Jr., and one section of Captain Charles H. Lamphere's Michigan Battery, under command of Lieutenant George L. Stillman. Keigwin marched the detachment on the Lake Saint Joseph road approximately four miles. Arriving at Holt's Bayou, the detachment's advance party observed that the Rebels had burned the bayou's bridge. Colonel Keigwin detailed 100 soldiers from each of the infantry regiments to assist Lieutenant Colonel John W. Beekmamn of the 120th Ohio Infantry, who had been sent with the expedition for the purpose of supervising bridge building.

Soon the soldiers performing engineer-pioneer duties were at work. In a few hours they had a replacement bridge across the 80-foot-wide bayou. Colonel Keigwin ordered the cannon moved across and marched the detachment along the road for approximately a mile. Arriving at Durossette Bayou, about 120 feet wide, they faced water, with a stiff current, which was overflowing the banks. Keigwin's detachment could not cross over because the Rebels had burned the bridge a few days before. Keigwin detailed Lieutenant James Fullyard, 49th Indiana Infantry, to supervise the reconstruction of the bridge, which had to be well built because of the strength of the current and the width of the stream. Brush fires furnished light to permit the soldiers to carry on their work during the night. To stop the bridge from sinking in the quicksand, the bridge builders tore down houses in the vicinity and laid layers of half-inch boards crosswise and lengthwise, layer upon layer, until there was enough buoyancy to make the trestle bridge into a floating bridge. Through skillful management and industry, Lieutenant Fullyard and his soldiers completed the reconstruction of the bridge during the night, and it was ready for the crossing of the detachment

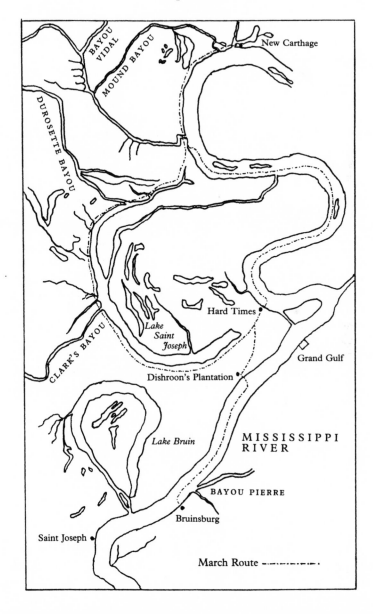

McClernand's March from New Carthage to Bruinsburg (Adapted from *The War of the Rebellion, A Compilation of the Official Records of the Union and Confederate Armies*).

in the morning. Colonel Keigwin left a guard of one sergeant and ten soldiers at each bridge to prevent any small party of the Rebels from attempting to destroy them.

(Fullyard's bridge-building tasks are examples of how all the officers and soldiers were required to perform engineer-pioneer duties. There were no engineer officers or engineer-pioneer units with the division detachment. Their improvisation in the field confirmed that soldiers could be found to undertake difficult work.)

General Hovey reported that on the four-day march from Gilbert's Bayou to Perkins' Plantation, his Twelfth Division, with the aid of Captain Patterson's Company of Mechanics and Engineers, built four bridges over about one thousand feet of water and cut two miles of road through the woods, thus opening up "a great military route" through overflowed lands from Milliken's Bend to the Mississippi River. Hovey noted: "During this severe task many of my men worked for hours up to their necks in water, and I take this occasion to thank them for their devotion and energy there displayed. To Captain George W. Jackson, 34th Indiana Infantry and his pioneer corps particularly due thanks for the performance of their herculean task."

In his report to Stanton, Dana stated:

> Grant's reconnaissance of Grand Gulf convinces him place is not as strong as Porter supposed. Key to place is first bluffs descending to Mississippi river. Enemy fortifying but no guns there yet. Landing to be made there when batteries there; if found, are silenced. Tomorrow or next day when troops can be readied.
>
> I am sorry to report there is much confusion in McClernand's command, especially about his staff and headquarters; movement delayed by that cause.
>
> Though it is ordered officers' horses and tents are to be left behind, McClernand carries his bride along.

Major F. C. Deimling, 10th Missouri Volunteer Infantry Regiment, reported that the regiment marched from Richmond to Holmes' Plantation ten miles. Colonel Buehler, 67th Indiana Volunteer Infantry, reported that his regiment embarked on the transport *Empire City* at Smith's Plantation and sailed down the bayou into the Mississippi, arriving at Perkins' Plantation at 9 P.M. in a severe storm.

Many comments in the soldiers' diaries and letters also reflect the march resulting from Grant's orders of April 20.

Captain Patterson reported in a letter to his wife that his company marched ten miles. "We are to go on boats. Killed several crocodiles twelve feet long. Hot weather here." Allen Geer wrote in his diary: "10 A.M. marched toward Carthage warm day; march heavy and exhausting. Left all equipment & property. Suffered fatigue and heat."

Sergeant Snure, Company A, 48th Indiana Infantry, wrote home: "Started in direction of Grand Gulf. Passed through some of as good country as I have seen in Dixie. Cleared land seemed to be almost an uninterrupted cornfield and corn knee high. Little cotton planted this year. Roads generally, with exception of about three miles of which I can give you no better idea of than by giving you the number of wagons stuck in the mud, which was 28 including supply, caissons, and artillery. Crossed a number of bayous on pontoon bridges. Saw two alligators."

Frank Leslie's Independent Newspaper reported: "Richmond [Virginia] papers say union troops withdrawing from peninsula opposite Vicksburg. Tents struck on April 6th."

April 26. Colonel Keigwin's detachment crossed the bridge at Durosette Bayou and marched about five miles down a beautiful road to arrive in sight of Phelps' Bayou. The soldiers observed that the bridge over the bayou had been burned just prior to their arrival. A Rebel picket stood on the opposite side of the bayou. On a strip of land about 400 yards in length separating Phelps' and Clark's bayous, Colonel Keigwin discovered Major Harrison's Confederate soldiers posted. He estimated Harrison's command was made up of 400 cavalrymen and 4 pieces of artillery. Keigwin ordered his advance guard to fire a few shots at the Rebels, and this action successfully drove them from the neck of land between the two bayous. Keigwin then ordered the artillery to move forward and to throw a few shells into the Rebel camp, which caused them to saddle up and leave in the greatest confusion. Major Harrison left a few dismounted men under the cover of a hedge near the bank of the bayou, and these soldiers kept up fire on the Yankee detachment until Colonel Keigwin sent two companies of infantry across to drive them away. The companies skirmished with the enemy for about an hour and drove the Rebels from their cover.

With the retreat of the skirmishers, Keigwin immediately

prepared to build the two bridges. He concluded it would take a longer time to build these bridges than the two previous bridges because the bayous were much wider and the current much stronger. He detailed Captain Peckinpaugh of the 48th Indiana Infantry to supervise the building of the two bridges.

All the timber for their construction came from barns standing near the construction sites. Large dry beams 50 feet long by 18 inches square were used to hold the flooring, which was taken off the side walls of barns. The flooring was kept in place by using 6"×6" timbers. Where the banks of the bayous were steep, the bridge builders dug out the dirt and replaced it with logs for a corduroy road to prevent soldiers and animals from slipping.

Upon completion of the two bridges, Colonel Keigwin complimented Captain Peckinpaugh for the good judgment he displayed in working the soldiers to the best advantage. The detachment was not as well supplied with tools as it should have been for the task and lacked rope or anything in the way of tools necessary for building the bridges. Colonel Keigwin detailed a few soldiers from the cavalry, who from their experience in foraging, soon had a supply of ropes and tools. It took the detachment two days to complete the two bridges.

Colonel Keigwin then sent Major Arthur J. Hawhe with two companies of the 49th Indiana Infantry and two from the 114th Ohio Infantry to cross Clark's Bayou to make a reconnaissance a few miles in the detachment's front. Major Hawhe completed his mission successfully. He found that Harrison had left the road to Hard Times Landing and had crossed Choctaw Bayou, which emptied into Lake Bruin approximately two miles from the road the detachment was to march on the next day.

General McPherson, 17th Corps, reported his corps marched per Grant's orders from New Carthage to Perkins' Plantation; the eight-mile route turned out to be 15 miles for the leading echelon. The march from Milliken's Bend to Perkins' totaled 43 miles. McPherson noted in the record, "Heavy rains had rendered the roads across the rich alluvial bottoms almost impassable, and it was only by the most strenuous exertions on the part of the men, and by doubling teams, that the artillery and trains could be got along. This however was successfully accomplished and the Third Division reached Perkins' at 9:00 P.M."

General McClernand, 13th Corps, issued orders that on the

march to Hard Times troops would bivouac on field; one tent per company was authorized for the protection of rations, one for a hospital, and one for the headquarters. A corps hospital was to be located at Perkins' Plantation. His order also stated divisions were permitted to organize fatigue corps from able-bodied Negroes. McClernand ordered that there would be no insulting or provoking language to citizens and no wanton destruction of property or going into houses. Negro women and children were not to follow the army.

General Osterhaus published a memorandum to the troops: "The commanding general pained to notice the neglect from former orders in regard to digging of sinks. This is the last time attention will be called to regimental commanders to this subject. In future any commanding officer who shall neglect to have sink trenches dug immediately on arrival in camp and to compel men to use them will be placed under arrest and charges preferred against." Osterhaus also sent an order to his troops: "I have observed with deep regret violation of orders issued on March 2 persons found gambling or playing games of hazard will be arrested and punished and money confiscated for purpose of the hospital fund."

Brigadier General Stephen G. Burbridge, First Brigade, Tenth Division, 13th Army Corps, whose brigade had been marching and camping since April 14, arrived at Smith's Plantation on April 24. After camping for two days, the brigade embarked on transports in Roundaway Bayou, followed the waterway to the Mississippi River opposite New Carthage, and thence proceeded down the river to Perkins' Plantation, arriving about 9 P.M. during a very severe storm. Burbridge's brigade was one of the few that provided evidence that troops were transported through the bayou canal on boats and barges.

Sergeant Onley Andrus, 95th Illinois Volunteer Infantry, in a letter to his wife wrote: "Regiment to break camp at Lake Providence, to be transported to Milliken's Bend. Colonel uses men for personal benefit, wanted combat, heroics, to fight. There are no cowards in the regiment but few rush into a fight on account of their patriotism. [Colonel Thomas W.] Humphrey looking for stars. Forgets comfort of men and sacrifices them."

Allen Geer wrote in his diary: "Marched at 7:00 A.M. Footsore, weak, and weary. Marched 10 miles to Hanes on Miller's Plantation. ¾ hour in camp when received orders to march. Marched 4 miles and camped. Nearly played out with cramps."

Digging a Sink (*Harper's Weekly*).

Alonzo Brown wrote in his diary: "Marched 10 miles to Smith's Plantation. Held up as division before us stopped, roads impassable. Camped in old cornfield, mud is awful. Rained all night."

April 27. Grant reported to Halleck: "Moving troops from Smith's has been a tedious operation; moreso than it should have been. I am now embarking troops for the attack on Grand Gulf, and expect to reduce it tomorrow."

The primitive roads and bayous complicated the troop movements. There were three ongoing steps to Grant's "tedious operation":

A contingent of soldiers in McClernand's Corps were being ferried, or had been ferried, by boats through the Bayou Vidal canal to New Carthage and the Mississippi River to board transports. When Grant discovered the New Carthage ferrying operation was inadequate to move the entire army, he ordered the remainder of McClernand's 13th Corps, followed by McPherson's 17th Corps to march over the road and bridges Captain Patterson's Kentucky Mechanics and Engineers and General Hovey's soldiers had built between Smith's and Perkins' plantations.

The troops that first reached Perkins' Plantation discovered a lack of facilities to camp or be transported by water, so Grant ordered them to march to Hard Times Landing following Colonel Keigwin's Ninth Division detachment, which built the bridges on the road around Lake Saint Joseph.

While the three steps of the operation, with the troops in three locations on the march, might have been tedious, they were in essence Grant's method of overcoming the terrain obstacles. The difficulty of the operation meant that Grant's statement to Halleck that he expected to reduce Grand Gulf on the 28th was overly optimistic.

Colonel Keigwin's detachment completed the bridge at Phelps' and Clark's bayous and received orders from General Osterhaus to be at Hard Times Landing early the next day.

Sherman wrote in the record that the road his corps marched over was very bad and that Grant suggested his corps reverse its march and make a feint on Haynes' Bluff. This was not an order, so it was possible to save face if the enemy reacted. "We had to fight the clamor in the north as well as determined foe in the south and obstacles of nature," Sherman noted.

Dana reported to Stanton:

> Movement against Grand Gulf is still delayed. Grant went by water to New Carthage and Perkins' Plantation where Osterhaus' Ninth Division and E. A. Carr's Fourteenth Division are encamped to order immediate embarkation of their troops. There are seven transports in good order.
>
> 7,000 troops could have been transported with artillery and ammunition; barges could have carried 5,000 more. First point struck us was (at points of embarkation) that steamboats and barges were scattered about in the river and in bayous as if there were no idea of the imperative necessity of their promptest possible movements.
>
> Arrived at Porter's flagship above Grand Gulf and Grant sent at once for McClernand; discussed point of attack, and ordered him to embark his men without losing a moment. Somehow not moved. Still at dark last night when a thunderstorm set in not a single man or cannon had been embarked. Instead, McClernand held a review of an Illinois Brigade at Perkins' Plantation at 4:00 P.M. When Illinois Governor Richard Yates made a speech to the troops a salute was fired contrary to orders (fire only against the enemy).
>
> McPherson arrived last night at Perkins' Plantation with Quinby's Seventh Division; held up until McClernand's Corps moves.
>
> Road injured by last night's rain and cut up by wagons. Without heavy storm can be depended upon. If they came upon us unexpectedly, as fall of river, army will be in straits.

Allen Geer wrote in his diary: "Moved out late. Clouded up and rained at noon. Road muddy, miry, many wagons stuck. Moved slowly indeed. Regiment detached to help along difficult wagons. Marched 7 miles and camped."

April 28. Colonel Keigwin departed with the detachment from its bivouac in the morning, leaving a sergeant and ten soldiers at each of the bridges as a guard. He sent two companies of cavalry under the command of Major Benjamin F. Marsh, Jr., to leave the road and find out whether Harrison was still in the position he held the previous evening. Keigwin soon received word from Marsh that he had found the enemy and that he could not move the Confederates from the point they held. Colonel Keigwin immediately sent Major Bush in that direction.

Major Bush had been gone only a short time when Colonel Keigwin heard artillery firing. He left the road with his detachment determined to drive the enemy troops away from the point they held. Keigwin was fearful that as soon as the detachment passed, the enemy would recross the bayou and destroy the two bridges the detachment had built. Keigwin moved on and soon came in sight of his cavalry, which were held at bay by the enemy's artillery. He halted his command and went forward to reconnoiter and find the position of the enemy. He discovered the enemy had four pieces of artillery in position.

Colonel Keigwin also discovered that Choctaw Bayou was a small stream about 60 feet wide. On the point of land into the angle where the bayou connected with Lake Bruin, the enemy had four pieces of artillery in battery. The only approach Keigwin had to the point was over an open field without stump or tree that would cover the Union skirmishers. Lake Bruin lay on the left and the backwater from the bayou on the right, which left a strip of land about 500 yards wide and narrowing down to about 200 yards at the point on the opposite side from the enemy's battery.

The enemy's battery was supported on the right and left by its cavalry, which made a formidable appearance. Keigwin found that he could not use his infantry or cavalry to any advantage. At first he had doubts whether he could move the enemy from its position with the two pieces he had.

Colonel Keigwin formed his two regiments in columns of divisions and deployed four companies forward as skirmishers. He placed one piece of artillery on the bank of Lake Bruin, where it had a fine range and lay in open view of the enemy's battery. The other piece he posted in the field, where it had an excellent range. He then ordered Lieutenant Stillman to open fire upon the enemy with his artillery and advanced his line of skirmishers. The enemy opened with its battery, but caused no injury to the division expedition soldiers because the shots passed over their heads. After a few shots from Stillman's pieces, Harrison moved his cavalry out of range of the Union shells. In about an hour from the time Stillman's artillery opened fire, the enemy limbered up and hastily left the ground.

Keigwin's soldiers followed Harrison as far as they could toward Choctaw Bayou and then halted. Keigwin had no orders to bridge Choctaw Bayou, which was off of the line of march of his detachment, and from all appearances the enemy had fled. He thus returned to the road with his command and bivouacked there for the night. He sent the cavalry on, however, to Hard Times to report to General Osterhaus, who he learned had arrived during the day.

The 24th Indiana Volunteer Infantry Regiment reported that it completed a 12-day march from Milliken's Bend to Perkins' Plantation "after most fatiguing and dangerous march without tents or baggage and short rations through swamp and over bayous through which we cut roads and built bridges."

General Burbridge reported he was ordered to embark the 16th and 17th Indiana Volunteer Infantry regiments, the 83rd Ohio Volunteer Infantry, and the 23rd Wisconsin Volunteer Infantry on transports and barges to proceed to a point as near Grand Gulf as practicable to serve under General Osterhaus as reserve. He embarked his troops as ordered on transports and barges, leaving behind all wagons and horses.

Alonzo Brown recorded in his diary: "6 A.M. division moved four miles through mud. Rained. One team with regiment. Empty wagons get stuck. 14 span of horses were pulling a caisson through mud. Step in tracks of men ahead. Wagon train left at Smith's Plantation."

General Pemberton sent a message to General Johnston: "The enemy in large force with barges and transports moving down the river indicating a purpose to attack Grand Gulf." Pemberton realized Grant viewed Vicksburg as his real target. He also cautioned Johnston he would have to depend upon the Confederate Army of the Tennessee to protect the approaches through northern Mississippi.

April 29. In response to Wilson's recommendation, Porter declined to move his fleet into the Big Black River. He agreed to make an effort to silence the batteries at Grand Gulf to permit Grant's soldiers to attempt to land for an assault.

In his records Grant noted: "At 8:00 A.M. Porter made his attack with his gunboats against the batteries on the high bluff at Grand Gulf for five and one half hours. No enemy guns were silenced; 10,000 soldiers of McClernand's corps in transports were waiting for the signal to land. I was on a tugboat and could see effects of battle. At 1:30 P.M. Porter withdrew his fleet. I asked Porter to run the batteries at night. He volunteered his fleet as transports. His fleet succeeded in running past the batteries at night. The army and the transports are now three miles below Grand Gulf."

At this time, Grant executed his alternative plan, which followed Wilson's recommendation to go farther down river. In the seventh attempt to take Vicksburg, he ordered his soldiers to disembark from the transports and barges and to march across a neck of land in front of Grand Gulf for one and a half miles to Dishroon's Plantation, which was out of range of the enemy's guns. There they were to bivouac for the night

With rising confidence, Grant also recorded: "Citizens told us of a landing at Bruinsburg, a few miles above Rodney with a good road leading to Port Gibson, 12 miles away. A landing will be effected on the east bank of the river tomorrow. I feel that the battle is now more than half won."

Wilson reported he was satisfied from the information he collected that there were no batteries or Rebel soldiers at Rodney, but there was an open road that led to the interior. He urged Grant to cut loose from Dishroon's with all the soldiers the transports could carry and upon landing on the east side, "to swing out into the open toward Jackson without waiting for the rest of the army to catch up."[40] Grant agreed to this proposal.

General Hovey, Twelfth Division, reported from a transport, "witnessed brilliant assault by gunboats on Grand Gulf." General Burbridge reported: "We stood out in stream our transport towed by gunboat *General Price* in constant readiness to avail ourselves of any advantage which might be gained by the gunboats."

Dana reported to Stanton from Dishroon's Plantation at 11:30 P.M.:

> Gunboats came safely through from Hard Times Landing this evening. The batteries at Grand Gulf were nearly as active

as in the morning, and Admiral Porter thinks that in one of the lower batteries a large gun had been mounted during the afternoon. No harm received in passage, either boats or men.

General McClernand's Corps ready to embark; doubtful if they will get on before daylight. Grant gave them urgent orders to do so. They will land above Rodney below mouth of Bayou Pierre; casualties on fleet today 22 killed, 55 wounded.

Colonel Keigwin's detachment continued its march to Hard Times Landing, where it arrived at 8 A.M. There he received orders from General Osterhaus to send the section of artillery to General Burbridge and infantry regiments to their division commanders; these orders were carried out in a short time.

Colonel Keigwin wrote in the record that he could not speak in too high terms of all the officers and men in the detachment. They were ever ready to assist in all the labors of building bridges and to obey any command. When they came in sight of the enemy, they all seemed to be ready for any emergency. He added he felt indebted to Lieutenant Stillman and his men for their bravery and artillery skill. "I scarcely ever witnessed," Keigwin wrote, "as fine artillery shooting." Captain William H. Peckinpaugh and Lieutenant James Fullyard, of the 49th Indiana Infantry warranted special praise; Keigwin said he was indebted to them for the speedy construction of the bridges across the bayous and for aiding him in all the duties he had to perform on the expedition.

Colonel Buehler, 67th Indiana Infantry, reported the unsuccessful attempts of the Union gunboats to silence the Rebel batteries at Grand Gulf that occurred while the soldiers watched from their transports. The troops were disembarked at about 4 P.M., marched three miles across the bend to Dishroon's Plantation below Grand Gulf, and bivouacked for the night.

Allen Geer wrote in his diary: "Lay on damp ground till after sun rose then moved on down levee along a lake or bayou. Made several stops while bridges repaired. Passed one splendid mansion recently deserted, furniture worth $10,000. Our road lay along the highest and wealthiest section we have seen in Louisiana along the whole border of lake Saint Joseph; camped two miles from it. Heard of gunboats firing on Grand Gulf. Troops disembarked transports that ran blockade, engaged batteries after dark. Issued free beef and salt, slept soundly."

General McPherson's 17th Corps followed General McClernand's 13th Corps, and his soldiers marched directly from
Milliken's Bend to Hard Times Landing over the roads and bridges
built by McClernand's division pioneers, Captain Patterson's Kentucky Company of Mechanics and Engineers, and Colonel
Keigwin's infantrymen. Reporting on his forced march, McPherson
noted that the leading element of his corps left Milliken's Bend on
April 24. By strenuous exertion on the part of his infantrymen and
by doubling the animal teams pulling the supply trains and artillery
pieces, his corps' advance party arrived at Hard Times at 4 P.M. on
April 29 after marching for almost six days.

General John A. Logan, commander of the Third Infantry
Division, 17th Corps, marched this distance of approximately 70
miles in five days. He reported he had made the march over the
worst kind of roads, with the axles of the supply wagons and artillery
pieces often scraping the ground.

A Michigan farm boy who made the march recorded in his
diary that he thought the country "the most beautiful he had ever
seen and the plantation mansion grand." The only complaints he
had were the bad roads and the hot weather in late April. Along the
banks of the bayous, the soldiers found alligators, turtles, and snakes
in abundance. Shooting alligators became the soldiers' pastime, and
the accuracy of their marksmanship was measured by the number
of dead alligators floating in the bayous.

On the last step of the march to Hard Times Landing, another
soldier wrote that he passed through a countryside with magnolia
groves in full bloom and miles of blossoming rose hedge beautiful
and fragrant beyond description. Not so pleasant was the sight of
many dead mules and horses scattered along the roadside and the
smoking ruins of many plantation buildings. After completing the
same long march to Hard Times Landing, an infantry regimental
commander declared, "A worse march no army ever made in the
history of military operations."

Lieutenant Colonel Ezekiel S. Sampson, commander of the
5th Iowa Volunteer Infantry, Seventh Division, 17th Corps, wrote:
"self sacrificing spirit of my men was uncomplaining. Many of them
without shoes, all frequently without provisions, except sugar and
meat, pushed through rain and sunshine, without a murmur or
complaint, with a will to endure every hardship and peril for the success of their cause."

General Sherman reported that his force of ten regiments from Blair's Division embarked at Milliken's Bend at 10 A.M. and proceeded north up the river to the mouth of the Yazoo River, where he found Captain Breese's flagboat *Black Hawk* with the ironclads *Choctaw* and *De Kalb*. They were steamed up ready to go and were prepared to cooperate in the proposed foray against Haynes' Bluff. Sherman noted that the ships were managed admirably by Breese. The expedition laid up at the mouth of Chickasaw Bayou on the Yazoo River.

Pemberton reported to Johnston that six gunboats with ten guns each opened fire on Grand Gulf at 7 A.M., kept up their fire for six and a half hours, and then withdrew.

April 30. Dana reported to Stanton from Dishroon's Plantation: "P. J. Osterhaus' Ninth Division, A. P. Hovey's Twelfth Division, and E. A. Carr's Fourteenth Division landed safely without opposition at Bruinsburg, Mississippi at Mouth Bayou Pierre 11:00 A.M. Divisions of A. J. Smith, Tenth, 13th Army Corps and J. A. Logan, Third, 17th Army Corps will be landed before night. All seems to be going well."

Colonel Buehler, 67th Indiana Infantry, Tenth Division, reported that after muster his troops embarked at 2 P.M. on the gunboat *Carondelet* for Bruinsburg. General Burbridge, First Brigade, Tenth Division, reported that his brigade boarded the transports at Dishroon's Plantation and proceeded across the Mississippi to Bruinsburg. After debarking on the eastern side of the river and assembling, the brigade drew rations for six days. Buehler then ordered his regiment to take up the line of march to Port Gibson.

Allen Geer, 20th Illinois Infantry, Logan's Third Division, wrote that his regiment marched out after daylight to the boat landing at Dishroon's. His regiment waited for Hovey's and Carr's divisions to embark on the Mississippi. It was dark before the 13th Corps completed its crossing. The Third Division, the first in McPherson's 17th Corps to cross the river, landed on the east side of the Mississippi in the dark; after debarking it camped.

Alonzo Brown wrote that his 4th Minnesota Infantry Regiment completed its 21-mile march to Hard Times on a clear, hot day. He was prompted to remark that the roster of the regiment listed 694 enlisted men, but only half of them, 347, were present for duty, plus 22 officers. The present-for-duty rate in Brown's regiment was below the estimated 65 percent effective rate that generally prevailed

in the army. The 4th Minnesota Infantry, like many other regiments, faced the additional impediment of being 306 soldiers below
its authorized strength of one thousand.

Sherman reported on the feint on the enemy's right flank:

> The expedition proceeded up the Yazoo river within range
> of the enemy's batteries. The *Choctaw* followed by other gun-
> boats and our transports approached Haynes' Bluff. We kept
> up a heavy fire which was returned by the enemy. *Choctaw* was
> struck 53 times, but her injuries not in any vital part. Strange
> to say no one hurt. A very pretty demonstration. Used ten
> regiments from Blair's Division to make show of force and it
> worked. Pemberton pulled forces from Grand Gulf and Port
> Gibson, sent on a forced march to meet us. I disembarked
> command at Blake's Negroes' quarters and made disposition
> as for attack, which was kept up till after dark, drawing heavy
> fire from enemy nearby watching us.

General Bowen, at Grand Gulf, reported to Pemberton:
"Camp and fleet of enemy three miles below. Their troops moving.
I don't know if will attack our left or front. They may move to
Rodney and not renew attack on Grand Gulf."

Retrospection

As the month drew to a close, the Army of the Tennessee
marched to its objective in a state of increasing health. After four
grueling months of six attempts that failed, the seventh attempt to
take Vicksburg was reaching a successful climax. Led by Grant's
skillful generalship, the army achieved its long-sought goal of setting
foot on the eastern side of the Mississippi on dry ground and con-
fronting the adversary's army in a pitched battle at the metaphorical
Vicksburg Mountain alluded to by correspondent Galway of the
New York Times.

At the outset of the month, Galway had written poetically of the
sureness of change in the natural world. It was a change many of the
soldiers felt in their attitudes as they approached the spring campaign.

Unfortunately for the soldiers, the natural changes in their dis-
ease-inducing environment failed to diminish completely the illnesses

that burdened the army. The Army of the Tennessee with the Department of the Gulf remained afflicted with the highest rate of cases of diseases and deaths from diseases among the Union armies (see Tables 1, 2, and 3).

During four winter months, it had seemed as if a shadow hung over the soldiers of the Army of the Tennessee. In January and February, they lived in a mudhole. A high number of soldiers were afflicted with diseases, and the view of burial boxes and graves on the levees disheartened them. They labored on Grant's experiments in the hope they would succeed because the product of their labor was their only rescuer.

During March and April, the men's spirits began to lift as the unrelenting cycle of change in the natural world became obvious to the soldiers. The amelioration of their health and living conditions and the optimism of a spring campaign raised their morale.

Faced with a difficult terrain, the soldiers were affected by the acute shortage of soldiers who were trained as engineer-pioneers. This shortage meant that the ordinary soldiers had to build bridges, roads, canals, and defense works and to remove natural obstacles impeding their paths of reconnaissance and march.

Almost all the soldiers who remained well were detailed at one time or another to engineer-pioneer duties to work laboriously with shovels, axes, and other hand tools. As they performed such duties, they transformed their hands and feet into an engineer-pioneer's hands and feet. Their finger and toe nails cracked, and their skin became tough and blistered.

Amidst difficulties that might have overwhelmed them, most of the soldiers remained loyal to their country, the army, their fellow soldiers, and their officers. They persevered in their faithfulness to their labors and use of skills; they achieved the army's mission.

CHAPTER 6

April 30–May 22, 1863

The Other Side of the River

April 30. General Pemberton, the commander of the Confederate army at Vicksburg, found it difficult to assess Grant's intentions. He had in hand reports of many Union movements, but he misread Sherman's ruse of marching north to mean that Grant's soldiers were heading north on a new tactical move. The cavalry raid Grant sent Colonel H. B. Grierson on through northern Mississippi, which had been harassing the countryside and tearing up railroads and destroying depots since April 17, also turned the Confederates' attention away from Grant's march to Dishroon's Plantation.[1]

Grant and Wilson spent the night on a coil of rope on the ironclad *Benton*, "anxious to get the troops across," and they were awake at the break of day.

The first wave of soldier-filled boats from Dishroon's Landing headed across the Mississippi for Bruinsburg, 30 miles south of Vicksburg. After the boats dropped their anchors as near the eastern shore as the water's depth permitted, the soldiers debarked and waded ashore. To their surprise, there were no Confederate soldiers waiting on the edge of the river to open the critical battle between the contending armies. The Yankees trudged through the shallow water and the heavy brush on the river bank. McClernand's soldiers kept moving inland until they reached open ground. Their feet were on the first dry ground they had been on in months.

Wilson told Grant that with the army on good footing on Mississippi soil after four months of incredible labor, he should not wait but "swing out after the enemy." Grant and Wilson borrowed two horses from an Illinois cavalry regiment and were on the

Bruinsburg road to the front "to push the soldiers forward as fast as possible."[2] (Wilson, haunted by his experience at Antietam, was eager "to hurry.")

All day long the navy boats and army transports continued to ferry Grant's soldiers from McClernand's and McPherson's corps over the river. By nightfall an estimated 18,000 had been safely landed and were under marching orders. With the success of the amphibious operation, Grant declared he was overcome by a "degree of relief scarcely equaled since his army stood on dry ground on the same side of the river with the enemy."[3]

Grant oversaw the regrouping of his corps' soldiers into their companies, regiments, and divisions for battle formation. They drew a three-day supply of rations to carry. Supply wagon trains would not provide subsistence because Grant had ordered them to remain on the west side until his soldiers had crossed.[4]

The first objective Grant set for his soldiers was to move to the highlands three miles inland from Bruinsburg before the enemy could organize any resistance. McClernand's soldiers took up the line of march for the bluffs and arrived there before sunset. McClernand was intent upon surprising any enemy troops posted in the vicinity of Port Gibson and preventing them from destroying the bridge over the South Fork of Bayou Pierre on the road leading to Grand Gulf and Jackson. He ordered a forced march for his soldiers that night to cover as much distance as possible.[5]

May 1. At 1 A.M., when McClernand's soldiers approached Magnolia Church, four miles from Port Gibson, the soldiers in General Carr's Fourteenth Division came under light enemy rifle fire, follówed by artillery fire. Carr ordered a return of the fire, which silenced the enemy's fire. The soldiers of his division became the first to achieve the long-sought goal to engage the enemy on the battlefield. For the remaining hours of the night, McClernand ordered his soldiers to rest on their arms.

At dawn McClernand learned from a fugitive Negro that two roads diverged at Shaiffer's place and each led to Port Gibson, one to the right by Magnolia Church and the other to the left by the South Fork of Bayou Pierre, where the bayou was spanned by a railroad and an earth-road bridge. The two roads to Port Gibson were only separated by a distance of two miles; the land between them consisted of fields, thick woods, abrupt hills, and deep ravines where the enemy was posted in force and ready to contest the

Yankees' presence. McClernand verified this information by reconnaissance. McClernand ordered General Osterhaus to move his Ninth Division on the road to the left to relieve a detachment of General Carr's Fourteenth Division that was posted there to watch the enemy. Osterhaus was also given the mission to attack the enemy's right flank at a weak point and to create a diversion in favor of the corps' right flank prior to an attack on the enemy's strongest force.

When moving out at 5:30 A.M., Osterhaus soon met the enemy, which demonstrated considerable force and a determination to fight. Osterhaus' soldiers were at last in the midst of the fight they had sought. In an hour after a test in combat, Osterhaus' soldiers forced the enemy to withdraw. Osterhaus pressed his soldiers forward until formidable obstacles—terrain and enemy fire—halted their progress and demonstrated the impracticability of a frontal attack. At 2 P.M., General Logan's Third Division, 17th Army Corps, arrived and attempted to carry the enemy's position by an attack, but his division also failed.

Osterhaus decided on a flank movement to achieve his mission. To deceive the enemy, he threatened the right of the center of the line, and taking advantage of the effect of this tactic on the enemy line, he rapidly moved a force to the extreme union right flank. Leading a bold charge of his soldiers, he routed the enemy. General Smith's Tenth Division joined Osterhaus' men in pursuing the enemy to within a half mile of Port Gibson.

The Battle of Port Gibson

At 6:15 A.M., when sufficient time had elapsed to allow Osterhaus' first attack to create a diversion in favor of McClernand's right, McClernand ordered General Carr's division to attack the enemy's left. General W. F. Benton's First Brigade promptly moved forward to the right of the main road to Port Gibson through woods, ravines, and a light canebrake. He pressed his troops on until he found the enemy drawn up behind the crest of a range of hills intersected by the road. Upon one of the hills in clear view stood Magnolia Church. The hostile lines immediately opened fire on each other, and an earnest struggle ensued.

McClernand reported at the time that the action against the

enemy's left was taking a good turn, except at the center, where a continuation of the fields extending to the front of his line for more than a mile separated the combatants. The enemy troops concealed themselves in the fields, but continued to press McClernand's extreme right, expecting to envelop the Union force. At an opportune moment, General Hovey arrived with his Twelfth Division, and McClernand ordered him to form it in two lines near the fork in the two roads and to hold it there for further orders. After receiving these orders, General Hovey moved out to support Carr's division on the right.

To terminate a sanguinary contest which had been carried on for several hours, General Hovey ordered a charge with a portion of General Carr's division participating. The Yankee soldiers carried out the charge gallantly. They captured 400 prisoners, two stands of colors, two 12-pound howitzers, three caissons, and a considerable quantity of ammunition. McClernand ordered Carr and Hovey to attack the enemy with vigor and celerity, which they did, forcing the enemy soldiers back a mile and preventing their efforts to make an intermediate stand.

On the right, General Smith's Tenth Division marched up to Shaiffer's place about 7 A.M. All four of the 13th Corps' divisions were then in place on the battlefield. McClernand moved Smith's division into the field in front of Shaiffer's house, and this division, together with a portion of Osterhaus' division, held the center of the line and at the same time formed the reserve.

The enemy took up a stronger position on McClernand's right in a creek bottom covered with trees and underbrush. The approach to it was over open fields and ragged and exposed hill slopes. Hovey's and Carr's divisions advanced until they had gained a bald ridge overlooking the bottom land. At this point the enemy opened fire and a fierce engagement followed. McClernand discovered the enemy was massing a formidable force on his right front with the evident design to force back and turn his right flank. He ordered General Smith to send forward a brigade to support the flank. General Hovey massed his artillery on the right and opened an enfilading and destructive fire on the enemy. The two movements forced the enemy upon its center with considerable loss.

With a concentration of forces, the enemy renewed the attack against McClernand's right center. General Carr's division met and retaliated vigorously with infantry and artillery. Soldiers of Smith's

The Advance on Port Gibson (*Harper's Pictorial History*).

brigade and Hovey's division forced their way through cane and underbrush and joined General Carr's attack, transferring the battle from the enemy's left flank to its center. After an obstinate struggle, the Confederates were beaten back upon the high ridge on the opposite side of the bottom, which lay within a mile of Port Gibson. A brigade of General Logan's Third Division, 17th Corps, marched upon the battlefield to achieve the final result. "The shades of night soon after closed upon the stricken field," McClernand wrote, "which the valor of our men had won and held, and upon which they found the first repose since they had left Dishroon's Landing 24 hours before."[6]

Sherman's force made its way back to Chickasaw Bayou feeling for footing on ground that was underwater. When his soldiers were above the water on the levee at 3 P.M., the gunboats resumed their cannonading to prolong the diversion. The enemy's batteries replied with spirit, and enemy pickets moved back and forth as though they were ready to meet an expected attack.

Grant sent orders to Sherman to hurry forth to Grand Gulf. After prolonging his demonstration until night, Sherman reembarked his soldiers on the transports and quietly dropped back to Young's Point, where they arrived during the night. The expedition returned safely without incurring any casualties.

Allen Geer reported: "Marched at daylight with 15 days rations in haversacks. Day very hot, heard artillery firing. Men through [*sic*] away knapsacks, clothes. Reached scene of action at noon where McClernand's army had been engaged all morning. First brigade brought up on left to displace rebels in a stronghold among some houses on crest of hill surrounded by deep gullies, heavy cane brake and underbrush."

Sergeant Snure wrote to his family: "Company marched to Hard Times, crossed the river. Landed 7 miles below. Encamped near a bridge partly burnt. 50 of us hauled timber to help repair it. Rebels scadadelled [*sic*]. Grant said travel light. Ordered his soldiers to follow his example. He carried only a toothbrush, shared hardships of common soldier."

Captain Ankeny in a letter to his wife, wrote: At Milliken's Bend. Enclosed a list of money sent by express. I send you $400. News Grand Gulf is taken. This will place us in the rear of Vicksburg if pushed rapidly. We will operate on Yazoo. Blair up Yazoo on reconnaissance." (Blair was on Sherman's expedition to conduct a ruse.)

Frederick Dent Grant reported he went ashore and fell in with some wagons, where he observed artillery batteries and infantry regiments on their way to the front. He said he hid behind a tree because his presence on the battlefield was against his father's wishes. A shout, he said, announced a victory. Young Grant added that the horrors of the battlefield were soon brought home to him when he joined a detachment collecting the dead; he was sickened at sight. Another detachment collected the wounded. These were terrible scenes, he wrote, which made him ill. In summary, he said he became "a woebegone 12 year older" at the battle of Port Gibson.

General Bowen decided to meet the enemy on the south side of Bayou Pierre, but he recognized the water front of the Mississippi and Bayou Pierre was too extended for the strength of his soldiers and had too many vulnerable points to cover. He thus sent his force to block the two roads leading from Bruinsburg to Port Gibson. His advance engaged Union forces four miles south of Port Gibson. In a message he sent later in the day to Pemberton, Bowen reported that he had fought 20,000 of Grant's soldiers since dawn, and he was vastly outnumbered. "Under cover of dark will cross to other side of Bayou Pierre. Bacon removed out of Port Gibson; they will not get it. Will burn the bridges." He advised Pemberton he needed ammunition and reinforcements.

In the deployment of the Confederate forces, General Baldwin mistakenly believed a burning bridge on Bayou Pierre to be the suspension bridge. In reality it was the railroad bridge, but because of his error, he moved his force on the road due north through Port Gibson instead of on the Grand Gulf road. On the road that he took, he destroyed the bridge on the North Fork of Bayou Pierre, thus cutting off General Bowen's force and a wagon train of subsistence stores located between the two forks. Bowen had to resort to ferrying his soldiers over.

Bowen reported that he had a force of 5,500 against the enemy's strength of 20,000 to block passage through Bayou Pierre and that Grant's soldiers threatened to envelop his force. He said that he had heavy losses and that the Union forces would not let him visit his wounded or bury his dead. He proposed to retreat at sunset. He closed his report with the remark: "enemy landed 30,000 no exaggeration. We held them daylight to sunset." (His statement attests to the accuracy of the information Major Harrison passed on to his army leaders. Grant's strength on the battlefield at this point was approximately 30,000 soldiers.)

Bowen marched his force northeast of Port Gibson, crossed the South Fork of Bayou Pierre, and destroyed two bridges in the hope of preventing Grant from crossing the two forks of Bayou Pierre; he also wished to secure his left flank. Bowen recognized the need to give up Grand Gulf. At night he received orders from Pemberton to abandon his position and retreat north of the Big Black River.

With Confederate forces dispersed and unable to present a unified front, Grant had the opportunity to march his army to the northeast against an inferior opposition.

May 2. At dawn, Smith's Tenth Division leading the advance of the 13th Corps triumphantly entered Port Gibson. The enemy had hastily fled the preceding night, burning the bridge across the South Branch of Bayou Pierre to its rear.

The battle was admirably and successfully fought, declared McClernand, and if not decisive, it was a determining factor in the brilliant series of successes that followed.[7] It lasted 12 hours, with a total of 803 Union casualties: killed, 123; wounded, 680; and missing, 8.[8]

McClernand's corps remained at Port Gibson and infantrymen assisted the pioneers in constructing a bridge across the South Branch of Bayou Pierre under the direction of Colonel Wilson and

General Logan's Division Crossing on Hastily Built Floating Bridge
(*Harper's Pictorial History*).

Captain Patterson's Kentucky Company of Mechanics and
Engineers. Plenty of buoyant materials were collected by tearing
down the barns and cotton gins in the neighborhood. The engineers,
pioneers, and infantrymen then built a continuous raft bridge 160
feet long and 12 feet wide in 4½ hours. Layers of logs covered the
approaches over the quicksand. The corps also reconnoitered the
country north and east of the stream and skirmished with a detachment left by the enemy on the north side of the bridge to impede the
corps' work.

According to McClernand's report, Confederate reinforcements from Grand Gulf and Vicksburg met soldiers fleeing
from McClernand's soldiers and together they fled across the Big
Black River. The soldiers at Grand Gulf, seven miles from Port Gibson, also spiked their guns, abandoned the fort, and fled across the
river.

McPherson's corps crossed the bridge Colonel Wilson and
Captain Patterson had supervised building across the South Fork on
Bayou Pierre and marched eight miles east to the North Fork of
Bayou Pierre. At Grindstone Ford, they were forced to stop because
the retreating Confederates set the suspension bridge across the
bayou on fire.

With the help of local Negroes, Union soldiers put the fire out.
The roadway, side truss, and unseasoned timber ties on which the

road planks were nailed were burned out on the bridge for a distance of 120 feet, however.

Captain Patterson was innovative when challenged to overcome an obstacle; he quickly devised a way to repair the bridge. He told his engineer and mechanic soldiers to leave the charred cross ties in place. After searching around the area, Patterson's soldiers found 3"×7" timber planks. He had the soldiers lash the planks with wires cut from the telegraph line to the suspension rods that hung down from the chain that spanned the river.

Timbers for the cross ties were also collected. The engineers placed them at intervals of three feet and fastened them to the vertical planks they had tied to the suspension rods. Wedges were placed between the old burned ties and the new ones in the middle of the roadway. Over those cross ties, a road covering of boards of different thicknesses and qualities, ripped off nearby buildings, was put in place by spikes and lashings. To make the roadway safe, a rope loop was placed on the suspension cable and then around the end of the cross tie that extended out beyond the rail. Patterson placed a stick inside the loop rope and twisted the rope until it was tight and bore the weight of the roadway. The new roadbed was about ten inches above the level of the old one. Ramps were built at each end for traffic to move on or off. The bridge Patterson devised and supervised constructing was actually a suspension bridge within a suspension bridge.

Sherman reported that Blair's division broke camp and moved to Milliken's Bend to remain there as a garrison force until relieved by the 16th Corps troops from Memphis. Steele's division marched from Milliken's Bend and Tuttle's marched from Duckport on the road to Hard Times.

Frederick Dent Grant reported that although horses were scarce because of his father's orders to leave them on the west bank, he succeeded in finding a mount: a captured white Confederate artillery horse. He said soldiers made sport of him when he passed on the road on a big white horse.[9]

May 3. By five-thirty in the morning, Captain Patterson and his working parties had the bridge over the north fork of Bayou Pierre completed. After the soldiers of the two corps crossed, Captain Patterson, curious as to how well the bridge had withstood the traffic, examined it from end to end and found it free of any weak spots.

Grant sent his first message to Halleck since crossing the Mississippi.

> On April 30 the whole of the force with me was transferred
> to Bruinsburg the first point of land below Grand Gulf from
> which the interior can be reached and the march immediately
> commenced for Port Gibson. McClernand was in the ad-
> vance. About 2:00 A.M. May 1 four miles from Port Gibson we
> met the enemy; some little skirmishing took place before
> daylight but not to any great extent.
> The 13th Corps followed by Logan's Division of McPher-
> son's Corps which reached the scene of action as soon as the
> last of the 13th was out on the road.
> This army is in the finest health and spirits. Since leaving
> Milliken's Bend they have marched as much by night as by
> day, through mud and rain, without tents or much other bag-
> gage, and on irregular rations, without a complaint and with
> less straggling than I have ever before witnessed.
> Where all have done so nobly it would be out of place to
> make invidious distinction.
> Country here most broken and difficult to operate on I ever
> saw.[10]

(This was a strange statement from Grant after the west bank terrain
tied him down for four months.)

Grant's army then pursued the enemy to Hankinson's Ferry.
After struggling down the west bank of the Mississippi and then
crossing to the east, Grant planned to assemble his army and fill up
his supply wagons at Grand Gulf. At the same time, one corps
would be sent off to the south to help General Banks capture Port
Hudson. It was between Port Hudson and Vicksburg that the Confederates were carrying supplies from the west over the river. If
Banks and Grant joined forces, they would stop the enemy's supplies from moving eastward.

Sherman wrote in his memoirs that Grant marched down the
west side of the river to give the appearance of cooperation with
Banks.[11]

With the news that Grand Gulf had been evacuated and that
the advance part of his army was already 15 miles away from there
on the road his soldiers would have to take to reach either Vicksburg
or Jackson or any intermediate point on the Vicksburg-Jackson

Railroad, Grant decided not to turn his army back to Grand Gulf but to continue to march forward. Grant ordered Wilson and a small escort of 15–20 cavalrymen to accompany him to Grand Gulf to make the necessary arrangements to change his base of supplies from Bruinsburg to the nearer point at Grand Gulf, 30 miles below Vicksburg.[12]

Frederick Dent Grant wrote that his father met Admiral Porter at Grand Gulf, who handed him a message from General Banks that stated he could not arrive near Port Hudson until a week later and would only have 12,000 soldiers to augment Grant's army.[13]

Other news alarmed Grant. General Johnston was marching to Jackson and reinforcements were marching from the east under General Beauregard; they would attempt to join with the forces at Vicksburg.

Reviewing the tactical intelligence, Grant formed a clear estimate of the situation. He had to decide whether he could safely wait for Banks' 12,000 soldiers or whether he should move promptly with his present troops to stop the arrival of Confederate soldiers about whose movements he received information day by day. He believed he was in a favorable position to meet and defeat the Confederate soldiers at Vicksburg, and he did not want to lose time or let the opportunity slip by. Grant was on firm terrain and had the opportunity to strike, and strike quickly. All those factors, he wrote, "impelled me to the course pursued." He took it upon himself to ignore unilaterally the repeated reminders from Halleck that the president was interested in his coordinated movement with Banks and expected his wishes to be carried out. Grant instead ordered his army to start marching to the east to attack.

Grant ordered all wagons available to be filled. He also had his soldiers commandeer all the farm and plantation vehicles with free Negroes to drive them and to fill them with supplies and ammunition. The train was described as a "motley train of fine carriages drawn by mules, plow horses, with straw collars, rope lines, etc. and long coupled wagons with racks for carrying cotton bales drawn by oxen. Everything that could be found in way of transportation on a plantation either for work or pleasure."[14]

In a startling infraction of military doctrine, Grant cut his army loose from its supply route to the boats on the Mississippi. All supplies and equipment were piled into the vehicles. Grant's orders to his soldiers were to live off the wagons and nearby farms. Grant said he learned the lesson of living off the land at Holly Springs because the amazing amount of supplies the soldiers collected in the wagons from the countryside would have fed the army for two months.

Grant's actions also became a puzzle to Pemberton. He sought out Grant's line of communications in the belief that its destruction would bring about the defeat of the enemy. His efforts were to no avail, however; intelligence officers informed him that Grant's wagons were carrying his supplies and the crops in the region were feeding the enemy's army.

May 6. Grant reported to Halleck: "Ferrying and transportation of rations to Grand Gulf is detaining us on the Big Black River. Will move as soon as 3 days rations received and send back wagons for more."

Sherman reported that his troops arrived at Hard Times Landing at noon, after marching 63 miles.

Captain Patterson wrote to his wife from Willow Springs: "Through another terrible battle, Grand Gulf. First to enter Port Gibson, within 30 miles of Vicksburg. Rebels burnt splendid bridges but to no avail. We built floating bridge in one to two hours to go across. Grant and McClernand in thick of battle."

May 7. Grant commended the soldiers of the Army of the Tennessee:

> Thank you for adding another victory. One more to the long list of those previously won by your valor and endurance. Victory at Port Gibson one of most important of the war. Firm foothold gained on the highlands. We threaten line of enemy, the fruits of a brilliant achievement.
>
> The march from Milliken's Bend to opposite Grand Gulf was made in stormy weather, over worst of roads, bridges and ferries had to be constructed, moving by night as well as by day with labors incessant and extraordinary. Privations have been endured by men and officers as have been rarely paralleled in any campaign. Not a murmur not a complaint has been uttered. A few days continuance of the same zeal and constancy will secure to this army the crowning victory over the Rebels. More difficulties and privations are before us, let us endure them manfully. A grateful country will rejoice. History will record it with immortal honor.[15]

Sherman's corps arrived at Hankinson's Ferry. Grant had his men engage in activities on Hankinson's Ferry and Hall's Ferry to induce the enemy to think the Yankees would march on those routes to cross the Big Black River to Vicksburg. Grant also had reconnaissance conducted west of the Big Black River to within six miles of Warrenton.

At this point, Grant ordered an advance of his army. McPherson's 17th Corps was to march on the road nearest the Big Black River to Rocky Springs. McClernand's corps was to march on the ridge road from Willow Springs. Sherman was to divide and march his corps on two roads. All the ferries were to be guarded until the soldiers had advanced well beyond them.

McPherson met the enemy's soldiers near Raymond and after several hours of severe combat, drove the Rebels away with heavy losses. Many of the enemy deserted.

Grant stated it was his intention to hug the Big Black River as closely as possible with McClernand's and Sherman's corps and to deploy them to the railroad at some place between Edward's Station and Bolton. McPherson was to march by way of Raymond to Jackson, destroying the railroad, telegraph, and public stores, and was then to push west to join the main force.

Sherman marched forward on the Edward's Station road, crossing Fourteen Mile Creek at Dillon's Plantation. McClernand marched across the same creek farther west, moving one division of his corps by Baldwin's Ferry road as far as the Big Black River. At the crossings of Fourteen Mile Creek, McClernand and Sherman engaged in severe skirmishing to seize possession of the crossings.

General Hovey's Division, 13th Corps, led the advance to Fourteen Mile Creek, followed by Carr and Osterhaus. General Smith's division marched by way of Hall's Ferry on the Big Black River. He left a detachment there to guard the crossing and then marched on to Montgomery's bridge on the creek three miles below the point of General Hovey's approach.

An outpost of the Rebel force at Edward's Station that was concealed in the thick woods and underbrush lining the creek was first encountered by General Hovey's advance guard consisting of a detachment of 2nd Illinois Cavalry and then by his infantry and artillery, which boldly advanced across the open fields to the creek. Subduing the enemy resistance and driving the Rebels from their cover, General Hovey pushed forward a portion of his division beyond the creek and secured the crossing.

General Sherman's corps seized the crossing of Turkey Creek a few miles on the right of McClernand's corps. General McPherson's corps marched to Raymond on the army's right flank. General Blair's Second Division had remained behind at Milliken's Bend after the feigned attack upon Haynes' Bluff to guard the line of communications and to build a new road across the peninsula for the transportation of supplies to Grand Gulf. Blair now received orders to march with two brigades of his division to Grand Gulf and join Sherman's corps. He received further orders to escort a large supply train consisting of 200 wagons and the pontoon bridge train, which portended an arduous and time-consuming march.

Frederick Dent Grant reported that his father was constantly in touch with his corps commanders and ate with the soldiers; because of the foraging, the meals were good.

Captain Kellogg, Company B, 113th Illinois Volunteer Infantry, wrote in his diary that he was in the rear echelon of Grant's army, which marched out of Milliken's Bend. On the day's march, his company covered 14 miles and camped on a beautiful plantation. His soldiers procured raw cotton from a nearby gin to sleep on.

Captain Ankeny reported in a letter to his wife that he had arrived in the morning at Grand Gulf. "Today cold. No extra clothing, everything left behind. A shirt will be a luxury. No wagons. Health good; has to be to march with army."

May 8. Grant reported to Halleck

> I learn Colonel Grierson with his cavalry heard about ten days ago in Northern Mississippi. Then moved to Jackson, three miles east, and struck railroad. Moved southward. To Hazelhurst on New Orleans and Jackson Railroad, tore up tracks to southeast; last heard of making way to Baton Rouge. He spread excitement throughout the state. Damaged railroad trestles, locomotives, railway stock, stores of all kinds, took prisoners of war. My informant says, "Grierson has knocked the heart out of the state."[16]

Captain Kellogg wrote in his diary: "By noon reached banks of Woody Bayou. Halted for dinner. Night arrived at plantation of Confederate General Fiske; appropriated some of his fresh beef for supper. Marched 19 miles for the day."

May 9. Captain William L. B. Jenney, Sherman's staff engineer officer, received orders from Brigadier General Sullivan, commanding general of the military post at Milliken's Bend and Young's Point, to rebuild the eight-mile road across Bowers' Landing, on the west bank of the Mississippi, to enable the wagon trains to reach the boats on the river bank. The boats then proceeded across the river below the Confederate gun batteries at Warrenton to Grand Gulf. To rebuild the road, Captain Jenney employed an infantry regiment and a detachment of the pioneer company of Blair's First Division.

Captain Kellogg noted in his diary: "Pursued our march Roundaway Bayou through a beautiful country covered with fertile fields, corn, and other crops splendidly built up. We passed some streams on ponton [sic] bridges and saw first alligators in bayous. Saw many dead horses and mules scattered along roadside. Passed smoking ruins of plantation buildings. Ate dinner on grounds of Plantation of Judge Perkins."

Captain Ankeny wrote to his wife from a site on the Big Black River: "Arrived last night. Leave in morning. Country rough, broken timber, scattering of farms. Desolation after our army passes. Heart rending to see it, but it is said such is war. The magnolia is in bloom and the most magnificent tree I ever beheld. Flowers fragrant. Wish I could send one home to you. I think our corps moves tomorrow. Rebels all over. Grant probably knows what he'll do. 44 men in my company. Largest company in regiment. Big loss at Port Gibson."

Sergeant Onley Andrus at Smith's Landing wrote:

> I have been berrying, black ones, found plenty. Ate black ones and brought to camp red ones to "stew for sass." No tents but built shanties, but each time we stop we build new ones. Keeps us out of mischief. About sending money home, that I always intended to do. Your letter came down on me, kind of stirred me up a little and when I wrote that letter I wrote as I felt mean and ugly. I trust money in your possession than keep it in my possession. Use for what you want. Did not send as much last pay day as I wanted, loaned to boys who had leave.
>
> Little faith in Grant. One of core loyal and faithful to the obligation they assumed.

May 10. General Blair reported the arrival of his division's two brigades and the wagon trains at Hard Times Landing at 1 P.M. after a 63-mile trek.

Captain Kellogg recorded:

> We passed through magnolia groves in full bloom, and along miles of blossoming rose hedge, beautiful and fragrant beyond description. At night we arrived at Lake Saint Joseph. Out on surface of lake numerous old grey backed alligators lay sleeping and ever anon a musket would crack and one of those old gators would slap his hand on his side and go out of sight with a splash. A number of dead gators with bullet holes in their hides had floated ashore. Today we passed immense fields of grain, one corn field comprising 1,400 acres, and also passed the smoking ruins of plantation houses more frequently. At four o'clock we got to Hard Times Landing on Mississippi opposite Grand Gulf and encamped.

May 11. Halleck wrote to Grant: "If possible forces of yourself and Banks should be united between Vicksburg and Port Hudson so as to attack with combined forces; same has been urged on Banks."[17]

Major Tweeddale with three companies of the 1st Missouri Engineer Regiment and Captain Samuel W. Ashmead with the pioneer company of the Second Division, 15th Corps, reported to Captain Jenney to assist in rebuilding the road across Bowers' Landing.

Captain Kellogg wrote:

> Until 4 o'clock we laid off waiting for ferryage across the river and while some went fishing others spent the time in any amusement or recreation they chose but at that hour a gunboat arrived and we fell in and went on board of gunboat *Louisville* and were ferried across to Grand Gulf where we went into camp with our brigade at foot of high bluff. The camp was full of happy contrabands who "patted juba" and danced nearly all night to the music of a cone instrument unlike any other musical instrument I ever saw.

May 12. Captain Jenney reported that the building of the road across Bowers' Point was completed at 10 A.M. and the wagon trains began to pass over. By using the road, the wagon trains cut their route from forty to eight miles. Almost one and a half miles of the road lay in a swamp, but fortunately the water had run off enough to facilitate the building of a practicable road. The engineer and pioneer soldiers found it necessary to bridge or corduroy the entire distance of the road. A working party remained on the road to keep the wagons moving.

General Blair reported that after overcoming difficulties in obtaining transportation, he completed crossing his two brigades and wagon trains over the Mississippi River at 10 P.M. and began his march to Raymond. He and the providers of the boats performed quite a feat in 33 hours.

May 13. Grant rescinded his orders to McClernand to march his corps to Edward's Station and his orders to Sherman to march his corps to Bolton. Both commanders were ordered to march instead to Raymond. According to Wilson, Grant made his tactical changes on his advice because the Confederates were retreating to Jackson to their principal depot after their defeat by McPherson's corps at Raymond. If the Rebels were permitted to concentrate there, they could threaten Grant's rear and flanks. Another important factor was the intelligence Grant received that reinforcements were arriving at Jackson and that General Johnston had been ordered there by the Richmond authorities to take command of Confederate forces.[18]

Grant recognized the imperative need to take action to assure Johnston did not come upon his rearguard or flanks. He decided his action would be to deploy his army between the forces of Johnston and Pemberton, a bold move calling for skillful tactics and a cautious watching of the enemy's counter tactics. Grant ordered McPherson to move his corps to Clinton west of Jackson, to destroy the railroad tracks on the Jackson-Vicksburg Railroad. He ordered Sherman to move his corps onto the Mississippi Springs-Jackson road, and he ordered McClernand to move his corps to within four miles of Edward's Station east of Raymond.

To carry out the delicate and hazardous shift of his corps, McClernand ordered General Hovey to advance his division early in the morning a mile on the main road to Edward's Station and to form it in a line of battle across the road to make the enemy fearful of an attack. Osterhaus' and Carr's divisions crossed the creek and filed to the rear under cover of Hovey's line, crossed Baker's Creek a mile eastward on the road to Raymond, and halted. Hovey's division followed in successive detachments under cover of the woods.

The movement of McClernand's corps outfoxed the enemy.

Without an opportunity to prevent this movement, Confederate soldiers made a feeble attack on McClernand's rearguard troops, but were promptly and completely repulsed. McClernand's corps successfully crossed Baker's Creek.

"During these thirteen days," McClernand wrote, "my command subsisted on six days' rations and what scanty supply the country in the immediate vicinity of the route afforded; were wholly without tents and regular trains, and almost without cooking utensils, yet they were cheerful and prompt in the discharge of duty."[19]

General Smith's division received orders from Grant to destroy Montgomery's Bridge at Fourteen Mile Creek–Baker's Creek and march on the south side to Auburn to guard and bring forward the army's supply and pontoon bridge trains.

May 14. In torrential rains and on slippery and miry roads, McPherson and Sherman marched toward Jackson. The rains ceased about noon. Grant reported that his troops, in spite of weather and terrain conditions, "marched in excellent order, without straggling, and best of spirits, about 14 miles, and engaged the enemy about noon near Jackson."[20]

McClernand posted divisions at Clinton, Mississippi Springs, and Raymond. Smith's division with Blair's division escorted the wagon and pontoon bridge trains to New Auburn. Grant planned to hold McClernand's troops in their position for support in the event the enemy's resistance at Jackson proved tenacious. After marching his soldiers to their new positions, McClernand reported, "This was the most fatiguing and exhausting day's march that had been made."[21]

The Confederates marched the largest part of their force from Jackson west two and one-half miles on the Clinton road and engaged McPherson's soldiers. A small force of infantry and artillery took up a strong position in front of Sherman's corps the same distance south of Jackson, but Sherman's skirmishers forced the enemy back to their rifle pits outside the town.

Two divisions of McPherson's corps attacked the main force of the Rebels, although they were not entirely sure of its strength. McPherson did know there was a Rebel force on the south side to impede Sherman. Discovering the enemy's weakness, Sherman sent a reconnoitering party to his right; the enemy retreated.

After a heavy engagement of two hours with McPherson's corps, the badly mauled enemy marched out of Jackson to the north.

McPherson's soldiers pursued the enemy until dark, when the defeated soldiers were able to disengage from McPherson's troops.

During the evening, Grant learned that when Johnston had recognized he would be attacked, he had ordered Pemberton peremptorily to march out from Vicksburg to the east to attack the rear echelon of Grant's army.

Perceiving how the situation would develop with his army between two wings of the enemy's army, Grant immediately issued orders to McClernand and Blair's division of Sherman's corps to face their soldiers towards Bolton with the mission of marching on different roads to reach Edward's Station.

Wilson reported Grant's soldiers were heading for Pemberton's soldiers "to meet on fair and equal terms."[22]

May 15. Grant reported to Halleck: "A dispatch from Banks showed him to be off in Louisiana not to return to Baton Rouge until May 10. I could not lose the time. I sent message to Banks and asked him to join me as soon as possible."

Grant ordered McPherson to retrace his march on the Clinton road. He also ordered Captain Julius Pitzman of his topographic engineering staff to make a reconnaissance of Jackson and survey all the military facilities and resources. He ordered Sherman to march troops into the town to destroy the railroad, bridges, factories, workshops, arsenals, and any resources Captain Pitzman discovered of value to support the enemy. Sherman effectually accomplished his mission.

McClernand issued orders during the early morning to his division commanders to move the eight miles to Bolton Station to frustrate the designs of the soldiers retreating from Jackson to reach Vicksburg ahead of Grant's army. By 9:30 A.M., General Osterhaus' division had captured Bolton Station. General Hovey's division arrived later from Clinton, and both division commanders prepared for an enemy frontal attack. A reconnaissance was conducted seven miles west to Edward's Station, and three roads were discovered that led from Raymond and Bolton west to Edward's Station. The north road diverged one and one-half miles north of Raymond, the middle three and one-half miles, and the south seven and one-half miles from Raymond and one mile south of Bolton and the Jackson-Vicksburg Railroad. The three roads joined together two miles before Edward's Station.

By night, General Hovey's division arrived at the entrance of the north road, General Osterhaus' at the middle road, and General Carr's at the south road prepared to receive a threatened attack or to move forward on the converging roads to meet at Edward's Station. General Smith's division with the wagon trains arrived at night and bivouacked north of Raymond near General Carr's division. General Blair's division arrived at Raymond. During the afternoon, Grant proceeded as far west as Clinton. McPherson had marched through to within supporting distance of Hovey's division, which had marched west to within a mile and a half of Bolton on the north road.

Grant informed McClernand at 4:45 P.M. that the entire force of the enemy at Vicksburg had probably crossed the Big Black River on its march to the east and taken a position at Edward's Station; he ordered McClernand to march his corps the next morning to Edward's Station, proceeding to ferret out the enemy troops if they were in the region, but not to bring on a general engagement unless he was confident he was able to defeat the foe. Grant also instructed McClernand to order General Blair to march his division with the 13th Corps.

Lieutenant Grebe, 14th Illinois Volunteer Infantry, reported that on the three-day journey of his regiment to Young's Point, they were shot at one night by Rebels from the Arkansas shore with little damage. The next day they went ashore and burned all the houses in the town of Greenville.

Battle of Champion's Hill

May 16. Two employees of the Jackson-Vicksburg Railroad turned themselves in at Grant's headquarters about 5 A.M. They volunteered the information that they had passed through Pemberton's lines and that his force consisted of about 80 regiments of infantry and 10 batteries of artillery. They estimated the whole force of the enemy to be 25,000 soldiers. Grant said he also learned from them the positions being taken up by the Confederate troops and their intentions to attack Grant's rear. The information convinced Grant to cut short Sherman's mission in Jackson; he sent an order to Sherman at 5:30 A.M. to march with all possible haste to meet the main force at Bolton. Sherman started marching at 8:10 A.M.

Grant also ordered Blair to move his division to Edward's

Station with dispatch. He ordered McClernand to establish communication between Blair and Osterhaus and to move Blair to support Osterhaus. He instructed McPherson to join McClernand. He also ordered Colonel Wilson forward to communicate personally to McClernand the information on troop dispositions and to coordinate the deployment of his troops.

The one-day battle the two foes were preparing to engage in was complex in tactics, and the natural obstacles covering the terrain presaged costly casualties. Each contender recognized the importance of the impending battle.

From reading the reports of the battle, it is difficult to visualize in one's mind the extensive positions of the soldiers on the battlefield in the critical situations. To give the course of events some form, one must return to the dynamics of the inception of the battle and piece them together in the buildup of events.

The Confederate army and the Union army were marching to an area where there were three main features of the terrain. Edward's Station on the railroad marked the first one; it lay on the west side, approximately 22 miles from Vicksburg, and on the march route of Pemberton's soldiers. East of the station, Baker's Creek marked the second feature; it coursed north and south. East of the creek stood the third one, Champion's Hill, looming up on the Union soldiers' march route.

Acting on the intelligence received during the night, Grant immediately issued orders to Sherman to march his corps to join the army at Bolton. He ordered Blair to march his division to Edward's Station, ordered McClernand to continue his corps on the march route, and ordered Hovey, and McPherson to march their troops in the footsteps of McClernand. In response to Grant's orders, McClernand started his divisions marching on the south, middle, and north roads during the night and asked McPherson to provide support to Hovey's division on the north road, which constituted the army's right flank.

Early in the morning Grant rode out to Bolton and surveyed the situation of the impending battle at the crossing of the Jackson-Vicksburg and Bolton-Raymond railroads. To the troop commanders, he gave on the spot orders for tactical disposition. Grant then passed on to the front, where he arrived at Hovey's division, on the north road, where Confederate and Union soldiers faced each other.

The enemy troops in front of Hovey's division were in a strong position on a narrow, high ridge on the Confederates' left flank. The top of the ridge was a precipitous hillside. On the left side of the road, Hovey's soldiers were positioned amidst dense forest and undergrowth, and on the right side of the road was a valley and ravine.

At 9:30 A.M., Hovey reported to Grant that a strong enemy lay on his front. McPherson posted two divisions, Logan's and Crocker's, on the right side of the road. On the center of the Union line, two divisions of McClernand's corps were posted, and two of his divisions, Carr's and Osterhaus', were on an approach march to the battlefield.

At 11 A.M., Hovey ordered his soldiers into battle. In a fierce encounter with the enemy Hovey's soldiers bore the brunt of the combat, so Grant ordered McPherson to reinforce Hovey. Brigades of Logan's division struck the enemy's left flank, and because the north road that Logan's troops were on took a westerly course, they were in a position to strike the left and rear of the Confederate line. After three hours of continuous and severe combat, Hovey's soldiers were reaching the point of exhaustion. Logan asked Grant to order Hovey to make an attack and said that he would simultaneously surround the enemy on its left flank. Grant passed the order to Hovey, who implored his soldiers to rally to the attack; they responded and at 2:30 P.M. drove the enemy from the field.

On the Union's left flank, Smith's division forced the enemy troops, who offered little resistance, to withdraw.

Grant observed the enemy retreating on the Raymond road on the left. He also noticed on the ridge on his left flank a column of soldiers, which he discovered to be Carr's division, with McClernand; on Carr's left flank was Osterhaus' division. Grant ordered Carr to march to the Big Black River and to cross it, if he could, and ordered Osterhaus to follow this route in pursuit of the enemy.

In the aftermath of the battle, Grant stated that at the time of Hovey's attack he had expected McClernand to have Osterhaus' and Carr's divisions on the field when the battle commenced. They were two and a half miles away, however. McClernand reported their delay was due to the hilly ground, and he said that in the dense forest, his soldiers could not see the enemy front with its infantry and artillery. McClernand described Osterhaus' march route as lying through "broad field, thick wood, chaos of abrupt hills and yawning ravines."[23]

Grant's conclusion that of the three divisions that fought Hovey's bore the brunt of the battle is supported by the casualties incurred:

Division	Killed	Wounded	Missing
Hovey	211	872	119
Smith	51	239	27
Logan	128	528	15

If Grant implied criticism of McClernand because his divisions were not on the battlefield when expected, then another conclusion can probably be drawn. If Smith's division, which pressured the enemy on the left flank, and Logan's division, which reached the rear of the enemy on the right flank, had been promptly reinforced, the enemy's army might have been cut off. Grant's summary of the battle may have implied such a conclusion. As it was, a crafty and determined army escaped the battlefield to fight again. From the Union's viewpoint, Grant's skillful deployment of his troops confined Pemberton to Vicksburg and prevented him from joining Johnston.[24]

Grant sent a communication to Sherman of the outcome of the day's battle and ordered him to march his corps to Bridgeport, north of Grant's right flank. He sent orders to Blair to join Sherman's corps.

Battle of Big Black River Bridge

May 17. At daylight, McClernand's corps renewed the pursuit of the enemy, who had overnight thrown up strongly defended positions on both sides of the Big Black River six miles down the road. On Pemberton's front on the western side of the river, the bluffs extended to the river's bank. On the east side of the river grew an open cultivated bottom approximately a mile in width. A bayou of stagnant water from two to three feet in depth and from ten to twenty feet in width filled an area from the river above the railroad to the river below. On the inside of the bayou, the enemy had constructed rifle pits with the bayou as a ditch on the outside and immediately

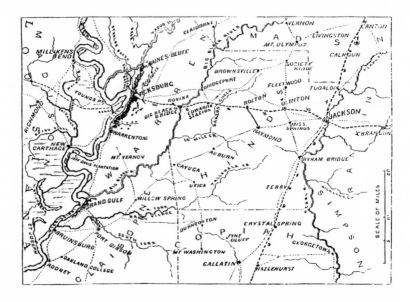

Grant's Vicksburg Campaign (*Harper's Pictorial History*).

in front. The enemy had been posted there since the first of the year
when Grant moved to Milliken's Bend. Pemberton's staff had had
time to anticipate Grant's tactics and build their defense works.

Carr's division attacked the Confederates in this position and
after a few hours skirmishing and passing over ground without cover
and overcoming obstacles, the Yankees were gallantly successful in
assaulting the enemy's position. The entire garrison and 17 pieces
of artillery were the Union's trophies from what Grant described as
a "daring and brilliant tactical movement." The enemy soldiers fled
to a steamer forming a bridge across the river near the railroad
bridge, and most of them escaped to the commanding bluffs on the
west side. The enemy on the west bank of the river immediately set
fire to the railroad bridge with cotton balls soaked in turpentine.
The bridge fire cut off an escape route for the remaining enemy
soldiers on the east bank of the river, however. By sunset, Grant's
soldiers dislodged those enemy soldiers.

Sherman's corps reached Bridgeport on the Big Black River.

Contemplating these last 17 days of battle, Wilson cherished the
memory: "The campaign east of the river more exciting than a picnic
excursion. The skirmishes and battles were gentle and joyous jousts."[25]

Bridge Building

Grant's Army of the Tennessee formed for battle on the east bank of the Big Black River. On the west bank, the Confederate Army of the Department of the Mississippi and Eastern Louisiana scurried to the safety of the defense works on the outskirts of Vicksburg.

The unbridged river remained as the obstacle to Grant's pursuit and the commencement of what his soldiers were looking to as the final battle to decimate the army they had cornered in the confines of the town. The skedaddling had reached an end. Every foot of ground Grant's soldiers had trudged over on the marches through Louisiana and Mississippi had been an obstacle, but their grit and resourcefulness overcame each problem and brought them face to face with the desired prize. They were Sergeant Andrus' "core of the faithful."

An engineer officer surveying the battlefield situation confidently announced that the Big Black River posed another opportunity to be innovative and imaginative in building bridges. Captain Lochbihler, Company I, 35th Missouri Infantry, who hauled the India rubber pontoon train all the way from Milliken's Bend, received his opportunity to build a pontoon bridge on the army's right flank. During the night his company built a bridge at Bridgeport for Sherman to cross his corps in the morning.[26]

On the left flank of the line, Captain Patterson and his engineer and pioneer soldiers of General McClernand's 13th Corps demonstrated again their ingenuity in bridge building. He had his soldiers fell tall pine trees from the river bank into the river. The engineer soldiers then stripped the trees of their limbs, floated them together to reach from shore to shore, and then anchored them. Soldiers collected timber from the burned-out railroad bridge and nearby houses and warehouses to place on the felled trees to reach across the river for a roadway.[27]

At the center of the army's front occurred what was perhaps the unique achievement of bridge building. As dusk claimed the battlefield, Captain Stewart Tresilian brought his horse to a halt on the river bank. Sitting in his saddle and staring at the river, he moodily thought of the job he was assigned to do. Grant had issued orders to the corps commanders to build bridges over the river. On the march to the river, Tresilian had rebuilt or built ten bridges. His new

Sherman's Corps' Floating Bridge Across Big Black River
(*Harper's Pictorial History*).

assignment would be to build his eleventh one, and it would not be
an impossible one. General McPherson stood ready to march the
17th Corps across the river in the morning.

The task of building a bridge for the 17th Corps in such a short
time weighed heavily on Captain Tresilian's thoughts because the
pioneer corps was without a piece of wood or a large assortment of
tools except their woodsmen's axes. An idea emerged, however,
while Tresilian was studying the surroundings. While looking at the
buildings along the river, an inspiration came to him when he noticed an immense warehouse filled with bales of cotton. Instantly, he
remembered that a bale of cotton would float.

With a mental image of a bridge quickly forming in his mind,
Tresilian hastened to the job. He had brush fires lighted for light and
put the tired soldiers from the 48th Indiana, 59th Indiana, 4th Minnesota, and 18th Wisconsin Volunteer Infantry regiments to work
helping the corps pioneers build the bridge. They tore down wooden
warehouses for timber and hauled it and the bales of cotton to the
river bank. They recovered nails from the wood.

A squad of pioneers first measured the width of the river and
then wove a guy line from rope used to tether the horses to the picket
line and to drag artillery carriages. They anchored this line on their
side of the river and then by use of a two-man raft carried it quietly

McPherson's Corps' Cotton Bales Bridge Across Big Black River
(*Harper's Pictorial History*).

to the enemy side, where they anchored the other end. The needed
bridge span was accurately measured by the guy line's length.

Under the supervision of Tresilian, the pioneers selected from
the timber moved to the river bank two thick beams 35 feet long and
laid them side by side 10 feet apart. They then joined the beams
together with 1-inch strips nailed 2½ feet apart. The structure the
pioneers fabricated looked like a wide ladder. Uprights were nailed
to the ends of each strip. Two cotton bales, one on top of the other,
were then placed on each cross piece and pressed against the end
uprights. The bales were kept tightly in place by nailing strips
crisscross in front of them. Additional bales of cotton were placed
and fastened in the same way until they filled the length of the lad-
derlike frame.

Next, 2"×4" uprights were nailed to the outside of the beams at
the end of the cotton bales and cut off about one inch short of the top
of the bales. To join the uprights, the pioneers nailed to them 2"×4"
cross pieces that pressed down on the bales. Five 2"×4" pieces were
then laid lengthwise and nailed to the cross pieces. The floor planks
were nailed onto these lengthwise pieces. When the pioneers finished their work, the bridge sections resembled crated bales of cotton.

In the light from the brush fires, Tresilian and his pioneers and line soldiers built three 35-foot sections of crated cotton bales and timber and dragged them into the 20 foot deep Big Black River, where they were floated into place. All three sections were fastened together end-to-end to form the bridge. The bridge sections were tied to the guy line the pioneers had strung across the river to keep them from breaking up and floating down the river. Logs and brush were used to make a fill upon which to construct the abutments and approach roads.[28]

In the morning, Grant, McPherson, Tresilian, and the pioneers watched the crossing of the 17th Corps on the bridge. They observed that the 20-pound Parrott gun sank the bridge only 14 inches, leaving an excess buoyancy of 16 inches. The bridge was 110 feet long and 10 feet wide, and it required 47 bales of cotton to build. After McPherson's entire corps had crossed safely, Tresilian and his pioneers relaxed.

Although Wilson did not file a report on the construction of the above bridges, he later wrote that when he reached the Big Black River, he became busy with "the duty of designing and supervising their construction. It turned out to be a simple task. While work underway General Rawlins, Dana, and I spent time together passing from bridge site to bridge site encouraging officers and men in their novel and necessary work and with admiration for the volunteer soldier and his unequaled capacity for practical bridge building."

Wilson also wrote, "Counting these improvised bridges on the Big Black river and those at Milliken's Bend and Bruinsburg, there were five to six thousand feet of such bridges." Still more noteworthy, he added, was the fact that most of them were built during the night so that no part of the army was compelled to delay its march while bridges were being built.[29]

McPherson's and McClernand's corps then marched to the outskirts of Vicksburg. Sherman's corps marched north to the Yazoo River, which emptied into the Mississippi River, and made contact with Porter's naval vessels and transports with soldiers aboard. A new supply base to receive the supplies brought down from Memphis by boats was opened to provide Grant's army with a secure supply line. To develop the storage facilities on the Yazoo, Captain William B. Jenney surveyed a road from the army's position to reach Johnston Place Landing. In a day, the road along Thompson's Lake was so far completed as to admit passage of wagons. At the landing the four companies of the 1st Missouri Engineer Regiment, which had been transferred from their duty of keeping the roads and bridges on the west bank of the river opened, built a pontoon bridge 350 feet long over the head of Chickasaw Bayou to complete the road. Later they built a permanent timber trestle bridge to replace the pontoon bridge because all the supplies and guns were brought to Vicksburg over it and the heavy traffic wore out the roadway.

May 18. On the other side of the Big Black River, the Yankee soldiers made a spirited effort in the morning to rush the enemy's entrenchments, but owing principally to the rough, unknown ground covered by fallen trees and entanglements, the assault was much too disorganized and dispirited to succeed. Grant's soldiers expected to find the enemy soldiers too discouraged and demoralized to put up an effective defense or too spread out to cover their entire line. Such a condition might have occurred the night before, but in the morning attack, the Yankees spent too much time finding and taking up their positions on strange terrain. In addition, they had been marching and fighting for three weeks. They were tired and deserving of rest while the roads were prepared, and supplies of rations, ammunition, and clothing were brought forward from the supply depot at Chickasaw Landing.[30]

Grant believed he had placed the army's three corps as their strength permitted to cover the ground in front of Vicksburg: Sherman's on the right to the north, McPherson's in the center, and McClernand's on the left to the south.

Captain Kellogg, Company B, 113th Illinois Infantry, reported that preparations had been made for the siege of Vicksburg. "A year before an attempt made and the Rebels said they did not know how to surrender to an enemy. Now we had arrived and proposed to teach them how to surrender to an enemy."

May 19. Grant began to plan the investment of Vicksburg. Continuous skirmishing took place during the day, and Grant expressed hope of carrying the enemy's works. Believing the enemy demoralized by the repeated defeats on the march to Vicksburg, Grant ordered a general assault on the enemy's line at 2 P.M. The 15th Corps, which was posted in a good position, carried out a vigorous assault. The 13th and 17th Corps only succeeded in gaining advanced positions covered from the fire of the enemy.

McClernand reported that early in the morning he had made a

personal reconnaissance to the brow of a long hill overlooking Two-Mile Creek, two miles from Vicksburg, which conformed to the line of the Vicksburg defenses in plain view on a similar north-south range a mile to the west. The enemy's defenses, he discovered, consisted of an extended line of rifle pits occupied by infantry and this line was covered by a multitude of strong works occupied by artillery arranged to command the approaches by the ravines and ridges in front and also to cover each other.

McClernand had been under orders since 4 A.M. to be in readiness to march forward and invest the enemy's defenses. He received his marching orders at 6:30 A.M. and in conformance with Grant's battle plan formed his corps behind the crest of the hill where he had been waiting. He deployed General Smith's division on the right of the Vicksburg road, General Osterhaus' division on the left, and General Carr's division along the base of the hill to be the reserve. Skirmishers were sent forward, and they engaged the enemy's skirmishers. The most commanding positions upon the enemy's works opened artillery fire. McClernand observed a body of Rebel infantrymen between the enemy skirmishers and his troops on his right flank. In a short time the enemy skirmishers fell back, and he ordered his line to advance across Two-Mile Creek to the hills on the opposite side.

McClernand received an order from Grant at 10:30 A.M. that directed corps commanders to gain as close a position as possible to the enemy's works before 2 P.M. At that time, all the corps were to fire three volleys from their artillery pieces in position to signal the start of a general charge of all the corps' soldiers along the line. McClernand reported:

> By 2 o'clock with great difficulty, my line had gained a half mile, and was within 800 yards of the enemy's works. The ground in front was unexplored and commanded by the enemy's works, yet, at the appointed signal, my infantry went forward under such cover as my artillery could afford, and bravely continued a wasting conflict until they had approached within 500 yards of the enemy's lines, when exhaustion and the lateness of the evening interrupted it. An advance had been made by all the corps and the ground gained firmly held but the enemy's works were not carried.

Captain Kellogg reported: "Beautiful May morning than that I had never seen. Pickets ceased firing. The birds sang sweetly in the trees, and the cool morning breeze was fragrant with the perfume of flowers and shrubs. Hard to believe such a beautiful morning would bring such an eve as followed. Giles A. Smith's Brigade of Blair's division, Sherman's Corps, under leaden hail from enemy blinding."

May 20. Grant reported the day was spent in improving the workings of the supply system. His soldiers had been marching and fighting for twenty days, most of them with only a five-day supply of rations drawn from the commissary department. Forage and meat were found in great abundance through the countryside, however, so there was neither suffering nor complaint in the army. While the men had not suffered from short rations, Grant noted that they had missed having bread.[31]

May 21. According to Grant's report his arrangements for the drawing of supplies of every description were completed. While he did not mention the details of the arrangements, his statement undoubtedly meant the supply boats from Memphis were able to change their destination from Grand Gulf to Johnston Place Landing on the Yazoo. Grant also made the decision to order another assault to carry Vicksburg, as he noted in his records:

> There were many reasons to determine me to adopt this course. I believed an assault from the position gained by this time could be made successfully. It was known that Johnston was at Canton with the force taken by him from Jackson, reinforced by other troops from the east, and that more were daily reaching him. With the force I then had, a short time must have enabled him to attack me in the rear, and possibly succeeded in raising the siege.
>
> Possession of Vicksburg at the time would have enabled me to have turned upon Johnston and driven him from the state, and possessed myself of all the railroads and practical military highways, thus effectually securing to ourselves all territory west of the Tombigbee, and this before the season was too far advanced for campaigning in this latitude. I would have saved the Government sending large reinforcements, much needed elsewhere; and finally, the troops themselves were impatient to possess Vicksburg and would not have worked in the trenches with the same zeal, believing it unnecessary, that they did after their failure to carry the enemy works.

Grant issued orders for a general assault on the whole line to commence at 10 A.M. the next day. Time pieces were to be synchronized to coordinate the assault.[32]

May 22. At 10 A.M. the three army corps in front of the enemy's works commenced an assault. Grant posted himself in a commanding position near McPherson's front, where he could see all the advancing columns from McPherson's corps and a portion of the commands of Sherman and McClernand. Soldiers from the commands of each corps succeeded in planting their flags on the outer slopes of the enemy's bastions, and they maintained them there until night.

"Each corps had many more men than could possibly be used in the assault over such ground as intervened between them and the enemy," Grant wrote. "More men could only avail in case of breaking through the enemy's line or in repelling a sortie. The assault was gallant in the extreme on the part of all the troops, but the enemy's position was too strong, both naturally and artificially, to be taken that way. At every point assaulted, and at all of them at the same time, the enemy was able to show all the force his work would cover."

The assault failed, Grant regretfully reported, with many men killed and wounded, but without any weakening of the confidence of the soldiers in their ultimate ability to succeed.[33] The unsuccessful assault did, according to Grant, prove the quality of the soldiers of his army. "Without entire success and without heavy loss, there was no murmuring or complaining. No falling back nor other evidence of demoralization."

Captain Prime, the staff engineer officer offered as a reason for the assault the demoralization of the Confederate army. Its strength had been underestimated, however. "Our troops buoyant with success, eager for an assault and would not work well if the slow process of a siege was undertaken." In his evaluation of the assault, Prime wrote that the attacks were gallantly made and that the men from each corps reached the enemy's line. In one instance, they even entered the enemy's works. The fire of enemy artillery and musketry and the losses sustained in moving over the rough and obstructed ground were so severe that the assault failed at all points. The troops took to the nearest cover, in some cases under the parapets of the enemy's works, and waited for night to enable them to fall back without exposure to the murderous fire.

The only soldiers to enter the enemy's works were Sergeant Griffith and 11 privates of the 22nd Iowa Volunteer Infantry Regiment. Only Sergeant Griffith and one private returned. The point they entered, Grant reported, gave his army no practical advantage unless other works to the right and left were at the same time carried and held.

The assault engendered a disconcerting brouhaha in the command relationship of McClernand and Grant. McClernand declared that his soldiers performed daring, heroic, and brilliant feats in carrying some parts of the enemy's works in the initial steps of the assault. McClernand informed Grant at 11 A.M. that he was "hot engaged," with the enemy massing upon his front from right to left. He suggested a vigorous assault by McPherson to create an alleviating diversion. McClernand sent another message to Grant at noon reporting he was in partial possession of two forts and suggesting in the form of a question whether a "vigorous" attack should be made all along Grant's line.

At 3:15 P.M., McClernand received a message Grant had sent at 2 P.M., directing him to communicate with Brigadier General John McArthur, Sixth Division, 17th Army Corps, who was marching to the battlefield, and to use his force to the best advantage. Grant believed his corps commanders had more than enough troops for the assault. McClernand also received information that General Quinby's division was on the march to his support. In a return message to Grant, McClernand reported that his troops were holding their ground and that he had gathered intelligence from prisoners that the works where his soldiers made lodgments were strongly defended in the rear. He concluded by saying that with the divisions on the march to support him, he was confident he would force his way through the hostile lines.

In his report filed after the assault, McClernand stated that obstacles intervened to disappoint him. Some of the reinforcements did not arrive, others arrived too exhausted to engage the enemy, and, finally, night set in, calling a halt to the battle. He concluded that historical facts would abundantly establish that his soldiers did "their whole duty manfully and nobly throughout this arduous and eventful campaign." McClernand spoke frankly and truthfully with these eloquent words on his soldiers attention to duty.[34]

Grant responded to McClernand's first message by ordering him to reinforce the hard-pressed line with his troops that were not engaged. In response to the second message, he ordered McClernand to call up McArthur's division and showed the message to Sherman, who ordered a renewal of the assault on his front. Grant then journeyed to McPherson to show him McClernand's message and his suggestion to make a diversion on the line. In reply to McClernand's third message, Grant wrote that from the position he occupied during the assault, he had a better opportunity to assess the action of the 13th Corps than its commander. He concluded in his report that he did not observe the possession of the forts nor did he see the necessity for reinforcements discussed in McClernand's message. With regard to McClernand's assertions, Grant wrote: "I expressed doubts of their correctness, which doubts subsequently, but too late confirmed." Grant added that he had not disregarded McClernand's repeated statements because they might possibly have been true and he should not let escape any possible opportunity to carry the enemy's stronghold.[35]

Grant reported to Halleck:

> Vicksburg is now completely invested. I have possession of Haynes' Bluff and the Yazoo; consequently have supplies. Today an attempt was made to carry the city by assault, but was not entirely successful. We hold possession, however, of two of the enemy's forts, and have skirmishers under all of them. Our loss was not severe. The nature of the ground about Vicksburg is such that it can only be taken by a siege. It is entirely safe to us in time, I would say one week, if the enemy do not send a large army upon my rear.[36]

(Grant's target date of a week turned out to be overly optimistic.)

Captain Ankeny wrote to his wife: "Leave for Dixie. Johnston has fallen back. Inspections and lots of reports to make out. In works in rear of Vicksburg. Fighting for four days. Enemy inside his works. We on hill within 300 yards of enemy. Enemy strongly entrenched in rifle pits. Charge on line today failed. Useless expenditure of life. Satisfied our generals Vicksburg cannot be taken by assault. Much hard work before this city taken. Soldiers met between the lines."

The correspondent of *Frank Leslie's Independent Newspaper* reported: "Siege of Vicksburg becoming a siege in fact as well as name. Terrible scenes of siege renewed. Terrible and fruitless assault on Pemberton's last line of defense. Massive assault made on grass covered fortifications. Chain of forts 800 yards apart connected by entrenchments, 7 miles."

In considering McClernand's claim of the day's success on the line, Wilson wrote that McClernand was blameworthy, but he placed the same judgment on McPherson and Sherman. He said they had not prepared contingency plans for follow-up action on a temporarily successful situation like McClernand's. "Generals," he wrote, "just assault but never trained to follow through weak points with reinforcements or cooperative movements or developed stratagems for countermeasures.[37]

McClernand's staff engineer officer, Captain Peter C. Hains, reported that since Grant had landed on the east side of the river, he had avoided committing blunders but he had committed some mistakes. He believed Grant's worst mistake was the day's assault on the enemy's line of works. He believed it was a tactical error to make the assault along the entire line. Three days earlier Grant had been repulsed in the same endeavor. Hains said that one soldier behind a field work equaled three in the open and that Grant risked his advantage of a higher number of soldiers by the attrition of another attack.

Hains believed Grant should have massed four divisions at one point on the line of works in the second assault. He believed the weak point to be where the right flank of McClernand's corps and the left flank of McPherson's corps interfaced on the Union line. A ravine was located in front of that position where troops could have been massed, and feint attacks on the line at other places could have increased the chances for success.

A second mistake of Grant, according to Hains, speaking from his position on the line as a staff engineer officer, was to give in to the importunings of McClernand for an assault along the line to support the alleged report of the capture of a part of the works of the enemy. Although Grant from his position on the line observing the entire operation did not believe McClernand's claim, he relented to his request.

Hains wrote that from his observations on the line he told McClernand, "We do not have possession of the enemy's works." Sergeant Griffith's exhibition of courage in seizing a part of a works of the enemy was an unfortunate incident because it convinced McClernand his soldiers had possession of an enemy's works, which in turn prompted him to send a request to Grant. But Hains conceded that McClernand was in bounds stating to Grant he held part of an enemy's works. The ditch McClernand's soldiers held was in reality a trap, however, because soldiers in it could not advance or retreat. Grant assumed McClernand had taken an important part of an enemy's works. What McClernand reported to Grant was open to misinterpretation, and Grant did misinterpret it.[38]

CHAPTER 7

May 23–August 1, 1863

Siege and Surrender

May 23. Grant announced his decision to conduct a siege by regular approaches against Vicksburg. A day before, he had ruled out a siege because his soldiers were impatient to possess Vicksburg; at that point they would not have worked zealously in the trenches because they believed it was unnecessary. Grant also expressed a concern that General Johnston would arrive in his rear to raise a siege.[1]

Grant's decision verified the prediction of the correspondent of *Frank Leslie's Independent Newspaper* at Milliken's Bend on February 28 that Grant's army was working toward a siege of Vicksburg like the historic one of Sevastopol.

The resort to a siege recognized two realities:

1. After three weeks of bold tactics and long-sought battle victories over the enemy on the march to the outskirts of Vicksburg, the Army of the Tennessee had failed on May 17 at the battle of Big Black River to close with and vanquish the Confederate army and had permitted it to escape to safety behind the defense works of the town.

2. To prepare the siege works, all the soldiers in Grant's army would again be required to equip themselves with axes, shovels, and hand tools to perform prodigious engineer-pioneer duties. It was ironic they had started the campaign laboring with the same tools to work their way to the battlefield and after swift victories over the enemy, they were again returning to manual labor.

The planning duties for the expansive siege works fell upon the engineer officers at army, corps, and division levels. Captain Prime, the army's chief staff engineer officer, was responsible for overseeing the entire siege operation. He laid out the plan of the siege works to be implemented by the corps' staff engineer officers. They in turn were to lay out the tasks for the division engineer officers and pioneer companies, as well as for the work details drawn from the infantry regiments. Prime decided to place the first emphasis on the works on the northern end of the Union line to protect the supply depot at Johnston's Landing on the Yazoo River. The second emphasis of the siege was to place the army's soldiers in the works in position and the siege guns in place ready to fire to ensure that a Confederate relieving force could not by a rapid movement effect a junction with the garrison in Vicksburg before the army's preparations were completed.[2]

In his survey of the ground before Vicksburg, Prime reported that the original 200'–300' elevation of the plateau around the town had been gradually washed by rain and stream until the plateau had disappeared. In its place remained an intricate network of level bottom ravines and sharp ridges. The ridges were steep enough that their ascent was difficult to a soldier unless he used his hands. The sides of the ravines were usually wooded. Near the enemy's line, the trees had been felled, forming in many places entanglements which under fire were impassable to an attacker.

The enemy's defenses were essentially an entrenched camp four miles long and two miles wide, with the oblique line of defenses seven miles long and well adapted to the ground. On the north the enemy's line of defense was anchored where the bluff joined the Mississippi; it continued southward on a high dividing ridge, crossed the valleys to two small streams, and reached the river bluff again two miles below the town, where the bluff had receded to a distance of a mile from the river. The line then followed the bluff up the river for a mile for fire to cover the river or any troops who might attempt an attack from the south by marching up between the bluff and the river along the river bottom.

The Confederate line was well located for observing the Union troops in its front. It consisted of small works on commanding points, necessarily irregular from the shape of the ridges where they were located. The works were placed at distances varying from 75 to 500 yards from each other and were located along a line of simple trenches or rifle pits.

Vicksburg, Prime observed, was an entrenched camp more than

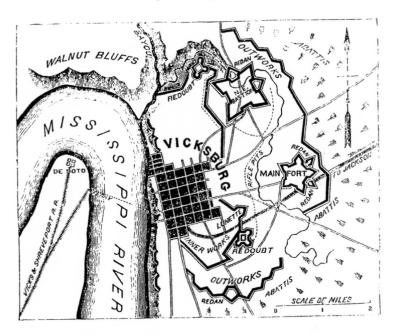

Vicksburg's Defenses (*Harper's Pictorial History*).

a fortified place and owed much of its strength to the difficult ground obstructed by fallen trees in its front which rendered the rapidity of movement and ensemble necessary in an assault impossible.

Prime believed the enemy's active defense lacked vigor, the object seeming to be to wait for a Union assault and to lose in the interim as few soldiers as possible.[3]

The Union soldiers in the ranks as well as the officers had settled the question of the practicability of carrying the enemy's camp by assault without previous preparation, Prime concluded, by their experience of May 22.

Before an assault could again be attempted with a reasonable prospect of success, Prime postulated, the enemy's artillery had to so far as practicable be disabled by Yankee fire and means had to be found to cover the soldiers from Rebel fire until they were close to the enemy's works. Long and continued exposure to enemy fire, he said, had caused the failure of the first assault.[4]

Planning was undertaken accordingly for the preparation of batteries and opening trenches for the commencement of the siege.

Engineer Organization

After assessing the engineer organization in the army, Prime deemed it to be deficient to construct the siege works. What he meant by "deficient" remains unclear, but he added that at the time there were only two officers besides himself of the Regular Army Corps of Engineers performing staff duties, whereas he estimated that he needed 30 officers. "A few officers," he added, "had been detailed from staffs of Corps or from line units for engineer duty." He cautioned that he could not himself superintend any point on the line because such a responsibility would cause him to neglect his staff superintendence of planning and coordinating the entire line.[5]

Prime failed to credit the recorded presence of 42 volunteer officers in the Army of the Tennessee who had performed engineer officer duties since the beginning of the campaign and were capable of picking up the tasks at the work sites. They had performed innovative feats in every aspect of military engineering—the construction of canals, roads, bridges, and defense works, and the clearance of obstacles on the march route to Vicksburg. In the words of a writer, "The western pioneers in Grant's army were handy with axe and the spade, and they built roads and bridges with an untaught competence that left the engineer officers talking to themselves."[6]

It was evident, however, that if Prime were looking for officers with experience in the construction of siege works, the volunteer officers probably lacked such experience. On the other hand, the three Army Corps of Engineer officers, who had pursued academic instruction in siege works at the U.S. Military Academy during the 1850s, lacked any war experience in the layout and construction of siege works.

It is a matter of record that there was a dearth of engineer units in the volunteer army. Every army commander registered a request for engineer units with General Halleck, who, with other general officers, petitioned Congress for authorization to form these units.

The Army of the Tennessee had available the battalion of Colonel Bissell's Missouri Engineer Regiment, which remained on the west side of the Mississippi River to repair and keep in order the roads and bridges for the troop and supply wagons until a new line of communications could be opened on the east side of the river. In addition, Captain Patterson's Kentucky Company of Mechanics and Engineers accompanied McClernand's 13th Corps. There were also the pioneer companies in the divisions and Lieutenant Loch-bihler's Company I, 35th Missouri Infantry, which was assigned to duty with the pontoon bridge wagon train.

Siege Approaches

A land area existed between the defensive lines of the contending armies. Grant's soldiers attacked on May 19 and 22 across the approximate mile of open land in the face of the opponent's gun barrels and were gunned down. Many Civil War battles were fought in such an unsuccessful manner with consequent heavy casualties.

The siege was a way of obviating the futility of an open assault across an open battlefield against an enemy entrenched in a well-fortified position. The tactics Grant's army developed were to cross the battlefield to the enemy's force by approaches composed of saps and parallels, which would be covered by the fire of artillery batteries and mortars. In saps, the soldiers could move through to an opening blasted through the Confederate defenses and engage the enemy soldiers in close combat.

On the ten locations that Prime selected for approaches, the engineer-pioneers were to build the saps by digging trenches jutting from the Union lines like fingers to the Confederate lines. From parallels, trenches in front of their positions, soldiers would move through to the saps.

As the construction projects progressed, engineer and pioneer soldiers dug the parallels and saps day and night. As saps approached enemy fire, the sappers were protected by sap rollers or parapets and by infantrymen and artillerymen.

Reports of the engineer-pioneer officers record the techniques and incidents related to building the ten approaches. Their ingenuity in devising field expedients as the need arose is apparent from these records. The ten approaches were located in front of the three army corps, whose staff engineer officers provided staff supervision. Engineer officers of the divisions, the pioneer companies, and infantrymen were assigned to perform the manual construction work and guard duties. The details from the line regiments varied from 50 to 250 soldiers a day. Negroes who came into the Union lines augmented several of the pioneer companies; they were paid ten dollars a month for their labor.

The ten approaches, each built with particular characteristics to conform to the terrain from the right flank northward to the left flank southward, were named after these unit commanders:

1. Brigadier General John M. Thayer, Third Brigade, First Division, 15th Army Corps (covered the right flank).
2. Brigadier General Hugh Ewing, Third Brigade, Second Division, 15th Army Corps.
3. Brigadier General Giles A. Smith, First Brigade, Second Division, 15th Army Corps.
4. Brigadier General Thomas E. G. Ransom, Second Brigade, Sixth Division, 17th Army Corps. Corps' right flank.
5. Major General John A. Logan, Third Division, 17th Army Corps.
6. Brigadier General Andrew J. Smith, Tenth Division, 13th Army Corps.
7. Brigadier General Eugene A. Carr, Fourteenth Division, 13th Army Corps.
8. Brigadier General Alvin P. Hovey, Tenth Division, 13th Army Corps.
9. Brigadier General Jacob G. Lauman, Fourth Division, 16th Army Corps.
10. Major General Francis J. Herron, Herron's Division, Department of Missouri (covered the left flank).

Because the building of approaches was an unfamiliar task, the soldiers had to be instructed by the division and company engineer and pioneer officers on the techniques for digging saps, employing sap rollers, and fabricating gabions and fascines. The men also had to be taught to build batteries, traverses, rifle pits, parallels, magazines, covered ways, and roads, and platforms for 30-pound Parrott guns.

As the Union sappers pushed their saps out the ten approaches toward the Confederate defenses, the enemy resistance stiffened to this frontal approach. Enemy soldiers stalked out of their lines to attack working parties. The corps engineer officers reacted by assigning infantry soldiers as working-party guards to push the enemy pickets back into their lines. The enemy then resorted to harassing sappers with 6- or 12-pound shell's with short burning fuses that

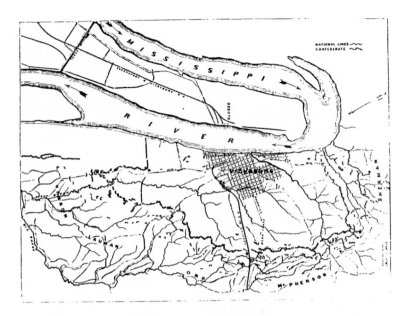

Troop Positions, Siege of Vicksburg (*Harper's Pictorial History*).

could be thrown like hand grenades; underground mines and field artillery shells were also used against the attackers. The enemy set the sap rollers on fire by lodging against them fireballs of cotton dipped in turpentine.

To counter enemy harassment, the Union soldiers retaliated with hand grenades, mortar shells, mines, and musketry fire. In a further protective measure, most of the work had to be shifted to nighttime, when it was harder for the Confederates to harass the working parties.

Faced by the large amount of construction tasks, the engineer and pioneer officers and soldiers responded with many innovations. The pioneer companies of the different divisions prepared the larger part of the fascines, gabions, and sap rollers. The material for the weaving of the gabions was in abundant supply. Grape vines were at first used, but they made the gabions too heavy to use conveniently. Captain H. C. Freeman experimented with cane for weaving material. He found that when one crushed the joints of a piece of cane with a mallet, the remainder of the cane split open sufficiently to permit pieces to be woven between the stakes of the gabions.

Because of their strength they made good and neat structures. Cane became in time the material to use to fabricate fascines because of its abundant supply.

In the early stages of the siege, difficulties were encountered with the sap rollers because they were vulnerable to the minié ball and were heavy to use on rough ground. Lieutenant Hains devised an innovative solution. He placed two empty barrels securely head to head and then instructed the pioneers to fabricate the sap roller with cane fascines around this hollow barrel core.

In an innovative feat, Captain Tresilian built wooden mortars by shrinking iron bands on cylinders of tough wood and boring out the center to set off 6- or 12-pound shells. His mortars, according to reports, fired well and caused sufficient damage at a distance of 100–150 yards.

In accordance with General McPherson's instructions, Captain Tresilian collected suitable lumber from cotton gins and put pioneers to work building scaling ladders varying from 16' to 22', light enough for one man to carry and strong enough to support two men when used in a horizontal position across a 10-foot-wide enemy ditch. The ladders saved the soldiers from approaching through a ditch and being trapped therein by enemy gunfire. Attached to the ladder was a rope three-quarters of its length to enable a soldier to lie on the ground and pull the ladder. The enemy was unable to observe what the soldier was doing until he successfully crossed a ditch and made an assault.

When Captain William B. Kossak's pioneer company of the Second Division was severely shelled by the enemy to prevent the advance of the sap rollers, he resorted to mining the enemy's position. He recruited 16 volunteers from the West Virginia 4th Volunteer Infantry who were coal miners by occupation before their army enlistment; they carried out this assignment very well.

To have some means of throwing shells into the enemy's fort, Hains instructed Captain Patterson to construct spring boards. Hains made a novel reconnaissance of the enemy's ditch by means of a mirror attached to a pole. He raised it above a sap roller and a little to the rear and then inclined it forward to obtain a perfect view of the enemy's ditch.

Harper's Weekly made particular mention of "two able officers," Captain Hickenlooper, city surveyor of Cincinnati, and Captain Merrit, a civil engineer from New York, who acted coolly in an emergency. Merrit was at his post on an advanced trench of Logan's approach with a working party where he was a target for enemy sharpshooters. When the Rebels threw a lighted shell into his working party, he picked it up and threw it back. It exploded among its senders.[7]

Such a massive siege project involved a myriad of problems to solve. Speaking of the work done in the 13th Corps, Hains reported that he believed Grant had made a mistake in ordering the siege when the army was ill prepared for the work. Also, the soldiers knew they had won the battles at Port Gibson, Jackson, Champion's Hill, and Big Black River, and they expected they would win again at Vicksburg. Another factor was that the hot weather brought a mounting number of cases of diseases that incapacitated many soldiers.

The first week the working parties started their tasks they lacked entrenching tools for the 250–300 soldiers assigned to strengthen the batteries that had to be thrown up hastily against enemy artillery fire. Hains reported engineer officers had to depend entirely on infantry soldiers for every shovelful of dirt thrown up. When these men were required to break "hard ground," they complained they were being worked too hard. The warm weather, Hains added, retarded the work because working parties could not work in the middle of the day.[8]

Hains also said there was a severe want of sappers as the work progressed. A different detail was sent out to work each day from the infantry regiments, and these men knew nothing of what work was to be done. Much valuable time was thus lost in repeating instructions.

Captain Prime reported from his perspective as the chief staff engineer officer:

When the enemy's grenades were most troublesome, it was impossible to keep working parties from the infantry regiments at their posts. Thus the pioneers had to be depended upon to do the dangerous work.[9]

Speaking of the labor performed by details from the regiments, Prime commented: "As is usual in such cases, it was light in comparison with that done by the same number of pioneers or Negroes. Without the stimulate of danger or pecuniary reward troops of the line will not work efficiently, especially at night after the novelty of the labor was worn off. The amount of night work done by a given detail depends very much on the discipline of their command and the energy of its officers. Under average circumstances such details do not in a given time accomplish half the work they have the capability to do."[10]

On the subject of the volunteer engineer officers, Prime commented that in the month he had worked with them on the siege works, he had developed a respect for their work:

> The siege work took on its own peculiar characteristic, namely that many times at different places, the work that should be done, and the way it should be done, depended on officers, or even on enlisted men, without either theoretical or practical knowledge of siege operations, and who had to rely upon their native good sense and ingenuity. Whether a battery was to be constructed by men who had never built one before, a saproller made by those who had never heard the name, or a ship's gun carriage to be built, it was done, and after a few trials, was well done. But while stating the power of adaptation to circumstances and fertility of resources which our men possess in so high a degree, it must be recollected that these powers were shown at the expense of time, and while a relieving force was gathering in our rear. Officers and men had to learn to be engineers while the siege was going on.[11]

One of the unusual problems the army encountered was the fraternization of the soldiers at night on some approach work sites. The enemy pickets entered into agreement with Union work parties not to fire on each other. The Union pioneers or regiment work parties were allowed to work in full view of the enemy without any attempt to stop them.

May 24. Grant in a message to Halleck reported that the troops of the army were well disposed, with the right flank resting on the Mississippi and a division on the left flank occupying the roads leading south and southeast from the city. He described his physical position to be as strong as one could conceive and well fortified. The strength of the enemy garrison was estimated at between 10 and 20 thousand soldiers. Grant also wrote:

> The enemy are now undoubtedly in our grasp. The fall of Vicksburg and capture of most of the garrison can only be a question of time. I heard a great deal of the enemy bringing a

Shirley House Headquarters of General Logan's Division in the Trenches (*Library of Congress*).

large force from the east to effect a raising of the siege. They may attempt something of the kind, but I do not see how they can do it. The railroad is effectually destroyed at Jackson, so that it will take 30 days to repair it. This leaves a march of 50 miles over which the enemy will have to subsist an army, and bring their ordnance stores with teams. My position is so strong that I could hold out for several days against a vastly superior force. I do not see how the enemy could possibly maintain a long attack under these circumstances.[12]

May 26. In a letter to I. N. Arnold, President Lincoln wrote: "My good friend let me turn your eyes upon another point. Whether or not Grant shall consummate capture of Vicksburg, his campaign from beginning of this month up to 22nd day of it is one of most brilliant in world."[13] (It is to be noted that the president limited his applause of Grant's generalship to his actions on the east side of the Mississippi River.)

May 28. Captain Patterson in a letter to his wife wrote:

Since 1st of April I have been pressed forward with the advance in order to prepare the way for our immense army which I have done successfully.

To resign is no longer a matter of choice to me. I will rejoice when my term of service is happily filled. And oh what joy to this heart of mine to be once more in the bosom of my dear little folks. Could you have seen what I have seen (but heaven forbid that I should tell you all the horror of this war).

There was I think on the 25th [22nd] a charge on the rebel batteries in the open field. Our troops were very near them when they started on the run, say 200 yards the rebels retreated, our men succeeded and planted our flag upon their fortifications. On the outside the rebels yet inside. Our pioneers were sent for to dig down the earth that our men might reach them without climbing the earth work. The rebels would light shells and throw them over. They would reach their bayonets over. Our men would break them. All the while our corps would dig away throwing up earth for their own protection until they were ordered to stop and soon they reinforced and dashed down upon our men with a great number when our men returned to our works.

To see these works and our flag upon the rebel forts!

My father went in the rear of our batteries and was there but 5 minutes when a rebel bullet struck him near the mouth moving along the jaw and lodged in the neck. Jaw fractured. He will get well though a bad wound. This is now truly the sunny south—so hot.

The men killed in this charge were allowed to remain on the field beneath the hot sun between the fire of both parties neither daring to venture until 2 days had passed to them a flag of truce to bury the dead. Both parties came together brothers, old acquaintances. All talked and laughed over the incidents of the charge and the battles fought.

The mingling was kept up until 8:30 that night. All slept that night, and were slow to begin next day.

Would you know what we are doing? Just imagine a man in a ditch earth thrown up in front of him watching intently an opportunity to shoot any one who may be so daring to show himself.

Men 6 miles in a line just in this condition and a battery every 300 yards and all day long wherever you may go, these are heard and at night shells from the mortar boats can be seen making their curves in the destruction of the town and often as I have watched them I have thought what screams might be uttered by those just beneath waiting its rapid approach. They often burst in mid air with an awful explosion we don't know but suppose terrible effect.

We have them completely surrounded. I never was in a

Battery Sherman (*Library of Congress*).

condition that I could not freely write all I feel and open my whole heart.

But now my dear you have trouble enough.

I will send you some money.

I can't say how long we be in this condition or whether I can ever get home.

Human life here is not more than mule life and to see a dead man about the same as to see a dead horse.

Soldiers part with their comrades readily whole regiments march into battle and are found upon the field in all possible conditions, such is war.

I sent a 100$ a few days ago. I will enclose a 100 now.

Joy to have your letter but pain to read your troubles.

My dear wife how I love thee. Pray I may once more join you safely.

May 29. Grant reported to Halleck that there was evidence of a Confederate force collecting near the Big Black River about 30 miles northeast of Vicksburg. In response, Grant deployed all the troops that could be made available from the 16th Corps in western Tennessee and sent a request to General Ambrose E. Burnside, Department of the Cumberland, to march what force he could to

Vicksburg. He advised Halleck he could manage the force in Vicksburg and an attacking force of 30,000 on his rear, but he might have to contend with a higher number. Grant informed Halleck of his conclusion that Vicksburg would have to be reduced by regular siege. He had an effective force present of 50,000 but could increase it 10,000 from troops in the Department of the Tennessee.[14]

May 30. Captain Hickenlooper, chief engineer officer, 17th Corps, received orders from General Grant to proceed to the Big Black River railroad bridge with 300 men detailed from General Ransom's division and a pioneer company from the Third Division. Hickenlooper reported that the detail moved out at 11 A.M. for the bridge. At 3 P.M. the detail started moving westwardly along the Bridgeport road, obstructing it by felling trees to impede any approach of General Johnston's army. From Tiffin he sent the pioneer company southwest on the Bovina Station road with orders to return on the Hebron road, obstructing this road in the same manner as they had the Bridgeport road. They also burned bridges on the Hebron road.

June 2. Samuel H. Eells, the 26-year old assistant surgeon, 12th Michigan Volunteer Infantry, wrote that he was on board the steamer *Luminary* on the Mississippi River, headed for the scene of active operations at Vicksburg. He noted that when the steamer tied up at a landing, the soldiers plundered and burned houses. "Made very pretty bonfires in night." He also wrote he did not object to plundering a house if it were deserted, because it was enemy property:

> I plundered myself, the house of a rebel doctor, a pair of saddle bags such as a country practitioner uses, some valuable medical books, and instruments. More available but could not carry away. This looks like stealing? I don't have any compunction about it as long as from secesh! They have done me and my family too much harm for me to be tender to them. I could steal us rich in a short time.
>
> Looked at fort on Yazoo where Sherman repulsed last year, no one would wonder at it.
>
> Grant blazing away at Vicksburg all the time. Hot, dusty.

June 9. Captain Patterson wrote to his wife:

> Such joy in your letter of May 24. Others had been of troubles, dreaded to open it. But you spoke of my perfect

delight of love and heart felt interest in the husband far away. Showed so much love, patience, forgiving, undying confidence. A new spring of love. Point of all my actions form around.

Rebel gun fire at night.

At night I have to go within 100 yards to see earthworks we are constructing. One night they opened fire on us, 2 to 5 minutes. One man shot dead close by me of my company.

I hear roar of mortars and what a crash the explosion.

How can rebels stand such constant fire. Truth is they live in ground caves excavated. [For description of this cave life, see the Appendix.]

We destroyed all their cattle, mules, horses.

June 11. Captain Patterson wrote to his wife:

Hard rain. Rolled cotton bales as saps, rebels through [*sic*] turpentine-balls torches to fire them.

Thunder-like tones of mortar. Wish you could see flashes, but hope you never will.

Mounting new guns every day and getting closer.

Father is still with me, suffered from wound, getting better.

So much to attend to. Many questions to answer but am well. Of war I am sick. Daily slaughter. Oh, God knows, is it that our land is so cursed.

We are performing an immense work. General McClernand in his report is giving us full credit for our work.

You will understand that to make the difference considerable is to enhance his own performance and the difficulty he gets into he called upon me to get him out. I have done well and when his report is published you will see in detail. You will see how your husband had treated heavy responsibility. A clerk has promised to slip me a transcript so I can send it to you.

You will see in *Harper's Weekly* a bridge suspension burned by the rebels and Logan's troops crossing on a bridge built by my men, but the credit swallowed by one Tresilian and Negroes, the drawing is all right but the construction is all wrong a simple falsehood and some steps will be taken to correct it, my boys are very mad. I should not wonder a dozen letters will be written if the mail goes out this morning.[15]

My aching heart can only be relieved by your smiles. Father improving. Heat awful. Troops in good health, spirits.

June 18. Captain Cyrus B. Comstock, Corps of Engineers, newly arrived at Grant's headquarters, was assigned chief staff engineer officer and assumed staff supervision of the siege works. He had previously served as General Burnside's chief staff engineer officer at the ill-fated battle of Fredericksburg in February 1862.

Grant issued an order relieving McClernand from command of the 13th Corps. He ordered him to return to his place of choice in Illinois and report his readiness to the army headquarters for further orders.[16] McClernand's relief from command had been in the making for some time; he had been persona non grata to the army's and navy's top leadership since the day he arrived on the scene for the Vicksburg campaign. When Grant reported to Halleck on the failure of the May 22 assault on Vicksburg, he wrote that McClernand's dispatches on the action misled him about the real state of facts and caused many of the casualties. "He is entirely unfit for the position of corps commander," Grant asserted, "both on the march and on the battlefield. Looking after his corps gives me more labor and infinitely more uneasiness than all the remainder of my department."[17]

What precipitated Grant's action was the arrival at the army's encampment of an issue of the *Missouri Democrat*, which had printed a congratulatory order from McClernand to his soldiers on the assault against Vicksburg. McClernand wrote effusively of the valor of his soldiers and the glory they had brought to the 13th Corps. The order excited the ire of Grant, McPherson, and Sherman, who believed his remarks on the May 22 assault to be false. The order also included disparaging remarks about McClernand's fellow corps commanders and vituperative remarks about Grant's generalship.

Grant and the other corps commanders were probably taken aback by McClernand's use of showy expressions to grab headlines. The order also repeated in detail the severity of the west bank camp life resulting from the terrain, climate, and disease, and alluded to the soldiers' hardships under Grant.[18]

Grant asked McClernand to verify that he had issued the order as printed in the newspaper. McClernand admitted to its authorship, but in an effort to justify himself, he attempted to engage Grant in verbal warfare on his relief from command and he defended the correctness of every word in his congratulatory order.

Grant wasted no time with McClernand in such a fruitless discussion. In the dynamics of bureaucracy, a quick course of resolution of the complex matter was open to him. McClernand had failed to deliver the order to the army's headquarters before its issuance per standing orders and regulations. Such negligence provided Grant with the grounds to take disciplinary action and relieve him from duty.

Wilson delivered Grant's orders to McClernand that relieved him of command. During the campaign, Wilson had made efforts to ameliorate relations between the two generals. He had asked Grant to commend McClernand for being the pathfinder on the route down the west bank of the Mississippi River and for his success in the first battle against the Confederates at Port Gibson, but Grant refused. When Wilson spoke to McClernand, who was irate at his relief from command, Wilson asked him to be conciliatory to Grant. McClernand refused, believing their differences were irreconcilable. Wilson was considerate of McClernand, but he knew that during his assignment in the army, he had not been well received. Wilson also wrote that from the day Dana joined the army, he was set on seeing McClernand ousted. Wilson resignedly said he was "tired of keeping peace between headquarters and political generals."[19]

McClernand protested to Grant, the secretary of the army, and his commander in chief, President Lincoln, that he should not be relieved from command based on the nit-picking reasons that his adjutant forgot to send his order to the army's headquarters and that the contents of his congratulatory order offended some of his fellow officers.

Other aggrieved generals relieved from duty for their failures had laid their cases on the president's desk, but he had given them little solace. For McClernand, he had a justifiable answer. Any investigation of McClernand's complex grievance would require a long absence of the commanders in the Army of the Tennessee from the battlefield to appear before a court of inquiry. The greater interest of the country required that the issue could not interfere with the conduct of the battle. Lincoln's decision also upheld the traditional military doctrine that a senior commander had the authority to relieve a subordinate commander as he saw fit and deemed necessary.

General Grant in a letter to General Thomas, the adjutant general of the army, stated he did not want to interfere with the president's prerogative of assignments of command, but he had tolerated McClernand long after he thought the good of the service called for his removal. "It was only when almost the entire army under my command seemed to demand it that he was relieved," Grant stated.[20] He urged that McClernand be replaced by Major General E. O. C. Ord, pending the president's approval.

In a perspicacious letter to Stanton, Dana stated that the congratulatory address became the occasion of McClernand's relief but not the cause: "Cause as I understand it is his repeated disobedience of important orders, his general insubordinate disposition, and palpable incompetence for position." Dana added that he had picked up in private conversations that senior officers did not want McClernand to be in the line of command if Grant were to become disabled.[21] What actions the senior officers did or did not take against McClernand remain undocumented.

June 21. Doctor Eells, assistant regimental surgeon, wrote home:

> Rumor Johnston coming. The armies are behind lines of double fortifications. When Confederates know General Johnston not coming they will surrender. Soldiers talk back and forth between lines:
>
> *Reb*: Yanks, why don't you pitch in and storm our works?
> *Yank*: We weren't brought up to pitch on prisoners.
> *Officer*: Fire on them!
> *Yank*: No! Not till warned. Rebs, hunt your holes we are going to fire.
>
> We impatient for surrender. Men work hard on fortifications. Over 90 for a month. No rain.
>
> Went black berry picking. Wake up with bites of little insects soldiers call jiggers. As large as eye of fine needle. Itching intolerable.
>
> People at home do not have slightest idea of magnitude of siege, each shot 30$ night and day.
>
> Done quit troubling myself about my chances of anything happening.
>
> Corn, peaches, plums plentiful. Newspapers cannot approach truth of life here. Wish I had daguerreotype.

June 22. Captain Patterson wrote to his wife:

> Anxious about money I sent. I just returned from the two saps, which I am running directly to the rebel forts.

Fear this letter may fall into rebel hands.

Tonight boys throwing grenades over high banks into their works making quite an explosion. Really it is one continual fire. If they open a gun our boys turn to it with 10 to 30 guns at once and the thunder how it rolls over these hills.

Grant had reported to Halleck in the past month that during the construction of the approaches he had brought forward Major General F. J. Herron's division from the department of Missouri and two divisions from the 9th Army Corps, under command of Major General J. G. Parke. "This increase in my force," Grant stated, "enables me to make the investment most complete, and at the same time left me a large reserve to watch the movements of Johnston."

Herron's division took up a position on the extreme left of the line, south of Vicksburg, and Lauman's division took up a position between Herron's division and the 13th Corps. Parke's 9th Corps and Smith's and Kimball's divisions were deployed to Haynes' Bluff, which Grant fortified on the land side to prepare it to resist a heavy force.

At the outset of the final Vicksburg campaign on May 1, the effective strength of Grant's army was approximately 31,000. The four divisions he called forward made up for the casualties in the months' campaign: 1,242 killed, 7,095 wounded, and 537 missing. A number of the wounded would at some time probably return to duty. There was also a decrease in the effective strength due to diseases, which occurred at the rate of 200 per 1000. It is also difficult to arrive at Grant's effective strength because regiments were below their authorized strength.

In his report to Halleck, Grant also stated that Johnston had crossed the Big Black River with a portion of his force and everything indicated that he would make an attack.

> Our position in front of Vicksburg having been made as strong against any sorties from the enemy as his works were against an assault, I placed General Sherman in command of all troops to look after Johnston. The force intended to operate against Johnston, in addition to that at Haynes' Bluff, was one division from each of the 13th, 15th, 17th Corps and Lauman's division. Johnston, however, not showing any sign of attacking, I determined to attack him the moment Vicksburg was in our possession.

Dr. Warriner, United States Sanitary Commission, wrote about the physical and moral condition of the soldiers in the siege. He reported that they were dependent on the water in the bottoms of the ravines, which was impure from the drainage into them from the camping grounds and insufficient in quantity. The camping grounds were unsanitary, and sickness was slowly increasing. (Dr. Eell, assistant regimental surgeon, said it was "trebling.") Dr. Warriner said the unwholesome lodgings and water were beginning to show the expected effects in cases of fever and malaria.

To put into perspective the sickness situation that Doctors Warriner and Eell reported, the following table compares the number of cases and deaths of Class I diseases (fevers, diarrhea, dysentery) in April, which had the lowest number for the time the army camped on the west side of the river, and May and June, the months the army encamped on the east side of the river[22]:

April		May		June	
Cases	Deaths	Cases	Deaths	Cases	Deaths
18,865	425	15,860	327	28,882	450

June 27. Captain Prime was forced to leave his assignment as Grant's chief staff engineer officer because of illness. His report recorded the following construction on the ten approaches and siege works:

> Fabricated 1,220 fascines, 1,000 gabions, and 6 sap rollers.
> Constructed 89 batteries.
> Constructed 3 magazines.
> Aggregate length of trenches constructed, 12 miles.
> Guns, field or siege, placed in position, 220.
> Wagon loads of lumber hauled, 370.

The engineer and pioneer officers and the enlisted men merited the recognition Prime wrote into his report concerning facility to learn, the quality of their work, and the fertility of their individual resources.

Some writers on the siege misread Prime's statement that at the outset of the siege there was a lack of engineer officers to mean that there was a lack of an engineer organization. This misimpression

Engineers' Work Site for Construction of Gabions and Sap Rollers (*Library of Congress*).

was reinforced by statements Danà wrote in a letter to Stanton: "After a month of the construction of the approaches several activities conspired to produce a sort of listlessness among various commands." One of the activities Dana mentioned was "the absence of any thorough organization in the engineer department."[23]

Dana's facile generalization was totally in error, but a number of writers on the Vicksburg campaign perpetuated this error. Prime's closing remarks in his report belie Dana's denigrating remarks. The competence of the engineering work is evident because the siege succeeded in time, and without the cost in casualties another assault would have incurred.

Grant reinforced Prime's remarks and set the record straight that the only source of initial concern was the absence of Regular Army Corps of Engineers officers. There was a scarcity of engineer officers in the beginning, Grant wrote, but under the skillful supervision of Captain Prime, Colonel Wilson, and Captain Comstock, "such practical experience was gained as would enable any division

Chevaux-de-frise and Fascines (*Library of Congress*).

of this army hereafter to conduct a siege with considerable skill in the absence of regular engineer officers."[24]

Captain Patterson witnessed the agreement Union and Confederate pickets entered into not to fire on each other one night when he went out with a work detail. He related the incident in a letter to his wife:

> What Reb said last night.
> Colonel marches his men out to where reb pickets stood. Colonel, halloo, reb. Reb wakes up. I am going to work here to dig a rifle pit. Sit still we wont fire at you. Only if you think we are too close you can move back a little.
> Reb mutters indistinctly. Wakes up his company. Get up boys. Wake up. Wake up. The Yankees want to dig a rifle pit. We must out of the way. Wake up.
> Our Colonel went to digging, leaving the reb to move men.

July 1. Captain John M. Wilson, Corps of Engineers, one of Grant's newly arrived staff engineer officers, per Grant's orders completed an inspection of the ten siege approaches from the army's right to left flank. The work of the approaches continued steadily forward and Thayer's and Lauman's approaches (1 and 9) were within 30 yards or less of the enemy's ditch; Herron's (10) was within 120 yards. Ewing's, Ransom's, Logan's, and A. J. Smith's approaches (2, 4, 5, and 6, respectively) were up to or in the enemy's ditch.

In the closer approaches Giles A. Smith's, Carr's, and Hovey's (3, 7, and 8), the enemy seriously harassed the Union working parties with hand grenades, making it difficult to keep them at work and slowing down the progress of the construction. Captain Tresilian's mortars were more effective in retaliating from a longer distance of 100 to 150 yards.

Mines had been constructed from Ewing's, Logan's, and A. J. Smith's approaches (2, 5, and 6) with the expectation of exploding

Mine Explosion by Logan's Division Under Confederate Fort
(*Harper's Pictorial History*).

them before an assault, but the enemy constructed counter mines. This enemy action caused the Union to fire a charge of 1,800 pounds under Logan's approach (5). The explosion completely destroyed the enemy's parapet at the point, creating a crater 30 feet in diameter. It also blew some half dozen of the enemy's soldiers, one alive, into Logan's lines. No attempt was made to occupy the crater. The enemy used mines at several points, but they were feeble and damage was limited only to the crushing of some galleries.

The hand-to-hand character of the fighting in the closer approaches demonstrated that little more progress could be made by digging alone. The enemy's works were weak and at ten different points, Captain Wilson reported, heads of regiments could be maneuvered within 5 to 120 yards of the enemy's line.

Captain Wilson concluded, however, that the assault would be easier if the army waited ten more days.[25] After studying Captain Wilson's report, Grant, without stating any reason, rejected the recommendation of ten more days of work. He issued an order to besiege the enemy's works on July 6.

Orders were issued to widen the main approaches necessary to permit the movement of soldiers by fours with ease and to permit artillery to move along some of the approaches. The units were also ordered to prepare planks and sand bags stuffed with cotton for crossing ditches and to arrange the heads of saps for the easy debouch of soldiers.

Grant notified Sherman that he would again make an assault on Vicksburg at daylight on the sixth and instructed him that he was to have supplies of all descriptions ready to move his corps upon receipt of orders, if the assault should turn out to be successful.

July 3. Grant, during the afternoon, received from General Pemberton a letter proposing an armistice and the appointment of a commission to arrange terms for the capitulation of Vicksburg. Grant sent his answer to General Pemberton by Colonel Wilson. Later in the day Grant and Pemberton met between the lines and engaged in a personal conference on the subject of the capitulation. Pemberton asked for a commission to discuss terms, but Grant refused, declaring there were no terms other than unconditional surrender.[26]

Lieutenant Balazar Grebe wrote in his diary: "Bombarded rebs severely intensely, ran up white flags. Our troops mixed with Rebels, shook hands. Pemberton asked for terms of truce. All still."

Frederick Dent Grant wrote: "Siege not much excitement. Fear of Johnston in rear. White flag."

July 4. Grant wrote to Halleck at 10:30 A.M.: "The enemy surrendered this morning. The only terms allowed is their parole as prisoners of war. This I regard as of great advantage to us at this juncture. It saves probably several days in the captured town; leaves troops and transports ready for immediate service. General Sherman with a large force will immediately face on Johnston and drive him from the state. I will send troops to the relief of General Banks, and return the 9th Corps to General Burnside."[27]

Frederick Dent Grant was the first to hear from his father of the surrender of Vicksburg. He ran outside to tell everybody, which, he later wrote, he was not supposed to do.

Casualties from May 18 to July 4 were reported to be 8,875 (1,243 killed, 7,095 wounded, 537 missing). In addition there were 4,965 deaths from all classes of diseases for the six months ending June 30, 1863. The siege lasted 42 days; two days over the number prescribed as allowable in the book of military doctrine.[28]

Captain Patterson wrote to his wife:

> What shall I say of today? I have had headache. You will see by paper we have the place. Taking Vicksburg July 4 calculated to make one happy. They were reduced to mule meat. Poor fellows were glad to be captured.
>
> A charge upon their works was ordered by own men. The slaughter must have been great. Johnston is in our rear.
>
> We march tomorrow for him and return here in a few days and then the word is up the river and I hope for my home and dear little wife.
>
> I have had some money stolen from me which will require you to be as careful as you can. I send what I can. I would have sent you more if I had been allowed. [Many of his letters referred to the money problems that plagued his wife.]
>
> We captured near 30,000 men, large amount of artillery and ordnance.

Charles Calvin Enslow, Tenth Division, wrote home from the hospital: "We are all in anxious suspense. Flag of truce yesterday. At 3:00 P.M. went up to front works within 15 feet of rebel works. We all went outside of our works and rebs came out also. We had a good talk with them face to face."

Frank Leslie's Independent Newspaper correspondent wrote: "Vicksburg surrendered. Pemberton unconditionally. Asked to march his men. Grant said, no. Surrender unconditionally. Official intelligence sent by Porter from his Flagship *Black Hawk* to Secretary of Navy."

July 6. Grant reported that the preparations he ordered Sherman to make to be ready to march had been immediately made. When Vicksburg surrendered two days earlier than Grant had fixed for the attack, Sherman was ready and moved at once with a force increased by the remainder of both the 13th and 15th Corps; they invested Jackson, where Johnston made a stand.

Charles Enslow wrote from Clear Creek, Mississippi, "Broke camp 5th and came here, 12 miles east of Vicksburg. Had hot and dusty time yesterday. The rebs stronghold is fallen. We should allow July 4, 1863 to become day of veneration like we hold July 4, 1776. Went to chapel service but would not as Baptist take communion from chaplain of another denomination."

July 7. Halleck to Grant: "I have the pleasure to inform you appointed Major General, Regular Army, rank from July 4."

July 8. Port Hudson, the last vestige of Confederate control of the Mississippi River surrendered to Major General Nathaniel P. Banks' Army of the Gulf. Major General Frank Gardner, the Confederate commander of the fort, declared emphatically that the surrender of Port Hudson did not result from the surrender of Vicksburg, but from the exhaustion of his troops.

July 13. President Lincoln stated in a letter to General Grant:

> Write from greatful [*sic*] acknowledgement for almost inestimable service you have done for country. When you reached Vicksburg I thought you should do what you did, march troops across neck, run batteries with transports and then go below. I never had any faith except a general hope you knew better than I that Yazoo expedition and the like could succeed. When you got below and took Port Gibson and Grand Gulf and vicinity I thought you should join Banks. I feared a mistake to go northeast of Big Black. I wish to say you were right. I was wrong.[29]

Captain Patterson wrote to his wife:

> I thought since Vicksburg fell we would go up river but the whole force is employed in capture of Johnston about 45 miles from here.
>
> I will remain here but send effective men with main corps.
>
> Met daughter of an old friend, my old Preceptor. [He] Went off with their soldiers, not known where. Secesh bitter. I told them bayonets make most beautiful order and law. Cold to me, told them not personal fight. Father well again and busy clerking for me. Many stories to tell when I get home. I thought I should write details for so many letters will be published about this place and that you would have everything of interest.
>
> The mortar shells so dreadful to all appearances prove to be of trifling importance. Our small cannon and bullets they dreaded and well they should for many of our bullets traveled quite a mile, and surrounding as we did the whole town, every shot that passed high sought at once for center of town innocent people were killed, some women and children nearly all the animals were destroyed.
>
> Today the rebels left the place the very best feelings prevail among our troops. Kindness was the ruling spirit.

Sent money by express. Figs and peaches are about ripe, wish I could send you some.

I hope to be home soon, but do not look for me until I write I am coming. Your own Frank.

August 1. Halleck notified Grant:

Received your report of capitulation of Vicksburg. Your narrative of campaign operations, like themselves, is brief, soldierly and in every respect creditable and satisfactory. [He referred to Grant's report dated July 6.]

In boldness of plan, rapidity of execution, and in brilliancy of results these operations will compare most favorably with those of Napoleon about Ulm.

You and your army have well deserved the gratitude of your country and it will be the boast of your children that their fathers were of the heroic army which reopened the Mississippi.[30]

Retrospection

There were many judgments about why Pemberton and Johnston failed and Grant succeeded. Authors have said Johnston lacked the "divine fire" which leads to boldness and vigor and Pemberton conducted an "ostrich defense."

Judgments were also offered on Grant's generalship that were broad ones containing words like "brilliant" and "genius." The record will bear out that Lincoln confined his applause of "brilliant generalship" to the battle on the east side of the river from May 1 to 26 and General Halleck confined his applause to the "brilliancy of the results of the campaign."

If it can be hypothesized that Johnston lacked divine fire, it can also be hypothesized that Grant had a quality of divine fire that led to success: a dogged, unwavering determination to accomplish what he decided his soldiers should do. In January 1863, Sergeant Boyd said that a soldier in Grant's army had to have grit to live or he would die. Grit epitomizes Grant's indomitable spirit and quality. He held fast to his determination to extricate his soldiers from the difficult environment in which his seemingly unwise decision encamped them for four months.

Grant was supported in his determination by what Sergeant Andrus called the "core of the faithful," soldiers who adhered to their oaths, convictions, or personal reasons to support Grant until the battle was won. The core of the faithful may not have given Grant the battlefield victory they all sought, but their loyalty to their duty forced the enemy to surrender.

The victory taught the army as a living organization a number of lessons, among them, the futility of assaulting an enemy posted behind strongly built fortifications, the important role of engineer-pioneer soldiers, the need for terrain reconnaissance, coordination with naval forces, and strategical and tactical planning.

Grant credited Providence for the successful course of the Vicksburg campaign, but Captain Hains declared that he believed Grant spoke from unnecessary self-effacement. In Hain's assessment, Grant's merits led the army to a successful campaign and he should not have hesitated to take the credit. If the campaign had failed, Grant would have spoken out and placed responsibility for it on himself.[31] Some idea of Grant's attitudes can be derived from his May 2 congratulatory message to his officers and soldiers of the Army of the Tennessee; he remarked that it would not be proper to make "invidious distinctions." In a noble gesture, he declared the army's success to be providential. Today's reader could broaden Grant's declaration and conclude that Colonel Wilson, Grant's topographical staff engineer, had filled the role of a messenger from Providence. A thread of his advice, counsel, military knowledge, and influence coursed through the decision-making process of the Vicksburg campaign, and on occasion, Grant frankly acknowledged his contributions.

With the surrender of the Confederates at Vicksburg, the Army of the Tennessee achieved for the Union a number of major strategic objectives in the West:

1. The destruction of a Confederate army.
2. The cutoff of the Confederacy from its rich supply base west of the Mississippi and its states of Texas, Louisiana, and Arkansas.
3. The opening of the Mississippi River navigation to the northwest.
4. The severing of Confederate communications with foreign countries.

5. The rupture of the Confederate line of supplies to Mexico.
6. The demoralization of the Confederate citizens.
7. A contribution to the surrender of Port Hudson.

After the victory, President Lincoln poetically declared, "the Father of Waters then flowed unvexed to the sea."

Notes

Chapter 1

1. Benson Lossing, *Life, Campaigns, and Battles of General U.S. Grant*, p. 151. Logan had previously served as a representative to Congress from Illinois. He served under Grant as a Volunteer Officer.

2. U. S. Grant, *Personal Memoirs*, vol. 1, p. 24; Ledyard Bill, *Life, Campaigns and Battles of General Grant*, p. 19.

3. Robert U. Johnson and Clarence C. Buel, *Battles and Leaders of the Civil War*, vol. 2, pp. 22–24.

4. Richard Wheeler, *The Siege of Vicksburg*, p. 36.

5. U. S. Grant, *Personal Memoirs*, vol. 1, p. 420.

6. Wheeler, *The Siege of Vicksburg*, p. 33.

7. *Ibid.*

8. Francis V. Greene, *The Mississippi*, p. 59.

9. James H. Wilson, *Under the Old Flag*, p. 145.

10. Greene, *The Mississippi*, p. 2.

11. Grant, *Memoirs*, p. 424.

12. *The War of the Rebellion, A Compilation of the Official Records of the Union and Confederate Armies*, Washington, Government Printing Office, 1891, series 1, vol. 24, part 1, p. 426 (hereinafter cited as *Official Records*).

Chapter 2

1. U. S. Grant, *Personal Memoirs*, p. 437.

2. *Ibid.*

3. Benson Lossing, *Life, Campaigns and Battles of General U. S. Grant*, p. 167; William T. Sherman, *Memoirs*, p. 332.

4. Grant, *Memoirs*, p. 437.

5. Francis V. Greene, *The Mississippi*, pp. 88–89.

6. Grant, *Memoirs,* p. 437.

7. William T. Sherman, *Memoirs,* p. 333; *Official Records,* series 1, vol. 24, part 1, p. 8.

8. James H. Wilson, *Under the Old Flag,* p. 146.

9. *Official Records,* series 1, vol. 24, part 1, p. 10.

10. Grant, *Memoirs,* p. 437.

11. *Ibid.,* p. 12.

12. *Ibid.,* p. 13.

Chapter 3

1. *Official Records,* series 1, vol. 24, part 1, pp. 13–14.

2. *Ibid.,* pp. 371–72.

3. *Ibid.,* pp. 372–73.

4. *Orders Book,* Ninth Division, 13th Army Corps, February 3, 1863.

5. *Official Records,* series 1, vol. 24, part 1, p. 14.

6. *Ibid.*

7. *Official Records,* series 1, vol. 24, part 3, p. 36.

8. *Official Records,* series 1, vol. 24, part 1, pp. 371–90.

9. *Ibid.,* p. 371.

10. *Ibid.,* pp. 371–90.

11. *Ibid.,* p. 120.

12. *Ibid.,* p. 18.

13. William A. Hammond, *History of the United States Sanitary Commission,* p. 332.

14. *Official Records,* series 1, vol. 24, part 1, p. 18.

15. George W. Cullum, *System of Military Bridges in Use by the United States Army, 1863,* p. 5.

16. *Company I,* Muster-Event Report, MF 594, National Archives.

17. *Official Records,* series 1, vol. 24, part 1, p. 376.

18. Joseph K. Barnes, *The Medical and Surgical History of the War of the Rebellion,* part 1, p. 24.

Chapter 4

1. *Official Records,* series 1, vol. 24, part 1, p. 19.

2. *Official Records,* series 1, vol. 17, part 1, p. 710.

3. *Official Records,* series 1, vol. 24, part 1, pp. 409–11.

4. *Ibid.,* p. 19.

5. Benson Lossing, *Life, Campaigns and Battles of General U. S. Grant,* p. 198.

6. *Ibid.*

7. *Ibid.,* p. 19.

8. *Ibid.,* p. 143.

9. *Ibid.*, p. 122.

10. *Ibid.*, p. 387.

11. *Official Records*, series 1, vol. 24, part 3, p. 105.

12. Frederick Phisterer, *Statistical Record of the Armies of the United States*, p. 71.

13. Lossing, *U. S. Grant*, p. 198.

14. Charles J. Stille, *History of the United States Sanitary Commission*, pp. 331–32.

15. *Official Records*, series 1, vol. 24, part 1, p. 379.

16. *Official Records*, series 1, vol 24, part 3, pp. 113–14.

17. Lossing, *U. S. Grant*, p. 192.

18. *Official Records*, series 1, vol. 24, part 1, pp. 371–90.

19. *Official Records*, series 1, vol. 24, part 3, p. 109.

20. Stewart M. Brooks, *Civil War Medicine*, pp. 109–11.

21. *Official Records*, series 1, vol. 24, part 1, pp. 371–90.

22. *Official Records*, series 1, vol. 24, part 3, p. 112.

23. *Official Records*, series 1, vol. 24, part 1, pp. 431–32.

24. *Ibid.*, pp. 20–21.

25. *Ibid.*, pp. 432–33.

26. *Ibid.*, pp. 371–90.

27. *Ibid.*, pp. 119–25.

28. *Ibid.*, pp. 432–33.

29. E. B. Long, *The Civil War Day by Day*, March 20.

30. *Official Records*, series 1, vol. 24, part 1, p. 22.

31. *Ibid.*, pp. 371–90.

32. *Official Records, Union and Confederate Navies*, series 1, vol. 23, pp. 281–84.

33. *Ibid.*, pp. 248, 516.

34. *Official Records*, series 1, vol. 24, part 1, pp. 433–34; James H. Wilson, *Under the Old Flag*, p. 151.

35. *Official Records*, series 1, vol. 24, part 1, p. 435.

36. *Ibid.*, pp. 46, 430–37.

37. *Harper's Weekly*, April 18, 1863.

38. William T. Sherman, *Memoirs*, pp. 338–39.

39. *Official Records*, series 1, vol. 24, part 1, p. 46.

40. Richard Wheeler, *The Siege of Vicksburg*, pp. 18, 99; Earl S. Miers, *The Web of Victory, Grant at Vicksburg*, p. 133.

41. *Official Records*, series 1, vol. 24, part 1, p. 64.

42. *Ibid.*, p. 65.

43. *Official Records*, series 1, vol. 24, part 3, p. 147.

44. *Official Records*, series 1, vol. 24, part 1, pp. 407–8.

45. *Ibid.*, p. 144.

46. *Ibid.*, p. 145.

47. *Ibid.*, p. 166.

48. *Ibid.*, p. 14.

49. *Ibid.*, pp. 44–47.

50. Wilson, *Under the Old Flag*, pp. 154–55.

51. *Official Records*, series 1, vol. 24, part 1, p. 67.

Chapter 5

1. The *New York Times*, April 6, 1863, p. 1.
2. *Official Records*, series 1, vol. 24, part 1, p. 491.
3. *Ibid.*, p. 69.
4. *Ibid.*, p. 24.
5. *Ibid.*, p. 70.
6. *Ibid.*
7. *Ibid.*, p. 25.
8. James H. Wilson, *Under the Old Flag*, p. 218.
9. U. S. Grant, *Personal Memoirs*, p. 460.
10. *Official Records*, series 1, vol. 24, part 1, p. 492.
11. The *New York Times*, April 4, 1863, p. 1.
12. *Official Records*, series 1, vol. 24, part 1, p. 492.
13. *Ibid.*, p. 493.
14. Captain Patterson's Kentucky Company of Mechanics and Engineers, Muster-Event Report, April 1863, NARG 397.
15. *Official Records*, series 1, vol. 24, part 1, p. 71.
16. The *New York Times*, April 16, 1863, p. 1.
17. *Official Records*, series 1, vol. 24, part 1, p. 493.
18. William T. Sherman, *Memoirs*, pp. 342–43.
19. Wilson, *Under the Old Flag*, pp. 149, 151, 160; Peter C. Hains, "The Vicksburg Campaign," *The Military Engineer* 13 (May–June 1921): 189; William F. Vilas, *A View of the Vicksburg Campaign*, p. 27.
20. *Official Records*, series 1, vol. 24, part 1, p. 27.
21. *Ibid.*, p. 494; James H. Wilson, *Under the Old Flag*, p. 108; C.A. Dana, *Recollections of the Civil War*, p.73.
22. *Official Records*, series 1, vol. 24, part 1, pp. 493–94.
23. *Ibid.*, pp. 186–87.
24. *Ibid.*, p. 29.
25. *Ibid.*, p. 73.
26. *Ibid.*, p. 75.
27. Frederick Dent Grant, "With Grant at Vicksburg," *The Outlook* 59 (July 1898): 532–43. In March 1863, Frederick Dent Grant left school in Covington, Kentucky, and joined his father at Milliken's Bend.
28. Grant, *Memoirs*, p. 465.
29. *Official Records*, series 1, vol. 24, part 1, p. 126.
30. Wilson, *Under the Old Flag*, pp. 148, 164–66.
31. *Official Records, Union and Confederate Navies*, series 1, vol. 24, p. 552.
32. *Official Records*, series 1, vol. 24, part 1, p. 494.
33. *Ibid.*, p. 30.
34. *Ibid.*
35. *Ibid.*
36. *Official Records, Union and Confederate Navies*, series 1, vol. 24, p. 353.
37. *Official Records*, series 1, vol. 24, part 1, p. 31.
38. *The Medical and Surgical History of the War of the Rebellion*, p. 330.

39. *Official Records*, series 1, vol. 24, part 1, pp. 127–28; Wilson, *Under the Old Flag*, pp. 169–71.
40. Wilson, *Under the Old Flag*, p. 169.

Chapter 6

1. Francis V. Greene, *The Mississippi*, pp. 118–20.
2. James H. Wilson, *Under the Old Flag*, p. 171.
3. U. S. Grant, *Personal Memoirs*, p. 480.
4. *Official Records*, series 1, vol. 24, part 1, p. 142.
5. *Ibid.*, p. 143.
6. *Ibid.*, p. 145.
7. *Ibid.*
8. *Ibid.*, pp. 145–46.
9. Frederick Dent Grant, *The Outlook*, pp. 532–43.
10. *Official Records*, series 1, vol. 24, part 1, p. 34.
11. William T. Sherman, *Memoirs*, p. 347.
12. *Official Records*, series 1, vol. 24, part 1, p. 49.
13. Frederick Dent Grant, *The Outlook*, pp. 532–43.
14. John D. Billings, *Hardtack and Coffee*, p. 370; Wilson, *Under the Old Flag*, p. 196.
15. *Official Records*, series 1, vol. 24, part 1, p. 35.
16. *Ibid.*, p. 34.
17. *Ibid.*, p. 36.
18. Wilson, *Under the Old Flag*, pp. 198–99.
19. *Official Records*, series 1, vol. 24, part 1, p. 146.
20. *Ibid.*, p. 50.
21. *Ibid.*, p. 147.
22. Wilson, *Under the Old Flag*, p. 202.
23. *Official Records*, series 1, vol. 24, part 1, pp. 148–51.
24. *Ibid.*, p. 25; Wilson, *Under the Old Flag*, p. 204.
25. Wilson, *Under the Old Flag*, p. 207.
26. *Official Records*, series 1, vol. 24, part 1, pp. 125, 755; Billings, *Hardtack and Coffee*, pp. 383–84.
27. Captain Patterson's Kentucky Company of Mechanics and Engineers Muster-Event Report, May 1863, NARG 397. Captain Patterson Letters and Papers, Library of Congress, MMC 1180, F79 1802.
28. *Official Records*, series 1, vol. 24, part 1, Report No. 11, Captain Stewart R. Tresilian, pp. 203–6; *Harper's Weekly*, June 27, 1863, p. 1.
29. Wilson, *Under the Old Flag*, pp. 204–6.
30. *Ibid.*, p. 208.
31. *Official Records*, series 1, vol. 24, part 1, p. 54.
32. *Ibid.*, p. 55.
33. *Ibid.*, p. 56.
34. *Ibid.*, p. 156.
35. *Ibid.*, p. 56.

36. *Ibid.*, p. 37.
37. Wilson, *Under the Old Flag*, pp. 180–81.
38. Peter C. Hains, "The Vicksburg Campaign," *The Military Engineer* 13 (May–June 1921): 272.

Chapter 7

1. *Official Records*, series 1, vol. 24, part 1, p. 56.
2. *Ibid.*, p. 169.
3. *Ibid.*, p. 175.
4. *Ibid.*, pp. 176–77.
5. *Ibid.*, p. 177.
6. *American Heritage Pictorial History of the Civil War*, p. 293; *Official Records*, series 1, vol. 24, part 1, pp. 168–206.
7. *Harper's Weekly*, June 20, 1863.
8. Peter C. Hains, "The Vicksburg Campaign," *The Military Engineer* 13 (May–June 1921): 196.
9. *Official Records*, series 1, vol. 24, part 1, pp. 176–77.
10. *Ibid.*, p. 177.
11. *Ibid.*
12. *Ibid.*, p. 37.
13. Abraham Lincoln, *Speeches and Letters*, p. 449.
14. *Official Records*, series 1, vol. 24, part 1, p. 39.
15. *Harper's Weekly*, June 13, 1863, p. 369; *Official Records*, series 1, vol. 24, report no. 11 of Captain Tresilian, p. 204, mentions Captain Patterson's Company participated in the building of the bridge with the pioneers of the 17th Corps.
16. *Official Records*, series 1, vol. 24, part 1, pp. 164–65.
17. *Ibid.*, p. 37.
18. *Ibid.*, pp. 159–61.
19. James H. Wilson, *Under the Old Flag*, p. 183.
20. *Official Records*, series 1, vol. 24, part 1, pp. 158–59.
21. *Ibid.*, p. 103.
22. *The Medical and Surgical History of the War of the Rebellion*, p. 330.
23. *Official Records*, series 1, vol. 24, part 1, pp. 56–57.
24. *Ibid.*, p. 47.
25. *Ibid.*, p. 58.
26. *Ibid.*, pp. 57, 59; Wilson, *Under the Old Flag*, p. 226.
27. *Official Records*, series 1, vol. 24, part 1, p. 44.
28. Hains, "Vicksburg Campaign," pp. 193, 196. The siege officially started May 23. Some writers stated the siege lasted 47 days by including the assaults of May 19 and 22.
29. Abraham Lincoln, *Speeches and Letters*, p. 477.
30. *Official Records*, series 1, vol. 24, part 1, p. 60.
31. Hains, "Vicksburg Campaign," p. 194.

Bibliography

Unpublished Manuscripts

Eells, Samuel H., Assistant Surgeon, 12th Michigan Volunteer Infantry. *Letters*.

Enslow, Charles C., 77th Illinois Volunteer Infantry. *Letters to My Wife*.

Grant, U.S. *Headquarters Records from the Department of the Tennessee*.

Grebe, Balazar, 2nd Lieutenant, 14th Illinois Volunteer Infantry. *Autobiography and Civil War Diary*. Manuscript Division. Library of Congress, Washington, D.C.

Howe, Hiram P., 10th Missouri Volunteer Infantry. *Diary*. Manuscript Division, Library of Congress, Washington, D.C.

Jones, John G., Corporal, Company G, 23rd Wisconsin Volunteer Infantry. *Letters*. Manuscript Division, Library of Congress, Washington, D.C.

Kellogg, John J., *War Experiences at Vicksburg*. Alderman Library, University of Virginia, Charlottesville.

Miller, Allen Woods, Captain, 36th Iowa Volunteer Infantry. *Diary*. Manuscript Division, Library of Congress, Washington, D.C.

Patterson, William F., Captain, Kentucky Company of Mechanics and Engineers. *Letters and Papers*. Manuscript Division, Library of Congress, Washington, D.C.

Reichhelm, Edward P., Sergeant Major, 3rd Missouri Volunteer Infantry. *Diary*. Manuscript Division, Library of Congress, Washington, D.C.

Whitten, John, 5th Iowa Volunteer Infantry. *Letters*. Manuscript Division, Library of Congress, Washington, D.C.

Wilder, William F., 46th Illinois Volunteer Infantry. *Letters*. Manuscript Division, Library of Congress, Washington, D.C.

Wilson, James H., *Journal, Letters, Papers*. Manuscript Division, Library of Congress, Washington, D.C.

Archival Material

Civil War Records Group 94 Volunteer Regiments, Battalions, and Companies. National Archives, Washington, D.C.
Civil War Records Group 397 Muster-Event Report. National Archives, Washington, D.C.

Published Works

Andrus, Onley. *The Civil War Letters of Sergeant Onley Andrus, 95th Illinois Volunteer Infantry.* Fred A. Shannon, editor. Urbana, Ill.: University of Illinois Press, 1947.
Ankeny, Henry G. *Kiss Joey for Me. Letters to My Dear Wife.* [By a] Captain, Company H., 4th Iowa Volunteer Infantry. Florence M.A. Cox, editor. Santa Ana, Calif.: Friis Pioneer Press, 1974.
Barnes, Joseph K. *The Medical and Surgical History of the Rebellion.* Washington: GPO, 1870.
Beals, Carleton. *War Within a War—The Confederacy Against Itself.* Philadelphia: Chilton Books, 1965.
Bill, Ledyard. *The Life, Campaigns and Battles of U.S. Grant.* New York: Ledyard Bill, 1868.
Billings, John D. *Hardtack and Coffee.* Boston: George M. Smith, 1887.
Boyd, Cyrus F. *Civil War Diary.* Mill Wood, N.Y.: Kraus Reprint, 1977.
Brooks, Stewart M. *Civil War Medicine.* Springfield, Ill.: Charles C. Thomas, 1966.
Brown, Alonzo L. *A History [of the] 4th Regiment Minnesota Volunteer Infantry.* St. Paul: Pioneer Press, 1892.
Cadwallader, Sylvanus. *Three Years with Grant.* New York: Alfred A. Knopf, 1955.
Coppee, Henry. *Grant and His Campaigns.* New York: Charles B. Richardson, 1866.
Cullum, George W. *Biographical Register of Officers and Graduates of the United States Military Academy.* 7 vols. Boston: Houghton, Mifflin, 1891–1930.
_____. *System of Military Bridges in Use by the United States Army.* New York: D. Appleton, 1849.
Dana, Charles A. *Recollections of the Civil War.* New York: D. Appleton, 1898.
Dyer, Frederick H. *A Compendium of the War of the Rebellion.* 3 vols. Des Moines: Dyer Publishing, 1908.
Geer, Allen. *Civil War Diary.* Tappan, N.Y.: R.C. Appleman, 1977.
Grant, Frederick Dent. "With Grant at Vicksburg," *The Outlook,* volume 59 (July 1898).
Grant, U.S. *Personal Memoirs.* New York: Charles L. Webster, 1894.
Greene, Francis Vinton. *The Mississippi.* New York: Scribner's, 1882.
Guernsey, Alfred A. *Harper's Pictorial History of the Great Rebellion.* 2 vols. New York: Harper & Bros., 1866.

Hains, Peter C. "The Vicksburg Campaign," *The Military Engineer*, volume XIII (May-June 1921).

Hoehling, A.A. *Vicksburg: 47 Days of Siege*. Englewood Cliffs, N.J.: Prentice-Hall, 1969.

Hoffman, Wickham. *Camp, Court, and Siege*. New York: Harper & Bros., 1877.

Hoge, Mrs. A.H. *The Boys in Blue*. New York: E.B. Treat, 1867.

Johnson, Robert Underwood, and Clarence Clough Bud, editors. *Battles and Leaders of the Civil War*. 2 vols. New York: Century, 1887.

Kellogg, John J. *The Vicksburg Campaign and Reminiscences*. Washington, Iowa: Evening Journal, 1913.

Ketchum, Richard M., editor-in-charge. *The American Heritage Pictorial History of the Civil War*. New York: American Heritage, 1960.

Lincoln, Abraham. *Speeches and Writings*. New York: Viking Press, 1989.

Livermore, Mary A. *My Story of the War*. Hartford: A.D. Worthington, 1889.

Livermore, Thomas L. *Numbers and Losses in the Civil War in America*. Boston: Houghton, Mifflin, 1901.

Long, E.B. *The Civil War Day by Day: An Almanac*. New York: Doubleday, 1971.

Lossing, Benson J., editor. *The Life, Campaigns, and Battles of General U.S. Grant*. Hartford: Belknap, 1878.

_____. *Pictorial History of the Civil War in the United States of America*. 3 vols. Philadelphia: G.W. Childs, 1866–1868.

Miers, Earl S. *The Web of Victory—Grant at Vicksburg*. New York: Alfred A. Knopf, 1955.

Phisterer, Frederick. *Statistical Record of the Armies of the United States*. New York: Scribner's, 1883.

Russ, William A. Jr., "The Vicksburg Campaign Reviewed by an Indiana Soldier—Sergeant Samuel E. Snure, Company A., 48th Indiana Volunteer Infantry. *The Journal of Mississippi History*, volume XIX (October 1957).

Sellers, John R., compiler. *Civil War Manuscripts [in the] U.S. Library of Congress*. Washington: GPO, 1986.

Sherman, William T. *Memoirs*. 2 vols. New York: D. Appleton, 1875.

Stille, Charles J. *History of the United States Sanitary Commission*. New York: Hurd and Houghton, 1869.

Twain, Mark. *Life on the Mississippi*. New York: Harper & Bros., 1906.

U.S. Naval War Records Office. *Official Records of the Union and Confederate Navies in the War of the Rebellion*. 30 vols. Washington: GPO, 1894–1922.

U.S. War Department. *The War of the Rebellion: A Compilation of the Official Records of the Union and Confederate Armies*. 128 vols. including 1 vol. index and 3 vols. of atlases. Washington: GPO, 1880–1901.

Vilas, William F. *A View of the Vicksburg Campaign*. Madison: Wisconsin History Commission, 1908.

Warner, Ezra J. *Generals in Blue*. Baton Rouge: Louisiana State University Press, 1964.

Wheeler, Richard. *The Siege of Vicksburg*. New York: Thomas Y. Crowell, 1978.

Wilson, James H. *Under the Old Flag*. New York: D. Appleton, 1912.

Wood, William. *Captains of the Civil War: Chronicles of Blue and Gray*. New Haven: Yale University Press, 1921.

Woodward, W.E. *Meet General Grant*. New York: Horace Liveright, 1928.

Journals, Newspapers, and Periodicals

Frank Leslie's Illustrated Weekly
Harper's Magazine
Harper's Weekly
The Journal of Mississippi History
Military Affairs
The Military Engineer
The New York Times
The Outlook

Index

negative opinions on Grant's
expedients 101–102; advice on
seventh attempt to take the
mountain 112–113; recon-
naissance for road 139–141;
surveyed mouth Big Bogasha
and Big Black River 154; advice on landing east shore 166;
accompanies Grant on Bruinsburg road 173; bridge South
Fork of Bayou Pierre 179–180;
with Grant to Grand Gulf
182–183; bridges Big Black

River 197–201; comment on
assault 207; relief of McClernand 225; Grant's emissary to
Pemberton 232
Wilson, Capt. John M.: inspects
siege works 230–231
Wood, Col. R.C.: inspects
medical services 15th Corps
74

Yates, Governor Richard: reviews
Illinois brigade 163